The Quest for Authority

The Quest for Authority

An Ecclesiological Pursuit
from a *United* and *Reformed* Perspective

MATTHEW PREVETT

Foreword by
JOHN P. BRADBURY

☙PICKWICK *Publications* • Eugene, Oregon

THE QUEST FOR AUTHORITY
An Ecclesiological Pursuit from a *United* and *Reformed* Perspective

Copyright © 2021 Matthew Prevett. All rights reserved. Except for brief quotations in critical publications or reviews, no part of this book may be reproduced in any manner without prior written permission from the publisher. Write: Permissions, Wipf and Stock Publishers, 199 W. 8th Ave., Suite 3, Eugene, OR 97401.

Pickwick Publications
An Imprint of Wipf and Stock Publishers
199 W. 8th Ave., Suite 3
Eugene, OR 97401

www.wipfandstock.com

PAPERBACK ISBN: 978-1-5326-8047-2
HARDCOVER ISBN: 978-1-5326-8048-9
EBOOK ISBN: 978-1-5326-8049-6

Cataloguing-in-Publication data:

Names: Prevett, Matthew, author. | Bradbury, John P., foreword.

Title: The quest for authority : an ecclesiological pursuit from a *united* and *reformed* perspective / Matthew Prevett ; foreword by John P. Bradbury.

Description: Eugene, OR : Pickwick Publications, 2021 | Includes bibliographical references and index.

Identifiers: ISBN 978-1-5326-8047-2 (paperback) | ISBN 978-1-5326-8048-9 (hardcover) | ISBN 978-1-5326-8049-6 (ebook)

Subjects: LCSH: United Reformed Church (Great Britain)—History. | Authority.

Classification: BX9890.U255 P73 2021 (print) | BX9890.U255 (ebook)

To G. J. H.

The last authority is not demonstrable, it is only realisable, as *the* religious experience of the conscience.

—P. T. Forsyth, *The Principle of Authority*, 365

Table of Contents

Foreword by John P. Bradbury ix

Acknowledgments xv

Abbreviations xvii

Introduction: The Quest for Authority 1

1. Understanding Authority 11

2. A United and Reformed Church 32

3. Theological Authority of the Word of God 59

4. Authority Rooted in Identity 83

5. Structural Authority within a United Ecclesiology 112

6. Personal Authority in a Conciliar Polity 146

7. Deciding with Authority 160

Conclusion: The Contemporary Quest for Authority 187

Bibliography 213

Index 221

Foreword

Revd. Dr. John P. Bradbury,
General Secretary, United Reformed Church

AUTHORITY IS A FUNNY thing. It is wrapped up in rules and procedures which define it legally, practiced in a web of traditions, customs and practices, given and withheld to individuals because of, or in spite of their roles, and is all together difficult to pin down. That one must *Quest* for authority, either to discover where it lies, or to exercise it, speaks of the layers of complexity that surround the very idea of "authority." Matthew Prevett has in this work laid out the multi-dimensional nature of authority within one denomination, the United Reformed Church, which exists in the three nations of England, Scotland and Wales.

At the time of writing I am a relatively new General Secretary of the United Reformed Church. Experiencing the reality of its theory and practice of authority from that vantage point is a fascinating experience. Some people assume I have an authority I simply do not. I cannot determine policy, or give people what they want, when they want it. Others go out of their way to ensure that I am aware that I have no authority and am merely the "servant of the Church." "Authority," whatever it is in terms of this specific role, is exercised first and foremost in the qualities of the relationships that one develops. To say that the role, or indeed myself in that role has no real authority would be misleading. One has knowledge of how things operate. One has the possibility to sit around every national table within the denomination where matters of weight are discussed. One has the chance to set agendas. One line-manages several staff. Others place in one a measure of authority and might particularly look for it in a moment of crisis. Not to acknowledge all of that would lead towards the situation where the abuse of that authority became likely.

There is a fine line a General Secretary treads between being invited to offer support when issues arise within a provincial or national Synod and attempts to be supportive which are experienced as wholly inappropriate interference "from London." In terms of Local Churches things look different again. Within one of the village congregations I was serving immediately prior to taking on this role, the Sunday morning my new appointment was announced, the visiting worship leader had to explain what the General Secretary was; it was not a role anyone had ever heard of before. If I were to think I had any authority whatsoever over a Local Church as it decided how best to worship, witness and serve, the echoing laughter would soon relieve me of any false understanding. The *Quest for Authority* helps unravel the multiple layers of the theory and practice of authority within the United Reformed Church that goes some way to understanding why this might be the experience of a General Secretary.

The United Reformed Church brings together four different predecessor denominational traditions. Part of English and Welsh Congregationalism, and later, Scottish Congregationalism (with rather different historical roots), English Presbyterianism and the Churches of Christ. All broadly reformed, all committed to processes of decision-making that were collective rather than individual. Within them, one could roughly speaking say that Presbyterianism functioned "top-down," the General Assembly being the highest "court" of the Church. Congregationalism was "bottom-up," local congregations being essentially autonomous, collaborating in wider structures when helpful. The United Reformed Church was carefully constructed so that each "layer" of Church life has functions that are its rightfully to exercise. Each Council of the Church (Local Church, District, Synod, General Assembly) has authority over the functions they possess, and interference from other Councils over the exercise of those functions is foreseen in only limited ways. In some respects, the *Quest for Authority* tells the story of the theological, constitutional and practical outworking of this way of inscribing authority within an institution, which is both *United* and *Reformed*.

What a constitution says, and how authority is really exercised, are two different things. One of my predecessors, the Revd. Dr. David Cornick, has spoken of the United Reformed Church as "Presbyterian in Government; Congregationalist in ethos." That strikes me as about right. Quite often custom and practice has remained staunchly Congregationalist regardless of what the governing documents of the Church might say. A brilliant example is that almost everyone in the

United Reformed Church will tell you that only a Local Church can close a Local Church. In every Synod, when a Local Church closes, it is by resolution of that Local Church Meeting. If one pays attention to the *Structure* of the United Reformed Church (the constitutional document which sets out the functions of each Council of the Church) it is quite clear that the function to dissolve a local congregation rests with the Synod, not the Local Church. This is upheld almost universally in the breach, not the observance. Tradition is a living thing, and as the United Reformed Church lived into the traditions it forged for itself and this is part of the reality which emerged.

Being *United* has been a long-cherished part of the identity of the United Reformed Church. We proudly understand ourselves as an ecumenical people, both in the unions we embody and in our continued ecumenical engagement and intent. We are however, particularly at denominational level, a frustrating ecumenical partner, I fear. This is perhaps rooted in this sense of the tension we hold between the different strands of the polity we inherited from our predecessor traditions, and in the sense that who we are we are on paper, and who one encounters in reality can be different things.

If the tension between our formal governance and the ethos of our exercise of authority is shown up in our ecumenical engagement, the tensions also become visible in response to the impact of numerical decline, which has been the reality of the United Reformed Church throughout its fifty year history. Facing that reality square on is, it seems to me, the truly faithful response to the situation that we believe, for whatever reason, God has placed us in. As numbers decline, and structures constructed to exercise authority for an overall body three to four times the size we are now fail, we must face squarely what the exercise of conciliar authority is going to look like as a small, not a large, organisation. I observe that as the organisational structures creak under stresses and strains they have never before imagined, and complicated and difficult governance questions arise in forms never thought of previously, the tension between our governance and our culture is going to become marked. Good governance may require actions that run absolutely counter to what has been assumed to be the ethos of the United Reformed Church. If a local congregation cannot find officers to oversee its life, cannot keep its buildings safe for their users, cannot operate a safeguarding policy or provide a safeguarding co-ordinator, and cannot produce accounts satisfactory to the Charity Commission, can a Synod any longer refrain from exercising its authority to dissolve a local congregation without resolution of the Local Church Meeting? This is a question which currently begins to become pressing in places, and I suspect we are going to need to find the answer multiple times over in the period to come.

If one reads history generously enough, and with enough twinkle in the eye, one might say that we are descended both from those who cut the head off a King because he was interfering too much in religious affairs and that the State should know its rather limited place when it came to religion, and those who thought they might be the ones to fill the resulting vacuum with a new form of national Church. As *United* and *Reformed* people, we have at times an "interesting" relationship with secular authority.

If the first fifty years of the United Reformed Church have been about inventing the traditions of authority that have forged our identity to date, I suspect as we live into the middle of the twenty-first century, it is perhaps Church-State relations that will cause us most directly to grapple with questions of authority. It is not that successive governments wish to direct our worship, witness or evangelism, or even dictate our internal decision-making processes; they don't. It is that in a world of compliance of the varieties alluded to above, that which we are expected to comply with is shaped by a very different practice of authority than the one we inhabit. It is in such areas as safeguarding, employment and health and safety, one begins to see the tensions between a *United* and *Reformed* operation of authority, and that of the world in which we are situated.

As a conciliar Church, all authority formally rests within the Councils of the Church. We believe that we discern God's will better together than apart. That is foundational to us (and to all our predecessor traditions). Much of the world of compliance, however, operates with a very different dynamic of authority which tends to be heterarchical and individual, rather than collective and conciliar. One experiences these tensions in varying ways. One current example which arises more than we can be comfortable with is in the realm of safeguarding. If an individual is deemed to be a safeguarding risk all would agree that risk must be mitigated, and potentially by placing serious restrictions on what that individual may and may not do within the life of the Church. But if safeguarding advice demands such restriction, and the authority to make that restriction sits rightfully within the United Reformed Church within one of its Councils, can an individual make that determination? Does a

Synod Moderator have the authority to act on safeguarding advice when really it should be the Council that should act, but confidentiality makes it impossible to determine the matter on the floor of a Council that may have eighty members? Safeguarding professionals, rightly, cannot wait around in individual cases whilst the Church unravels its understanding of authority to meet the compliance need. Which is, of course, not really "compliance" at all, but about safeguarding vulnerable people and promoting human flourishing for all.

Employment law "encroaches" ever further into the life of the Church. Here, the Church finds itself in something of a "bind." It would often find itself on the side of enhancing workers' rights, and demanding justice in the workplace for all. And yet the Church holds onto its exemption from employment legislation for clergy tightly. There have been various moments cases have ascertained that an employment tribunal may have jurisdiction, to a limited extent. Again, employment tribunals work with an inherent conception of authority which is individual and hierarchical. The responsibilities of an employer, through its line management structures and policies are clear. But how on earth would that map onto the reality that at times a Church Meeting will withdraw the call of a minister to serve it? How would an employment tribunal ever judge whether that decision, discerned together in Council of the Church, was fair and just to the minister concerned? We probably need to recognise that sometimes it likely has not been, and yet also, can at times be exactly the right decision for all. It is not that the principles of treating employees fairly the Church would not wish to uphold, or that they would not wish fair and just treatment for its ministers in this way. The complexity comes when those principles are embodied in legal practices that assume an individual and hierarchical model of authority and encounter within the United Reformed Church a conciliar form of authority.

My suspicion is that it is in part out of these kinds of Church-State tensions that our practice of authority is going to be challenged in the years to come, and quite possibly for the good. Simply shouting "religious freedom" is not an adequate response, when much compliance is ultimately about seeking human flourishing—something deep-rooted in the Christian gospel. Yet at the same time, there is a danger that as we respond to the challenges of compliance, we find ourselves adopting an individual and hierarchical authority structure alongside, or in place of, a conciliar structure without really realising we are doing so, or stopping to think theologically about what that does to our identity as a people who believe that God's will is best discerned together, not apart. I suspect that as we respond to the twin realities of the massive numerical decline in the life of the Church, coupled with the rise of the compliance culture, we will be forced to reconsider the relationship between conciliar and individual authority. We may find ourselves needing to understand that our practice, as shaped by a compliance culture, will drive us further in the direction of individual authority than perhaps we might have imagined. This may call upon us to think about what conciliar oversight and accountability of individual authority looks like. This, in turn, may have interesting ecumenical implications, if we become more willing to speak instinctively of personal oversight.

We believe that the Church is always seeking to listen attentively to the ever-living Word of God, which is enlightened for us by the Holy Spirit. The context in which we engage in that process of discernment is continually changing, and forcing us to address new questions. The twin challenges of numerical decline and the emergence of what I have termed "compliance culture" will pose very specific questions and challenges to our understanding of authority in the years to come. They will, I suspect, force us to engage with the reality that our formal governance documents and our custom and practice of authority will need to converge rather more than they have in the first fifty years of our collective life as a Church. A faith rooted in the incarnation, God's close-up and personal engagement with the realities of life in the world, even at its most grisly, demands that we face such challenges square on. Doing so is part of what makes us faithful, seeking God's will in our ever ongoing *Quest for Authority*.

Acknowledgments

THE UNDERLYING STUDY WHICH formed the doctoral research and subsequently this book, was conducted through the University of Wales Trinity Saint David as an extension to my training for ordained ministry at Westminster College, Cambridge. The study was supervised by the Revd. Dr. Robert Pope and Professor Bettina Schmidt and was funded by the Education and Learning Committee of the United Reformed Church, the Coward Trust and the Westhill Endowment. Publication of this work has been part-funded by the James Donald Tract Fund. I express my sincere gratitude to the bodies and officers administering these funds for their generosity and support and to my supervision team and my examiners, Revd. Dr. David Cornick and Professor Densil Morgan, for their wisdom and insight which shaped the original thesis and its development into this book.

A number of individuals assisted with material used in this study. Access to the URC History Society archives at Westminster College was possible through the enthusiastic and encouraging support of Mrs. Helen Weller and Mrs. Margaret Thompson, while access to the URC Archive (located at Dr. Williams's Library, London) was made possible through the support of the Librarian, Dr. David Wykes, with the assistance of Mr. David Powell. Additionally, Dr. Carol Reekie, Librarian in the Cambridge Theological Federation, offered encouraging and supportive assistance through some challenging times for library access.

Thanks also to a number of colleagues around the URC who enabled and participated in the research. Participants in Local Churches, Synods and around the denomination provided access to meetings and documents and participated in interviews and focus groups, doing so with great sense of grace and welcome. They cannot be named, but I do offer my sincerest of thanks for such hospitality.

A particular mention is due to the General Secretaries who have supported the study and endorsed access to the denomination over the past decade: Revd. Roberta Rominger, Revd. John Proctor, and Revd. Dr. John Bradbury. I am especially grateful to John Bradbury for his foreword and for his many years of encouragement at Westminster College.

My sincere thanks to the team at Wipf and Stock, particularly Matt Wimer and Dr. Charlie Collier, who were kind enough not only to take on the project but have done such an excellent job at turning my manuscript into a published title. A first monograph is a significant moment for an author, and I have been well served by the team at Wipf & Stock.

I have been fortunate enough to be supported through this project by a number of friends and colleagues. People without whom this book wouldn't exist, include: Revd. Dr. Susan Durber, Revd. Carole Elphick, Revd. Hannah Hupfield, Revd. Anne Lewitt, Revd. Sue and Jamie McCoan, Revd. Neil Thorogood, Revd. Dr. Janet Tollington, Revd. Nigel Uden, Revd. Dr. Phil Wall, Revd. Sam White, and Mrs. Lyn Woodfield Many words of support, encouragement and improvement have been offered and the book is richer for it. Any errors that remain are of my doing. A special mention to friends in the Embassy Singers, Berlin, including Mr. Gareth Jones and Dr. Paul Talcott who provided support and much needed rest and refreshment.

Finally, my husband, Gary, has been tirelessly supportive of this project which has been absorbing my attentions since well before we met. While he had little prior knowledge of—or inclination towards—United and/or Reformed ecclesiology, his dedicated coaching and encouragement has guided me over the finishing line. I dedicate this volume to him.

Abbreviations

Basis	The *Basis of Union*; referenced as §A (Section A of the URC's *Manual*)
CCEW	Congregational Church in England and Wales
CUEW	Congregational Union of England and Wales
CTV	*Catch the Vision*
CYB	*Congregational Year Book*
GA Record	The Record of the Meeting of the General Assembly of the URC
GA Reports	The Reports and Resolutions for the Meeting of the General Assembly of the URC
MC	Mission Council of the United Reformed Church
PCE	Presbyterian Church of England
PCE Minutes	The Minutes of the Meeting of the General Assembly of the PCE
Reform	*Reform Magazine* (published by the URC)
Structure	The *Structure of the United Reformed Church*; referenced as §B (Section B of the URC's *Manual*)
URC	United Reformed Church in the United Kingdom

Introduction: The Quest for Authority

FROM THE POWERFUL PRESENCE and grandeur of Church buildings and ecclesial institutions, through to the local expressions of Church in communities, one universal constant in the life of the Church is the omnipresent influence of authority.[1] In matters of doctrine, structure, ministry, worship or finance, authority permeates all that is said and done, contributing significantly to the quality and outcome of discussions. Authority lies at the very centre of what it means to be called together in an ecclesial community and shapes how the Church understands its purpose and orders its activity.

Whether addressing fundamental questions of faith, the interpretation of Scripture, the priesthood of all, the unity of the Church, the process for decision-making, the authorisation of ministry, or any other matter concerning the Church, it is impossible to reach a position that is not impacted by authority beyond or within the Church. No issue, neither large nor small, is addressed or resolved without the inescapable presence of authority. Essentially, authority dominates Church life. To understand what makes a Church is to understand the authority in a Church.

Therefore, the quest for authority is an ecclesiological pursuit. Examining what it means for the Church today is to understand how the Church came to be and what values and principles were important in its formation and development. Authority is not just of the moment, but is historically contingent, formed and re-formed by the influences

---

1. It is a fundamental premise not only of this book but of my own ecclesiology that all contexts of the Church are manifestations of the Universal Church. I was grateful for an editorial footnote in Kennett, *Autonomy* which affirmed this conviction, and revised that journal's convention to provide for the capitalisation of "Church." Therefore, contrary to some publishing conventions (and with the consent of my editor) throughout this book I refer to "Church" in the capitalised form. To allow other authors' work to honour their ecclesiology, quotations retain their original capitalisation.

and challenges of doctrine and context. History sets precedent and tradition which casts a shadow over the Church, informs its ecclesiology and shapes its contemporary existence. To understand the authority in a Church is to understand the history of a Church.

Yet it is ecclesiological to understand not only what influenced the history of a Church, but to seek clarity on how the contemporary Church operates and functions. This is true for authority as it sheds light on the significant issues for contemporary Church life and gives a snapshot of the identity of the Church. The practice of authority demonstrates what makes the Church in the present, where it draws its strength and where it may struggle. In understanding what role authority has in the Church, how its authority speaks in the contemporary context and how this differs from the historical understanding, it's possible to understand not only how the Church functions but what challenges and opportunities face the Church. To understand the authority in a Church is to understand what makes a Church.

The one uncontested truth of ecumenical ecclesial authority is that it is grounded in Christ, its Head. Yet the understanding of how this is manifest alters across the denominational divides. While some traditions rely upon uninterrupted continuity in the succession from St. Peter to the present, Protestant Churches who inherit from the Reformation ground their understanding of the apostolic succession in a broader view of an "Evangelical" succession. Congregational theologian P. T. Forsyth wrote that apostolic succession:

> does not mean, at the one extreme, a historic line of valid ordinations unbroken from the Apostles to the last curate. Nor, at the other end, does it mean merely cultivating the spirit of the Apostles, or their precepts for sanctification. But it is the succession of those who experience and preach the Apostolic Gospel of a regenerating redemption.[2]

It is by nature of this evangelical zeal that the authority of Christ is inherited in the life of such Reformed Churches, not through a line of ordinations, but through living out the Word of God in the life of the Church. The grounding of this authority in the Word, with an openness to the ever-reforming presence of Christ, leads Churches of the Reformation to seek to hear where God is leading and what God is saying. However, the propensity of such Churches to fracture over disagreements about the

---

2. Forsyth, *Church and the Sacraments*, 110.

discernment of such authority demonstrates the extent to which history and context shape the understanding of authority held by a Church.

In some parts of the world, the understanding of a Reformed Church has a particular ecclesiology and theology. Elsewhere, the term is used more flexibly to relate to the "habit of mind" which underpins post-Reformation theology and ecclesiology in a group of Churches, some of which hold to the title of Reformed, while others are considered as Nonconformist, or Free Churches. Brian Gerrish regards such Reformed theology to have a number of characteristics:

> Reformed theology is an ongoing conversation into which the "fathers" of the Reformed Church are drawn, deferentially but not uncritically; in which openness to sacred and secular learning brings continual new light, always with an eye to the practice of piety and the transformation of human lives, both individually and socially; and in which, finally, the focus returns again and again to the meaning of the gospel.[3]

Under this broad umbrella, therefore, exists all manner of Churches which look to the Reformation (both European and English) for their theology and ecclesiology. It includes those who would be regarded as Baptist, Churches of Christ, Congregational, and Presbyterian, and those who may look to John Calvin, Friedrich Schleiermacher, Karl Barth, and Jürgen Moltmann with a critical yet deferential eye. Reformed, therefore, is less to be understood as possessing a specific definition, and more to be regarded as an understanding of thought and ecclesiology receptive, open and alive to a reforming Spirit, and the centrality of the gospel of Christ.

It has been rare, but notable, when divisions are reversed and union, rather than schism, become part of ecclesial history. Of the 232 members of the World Communion of Reformed Churches (WCRC) listed on their website in early 2021, twenty-nine have the world United, Uniting, or Union in their title, with a group of these bringing together unions of more than one type of ecclesiology. Instead of seeing a divergence in authority, United dominations have understood their calling to be one of coming together in a common vision and discernment of the Word of God. The authority which has led them to be disparate and apart at one time has also led to the movement towards union, and towards a coming together which unifies the denominational understanding of authority.

3. Gerrish, "Doing Theology," 8.

However, while it would be right to regard such new United denominations as forming a single ecclesiology, and therefore an institutional understanding of authority grounded in the unified denomination, to presuppose that this resulted in uniformity would be to ignore the distinct heritage of the constituent denominations and their impact on the resulting Church. Where the polity of one tradition is adopted while the other uniting polities are forfeited a clear understanding can be reached of ecclesial authority. However, where a uniting of polity takes place the authority modelled in one tradition, informed by cultural and ecclesiological history, will become interwoven with the polity of another tradition. In these situations, the United denomination is not a merger of its parts, but a unique manifestation of an ecclesiology, informed and reformed under the authority of the Word of God.

In these scenarios, it is important to consider the denomination not as a merger, but as an institutional body is that it is one system—one body—and is not defined by its constituent parts but by its whole. The model of unity in the one body can be found in the Bible, most notably in the Pauline assertion in 1 Corinthians 12:14 that the body is made up not one member but many. Read ecclesiologically, the passage emphasises the differing parts (hand, ear, eye, head, feet) but asserts that they are, ultimately, dependent upon one another to relate one to another for the sake of the body as a whole. Denominations are formed to be a single system consisting of their many parts and form themselves into a communion in such a way as to be "mutually dependent as they live the truth of their identity in Jesus Christ."[4] This approach to United and Reformed Churches helps to provide a method to be used in examining the structure of such bodies, recognising the uniqueness of a polity in which both particularity in the constituent parts and interconnectedness in the denomination is key.

Such United and Reformed denominations are therefore not a purebred ecclesiology, based on a model drawn up by Reformation Theologians, but are formed through the discernment process of uniting. Here they draw on the key authorities that have facilitated the union discussions and which are guided by commitment to denominational, cultural and eschatological authority. The guiding principles must be understood in terms of discernment of the Word of God (some theologians might call this "Scripture"), historically located authority (some

---

4. Ensign-George, *Between Congregation and Church*, 296.

theologians might call this "Tradition"), future context and eschatological fulfilment (some theologians might call this "Reason"), and cultural and empirical realisation (some theologians might call this "Experience").

Although United and Reformed Churches would regard their relationship to Anglican, Methodist and Roman Catholic theological method as sitting on opposite sides of an authority chasm, the commonalities in these principles of authority echo across the ecclesiological divide. Despite being guided by entirely different language to the ecclesiological sources and norms systematised in Anglican terms by Richard Hooker and Methodist terms by John Wesley, the *via media* approach to ecclesiology developed by United and Reformed Churches results in an understanding of authority that, while authentically Reformed, resonates with questions of authority also faced by Anglican, Methodist and Roman Catholic ecclesial expressions.[5] Irrespective of the methods involved, the mediation of the authority of Christ across the ecumenical landscape follows common principles of authority centred on Christ the Head. A United and Reformed perspective therefore draws on the history of the common ecclesiological pursuit of Christ's Church and informs the wider ecumenical landscape.

Although the pursuit of authority in a United and Reformed ecclesiology may suggest a focused insight into a particular area of the ecclesial vista, the wider scholarly and ecumenical impact of this examination is threefold. First, an ecclesial history gives insight into the context and concerns of other traditions which share the same polity or context. The English Reformation informed and inspired a number of identities later to form as denominations and their interconnectedness through a common history and context provides a useful counterpoint to alternative readings. Second, the process of union between Churches of two or more polities resonates with the *via media* approach adopted by other broad denominations. The experiences of United and Reformed Churches therefore provides a valuable insight into the concerns of all denominations that encompass a breadth of attitudes to theology, liturgy and authority. Third, the light shed on the significant issues of the contemporary Church highlights the concerns and struggles of other Churches. Thus, in considering the strengths and weaknesses of authority it is possible to reflect on the mission, identity and eschatological fulfilment of Christ's Church, and the particular challenges affecting United and Reformed

5. For an analysis of Anglican theological method and authority, see Avis, *In Search of Authority*.

Churches. However, the considerations for ecumenical ecclesiology go far beyond the United and Reformed Churches, and provide rich learning for Churches around the world.

Although these principles of authority in United and Reformed Churches can be shared across a number of international and ecumenical contexts, this book has grown as an examination of one example from a British ecclesial context. The Golden Jubilee of the formation of United Reformed Church in the UK (URC) marks an important stage in the life of the denomination and for the ecumenical movement. The URC had begun as a catalyst towards greater Church unity as part of the British Church context. However, after its formation in 1972 joining together the Congregational Church in England and Wales (CCEW) and the Presbyterian Church of England (PCE), the URC's movement of wider unity brought only further union with the Re-formed Association of the Churches of Christ (1981) and the Congregational Union of Scotland (2000). Rather than being the movement that would unite the Churches in Britain, the URC has found itself as a diminishing institution on the periphery of the ecumenical landscape. While facing the perennial challenges of an aging and reducing membership, the URC continues to strive to break forth yet more light and truth of Christ's ministry in the world.

As a Reformed Church the URC has, from inception, adopted a conciliar polity. The Local Church Meeting is the base unit of Council, with the Church Meeting electing Elders who meet together in an Elders' Meeting to be responsible for Local Church matters. Local Churches are grouped into thirteen Synods (a second unit of Council), and the General Assembly (a third unit of Council) which represents the gathering of the whole denomination. Representatives of the Local Church come together to form the Synod, while members selected by the Synod represent the Synod at the General Assembly. Members of Local Churches, present as representatives of the Synod, constitute the General Assembly, and this confirms the conciliar nature of the URC and its principally participatory nature where lay and ordained together take part in the denomination's governance. While there are other associated bodies (including Synod and Denominational Trust bodies) and there is a secondary committee level, the URC recognises three Councils of the Church: the Church Meeting; the Synod Meeting; the General Assembly. In 2020, the URC was made up of 1,331 Local Churches, thirteen Synods (eleven in England, one for

Wales, and one for Scotland), and the General Assembly, with a total membership of 43,208.[6]

Despite being part of the British ecumenical landscape for fifty years, the URC remains enigmatic to many in and out of British Church life, even to those who find themselves part of its life. In a land so influenced by established Anglicanism, the URC is less understood, documented, and explored as a mainstream Christian denomination than larger ecumenical cousins such as the Church of England, Methodist Church, and the Roman Catholic Church. Beyond Great Britain, the URC is part of a global Reformed Church family, consisting of Lutherans, Calvinists, Congregationalists, Presbyterians, and Churches of Christ, and is part of an international group of United and Uniting Churches. The denomination has been well served internationally and ecumenically by a number of its leading theologians and hymnwriters including David Cornick, Susan Durber, John Hick, John Huxtable, Colin Gunton, Michael Jagessar, Fred Kaan, Caryl Micklem, Leslie Newbigin, Erik Routley, Alan Sell, David Thompson, Kirsty Thorpe, Elizabeth Welch, and Brian Wren.

Previously published studies of the URC have been grounded on the particularity of the denomination's history or doctrine, focused largely on the way that this can be explained to those involved in the life of the Church. These books have been important and timely, meeting a need within the denomination's first three decades to explain and systematise the historical doctrine and ecclesiology which formed the URC as it was perceived and understood through its first thirty years. These studies give an initial stop for any further study, giving a solid and learned foundation for any further study. With these texts published by the denomination's communications department, the purpose of these books reflects a need to inform, educate and guide an audience of the denomination's own members and ministers. Little of these texts have left the sphere of the URC, and twenty to thirty years on, much of the denomination's history continues to be reimagined as social transformation, demographic change and increasing secularisation affects the place, role and rationale behind the URC.

The existence of the URC as both a United and Reformed Church provides a unique voice in the arena of British ecclesiology. It draws together the principles of the English Reformation, the nonconformist development of denominational ecclesiology, the movement of ecumenical

---

6. Statistics are published annually in the *URC Yearbook* and the URC website.

innovation, and the challenges of a digital age. The story of the denomination is the story of authority, navigated through the challenges of state ejectment, proposals for unity, virtual meetings, and through each decision and action of the Church. To understand what significance the URC offers to contemporary ecclesiology is to understand authority and its place in telling the story and shedding light on what it means to be United and Reformed.

The topic of ecclesial authority is one that has been on the radar for a number of years. The Human Sexuality debates which reached fever pitch in early 2000s saw a number of Christian denominations struggling with the question of authority. Although biblical authority and interpretation was a significant basis for such discussions, the question of ecclesial authority and the process for a Church to decide its view was not always easily navigated. Even in denominations which appeared to have a clear authority structure, cases occurred where authority was questioned and long-established process was being undermined.

In 2009, the Church of Scotland General Assembly debated the decision of the Presbytery of Aberdeen to concur to the call of minister Scott Rennie to Queen's Cross Church, Aberdeen. The Local Church had issued a call to Rennie and the Presbytery had concurred, in keeping with Presbyterian polity and practice. However, some Presbytery members objected to this concurrence due to Rennie's sexuality and sought to question the decision of the Presbytery to call Rennie to this Local Church. When this was heard by the Church of Scotland's General Assembly as the denomination's supreme court, the Presbytery's concurrence was upheld and Scott Rennie was subsequently inducted to Queen's Cross Church, Aberdeen.

Although the Church of Scotland's General Assembly ruling addressed Rennie's call to minister in the Local Church, the case stretched the established understanding of authority in the Church. On the one hand, Presbytery decisions are always open to be appealed to the General Assembly. In the Presbyterian structure of the Church of Scotland, the supremacy of the General Assembly remains final and there is little ambiguity about the sequential authority of the Church's courts. However, on the other hand, concurrence to call rests within the authority of the Presbytery. The decisions made by these courts hold the authority of the denomination.

The Rennie case showed that what had been regarded as practice and procedure could potentially be overturned and an alternative source of authority appealed to if a matter was sufficiently contentious. What it had questioned was to what extent this could be replicated in other situations and in other Reformed ecclesiologies.

The basis of this book is the doctoral research I conducted into the concept and practice of authority in the URC. In addition to drawing heavily on historic and documentary sources of significance to the URC, it uniquely draws on the largest ethnographic study of the denomination ever conducted to bring to light the never before uncovered empirical life of the URC in all its completeness. The study explored the full conciliar structure of the URC through an extensive variety of observations, interviews and focus groups which drew upon the spheres of the denomination including the General Assembly, Synod, and Local Church. Through observation of decision-making bodies in each of the spheres, and through extensive interviews and focus groups conducted with leaders and participants, it has been possible to demonstrate and describe the rich variety of the URC's life. Such illustrations are quoted throughout the book, demonstrating the richness of the empirical study in light of the denomination's contemporary reality.

While the depth and expanse of this ethnographic study is unique in URC terms, it is a significant ecclesiological study, providing a rich well from which to drink when carrying out investigations into United and Reformed ecclesial bodies. In this book, I bring this research together to demonstrate the understanding of authority through the lens of a specific denomination, but with significance for all United and Reformed Churches. In entwining historic and conceptual understandings of ecclesiology together with empirically observed understandings and perceptions of authority, this book embodies the present challenge for many of us in Churches; namely, to bring the theology, history, tradition and identity that is so important to our participation in ecclesial bodies, into dialogue with the practical and lived reality of being a Church in the early twenty-first century. The authority of a Church is most definitely told through its history, but its present and future rely upon what we can see, hear and experience of that Church in its contemporary expression.

This quest for authority, therefore, takes us on a journey. First, we consider how we understand authority, its challenge and facets, in laying the foundation for what we are to explore in ecclesiological terms. Second, in marking the first half-century of the URC, we explore in depth the historical basis which forms the understanding of authority in the denomination. Third, we explore a number of themes that are pertinent in understanding authority in an ecclesial setting. This considers the Word of God, historic identity, conciliarity and polity, personal authority, and discernment. In each chapter, the material draws on concept and practice, and brings together textual, theoretical and historical understandings of these topics and reflect how these are understood and reflected empirically in a contemporary United and Reformed ecclesiology. In conclusion, I draw out pertinent points from the study and from contemporary experience that consider the present and future challenges for authority in these United and Reformed contexts, and for the wider ecumenical landscape.

1

Understanding Authority

AUTHORITY IS LOST. It is missing from society. It is ignored by politicians. It is hidden in Churches. This, at least, is how it can seem. There is a perception that authority is lacking from our society, our politics, and our ecclesiology and that this deficiency is the cause of the challenges facing the world. If only there was more authority, then we could operate in a safe, fair, and just society. Conversely, there are those who say that authority is too overpowering. It is too prevalent in modern life. Politics and business are full of those who use authority to excess. Authority can be seen to oppress and suppress people, while corrupt authority leads to subjugation and injustice.

In addressing authority, it is difficult to gauge whether we are looking into the vacuum that leads to anarchy, or at authoritarianism which dominates life. We may find ourselves considering either—or both—as we view the world around, with neither being compelling solutions, while both seem preferable to the other. When taken to the extreme, authority becomes totally authoritarian or totally anarchic. Yet in most cases, we operate in a world in which authority is fused together in the people and contexts in which we find ourselves, with neither extreme dominating.

Within the many challenges that face our contemporary living, the loss of authority is something that many regard as the loss of a necessary lifejacket. This is not new. The German political philosopher Hannah Arendt wrote in the 1950s that there was a lack of authority in the modern world. This, she argues, had become manifest politically from the start of the twentieth century, evidenced by the decline of the party system and the rise of totalitarianism.[1] Such loss of authority shakes the foundations of what we know and, in doing so, emphasises the loss of "permanence and reliability."[2] It is perhaps of little surprise that the loss of authority feels like the world has changed, and that the rock on which our existence is built is no longer stable and secure. Authority, therefore, embodies both a permanence in holding fast to tradition and authenticity, and a reliability which is grounded on the sure foundation of an eternal truthfulness. It becomes both a historical afterglow and a lamplight pointing into the unknown future. Loss of authority makes us question what has brought us here and concerns us for what will—and can—reliably lead us onward.

As people, we find that the permanence and reliability of institutions provide for us security and authority. This is built on the permanence which is history, grounding solidly on the actions and behaviours of the past and providing assurance for the future. We have an understanding of what this permanence and reliability entails, and we're drawn instinctively to institutions which provide us with security. This is even more so in periods of uncertainty or when it seems that other factors are disturbing the reliability to which we have become accustomed.

We find certain institutions especially permanent and reliable. Monarchy has been the longstanding bedrock of Western secular society, supplemented in more recent centuries with elected parliamentary government, while the Church in its many manifestations has been the reliable permanence in Europe for much of the past two millennia. Other corporations, companies and institutions have established their place as reliable and permanent parts of not only national society but a global community, known for what services they provide and the authenticity of their presence. However, it is the loss of reliability in an institution—through public scandals or poor economic performance—which affects its authority. In demonstrating unreliability or a lack of permanence, institutional authority is undermined, eroded or made to feel distant or lacking.

However, permanence is not always to be attributed to a healthy application of authority. Authoritarian leaders argue for their permanence, while enormous architectural buildings, monuments and shrines are "symbols that the ruling order of power will last beyond the generation

---

1. Arendt, "What is Authority?," 89–95.
2. Arendt, "What is Authority?," 95.

which now rules and the generation which now obeys."³ Richard Sennett argues that such monuments of authority symbolise an end to history, whereby the old authority, in all its many ways, is to be sustained throughout time. Acts such as the pulling down of statues breaks links to the old authority and removes the permanence held in public monuments. The toppling of the statutes to Iraqi dictator Saddam Hussein in Baghdad in 2003 and to slave trader Edward Colston in Bristol in 2020 both symbolised turning points in the permanence of these authorities and provided opportunity to review the extent of authority given to such figures.

Yet authority in an institutional setting is not exclusively about the corporate "brand" having authority but is characterised by the interplay of the internal structures which manage and lead the organisation. Directors or Bishops have more authority than their Managers or Priests, with their role affording a greater authority in the structure of the organisations. Within organisational structures, whether that's corporations, governments or Churches, authority is the process by which sustainability is managed and through which change occurs.

It is perhaps little surprise, therefore, that the topic of authority has interested those from a vast number of disciplines. It is—amongst many things—a philosophical, political, anthropological, historical, sociological and theological subject, which relates to the entirety of our interactions, personal and corporate. While we may at times face authoritarianism, the majority of our encounters with authority are overshadowed by the question of legitimacy and validity. Such a question leads us to enter into the frustrating quest to locate authority. Yet it is the very fact that we have to search for authority, as Sennett argues, that "as long as we are frustrated, we keep our freedom from those masters of illusion who promise us that history is over, and that the search can come to an end."⁴ The need for a quest for authority is, therefore, something that reassures that where authority may seem distant, such a search is far from futile.

The Conceptual Challenge of Authority

Authority is needed, as Victor Lee Austin argues, so that we can be ourselves, and "is a manifestation of the glory of being human."⁵ Authority

---

3. Sennett, *Authority*, 18.
4. Sennett, *Authority*, 20.
5. Austin, *Up with Authority*, 1.

has the potential to offer not only human flourishing, for individual and society, but also to be part of a quest for freedom and equality. It can be a positive force within any given community and for each individual in it insofar as it provides a framework in which society can function. It is such a framework created by authority, Austin argues, that is necessary as members of a community grow in lifestyle, knowledge and power:

> For if growth in virtue and excellence, in potency and knowledge, does not result in a limiting of our choices but instead effectively multiplies them, then reason and good will alone will be inadequate to make necessary determinations among the multiple possibilities for human flourishing. Those determinations, therefore, will have to be made by authority.[6]

Austin, therefore, argues that authority is necessary for the well-being of society and the provision of human flourishing, recognising that the consequence of such will be that some views will be rejected as an inevitability of ordered social living. As such, authority has a clear place in the social world in which we live. However, authority has not always received such a positive reading and is frequently used interchangeably, even "haphazardly," with the terms "power," "might," and even "violence."[7] The way in which these terms have been used as synonyms has led to "the peculiar but interesting and important claim that the very concept of authority has been corrupted or even lost in the modern world, and that it is this loss of understanding that lies behind the confusion over authority prevailing in contemporary thought."[8] As a result, according to Hannah Arendt, "authority has vanished from the modern world" and "we are no longer in a position to know what authority really *is*."[9] She further describes the diminution of authority in terms of its impact on the world as a whole:

> Its loss is tantamount to the loss of the groundwork of the world, which indeed since then has begun to shift, to change and transform itself with ever-increasing rapidity from one shape into another, as though we were living and struggling with a Protean

---

6. Austin, *Up with Authority*, 26.

7. This interchangeability is recognised in Arendt, "What was Authority?," 82; also Sennett, *Authority*, 18; Höpfl, "Power, Authority and Legitimacy," 219.

8. Friedman, "Concept of Authority," 56.

9. Arendt, "What is Authority?," 91–92, italics original.

universe where everything at any moment can become almost anything else.[10]

This transformed and, indeed, corrupted understanding of authority, has led to identifying authority as a force of power and violence. Alongside this, "reason" has also been seen to counter the underlying rationale for authority. Arendt argues that "[i]f authority is to be defined at all, then, it must be in contradistinction to both coercion by force and persuasion through arguments."[11] Her position is Platonic in premise, arguing that Plato's consideration of authority in the *polis* was in contradistinction to the prevailing Greek approach to political affairs; these being characterised by Plato in domestic matters as persuasion, and in foreign matters as violence and force.[12] It is the realisation that where "force is used, authority has failed" and that persuasion "presupposes equality" which exempts these as two definitions of authority.[13] These two forms, consisting of violence and reason, are to be considered counter to authority, for if authority cannot command obedience by nature of its own existence, it cannot be authority.

The voluntary recognition and indeed adoption of authority, devoid of violence or the need to persuade, emphasises the importance of authority as a means of providing, if not also securing, human freedom and flourishing. The distinction implied by this free society relies upon the recognition of two different circumstances. First, that authority by force is not real authority and cannot be a mark of a free society; and, secondly, that any position where an authority has to gain its status through debate or argument cannot be real authority. The creation and prospering of free society necessitates, therefore, the voluntary recognition of authority and its lack of forcible compliance; the use of persuasion requires the application of reason while the use of force subjugates freedom in society. In both cases, therefore, any authority must establish its legitimacy without recourse to force or persuasion. This substantiates Austin's point that "reason and good will alone will be inadequate to make necessary determinations" for freedom and the benefit of a flourishing and prosperous society.[14]

10. Arendt, "What is Authority?," 95.
11. Arendt, "What is Authority?," 93.
12. Arendt, "What is Authority?," 93.
13. Arendt, "What is Authority?," 92.
14. Austin, *Up with Authority*, 26.

It is in the writing of sociologist Max Weber that a free, and voluntary, obedience can be observed. Weber regards authority in three categories: traditional; legal-rational; and charismatic. In Weber's view, traditional authority is that which is stable due to the length of time it has endured. Meanwhile, legal-rational is defined as that which is true by nature of the established order, and charismatic authority is where an individual has a sacred, heroic or exemplary nature that can create a following.[15] In each way, the authority is recognised as legitimate as demonstrated by voluntary compliance.

Yet, an argument may be made for an approach to the concept of authority that grounds it in the function it serves rather than in a utopian idealism. Such "functionalisation" of authority suggests, as Arendt poses, that "if violence fulfils the same function as authority—namely, makes people obey—then violence is authority."[16] However Arendt is quick to point out that she does not believe "that violence can become a substitute for authority."[17] Such functional descriptions can, therefore, obscure a direct definition and lead instead to the interchangeability of alternative or even contradictory terms. In common usage, authority is used interchangeably as both a term denoting the force used to secure obedience and also a term denoting a "mode of submission or subordination that excludes compulsion."[18] These contradictory understandings thus make authority a challenging topic to address. Authority may, at one and the same time, be responsible for securing obedience through force or without force, and with persuasion or without persuasion. R. B. Friedman points out: "Depending, then, on which sense of the word 'authority' is employed, it can be correct usage either to affirm or to deny that authority is exhibited in one and the same activity of compelling obedience."[19]

Thus, while authority has these apparently contradictory meanings whereby force is both indicative of authority yet counter to authority, its underlying purpose is to secure obedience. This could be regarded as the primary purpose of authority, and the basis on which its entire foundation is built. However, the prospect of compulsion suggests that authority may not, in this sense at least, hold to the Platonic ideals echoed by

---

15. Sennett, *Authority*, 21.
16. Arendt, "What is Authority?," 101–2.
17. Arendt, "What is Authority?," 103.
18. Friedman, "Concept of Authority," 62.
19. Friedman, "Concept of Authority," 63.

Arendt. Meanwhile, if authority's task is to secure obedience, the process of "securing" is itself an active process, whereby some form of act provides for obedience. It seems, therefore, that whether obedience is secured, or compelled, a Platonic, passive, authority cannot conceptually exist. While the need to compel questions its legitimacy and posits whether it does, ultimately, secure human flourishing, the role of authority as an agent or catalyst rather than an effect ensures that it must act rather than be seen to exist in a vacuum. It is, therefore, the pursuit of obedience without loss either to freedom or flourishing that makes such obedience the result of what can be understood to be *true* authority.

Such distinctions aside, however, it is clear that the concept of authority is burdened with understandings that inevitably invoke questions of force, coercion, power, trust and belief. Although Arendt's acknowledgement of "functionalisation" recognises the place these understandings have in definitions of authority, there is a tendency to regard such functional descriptors as counter to the Platonic understanding of true authority. While a concept of authority built upon Plato's conceptualisation distances itself from such an understanding, a functional understanding suggests a concept intrinsically linked with violence, force and coercion, and reliant upon trust and ideological homogeneity. Such conceptualisation constitutes a stumbling block that, in spite of philosophical discourse, gives authority in some contexts a wholly negative meaning, being associated not with freedom and equality, but as the bedfellow of tyrannical and totalitarian systems.

The concept of authority, therefore, is multi-faceted where both positive and negative connotations may be found. Thus when exploring authority in the Church there must be recognition of these different connotations of authority and the ways in which authority may be perceived in the life of the ecclesial community. While the criticisms directed towards secular authorities are applicable equally to ecclesial authorities, the authority offered within Church or society should provide a framework for freedom and equality, and for the flourishing of human beings.

The Subject and Object of Authority

Authority, in its quest to secure or compel obedience, has two foci for its work. These two foci are drawn from a simple logical position, namely, that authority has to possess both a subject and an object. This distinction is possible through recognition that in the relational sphere of authority there must always be a party who is the *subject* (locus) of authority while there is a party who must be the *object* (response) of authority. Yet, while authority requires both a subject and an object to exist, these foci are significant insofar as they are both distinct from one another and bound together in relationship. It is the interplay between these parties that provides nuance and alters the concept of authority into something more than an equation with predictable solutions. Both the authority of the subject and the reception of the object are open to differences. The relationship between these foci thus result in a diversity of practical expressions of authority.

In his essay exploring the concept of authority in political philosophy, R. B. Friedman succinctly outlines two ways in which a person (or party) exercises authority.

> For one, he may be said to be "in authority," meaning that he occupies some office, position, or status which entitles him to make decisions about how other people should behave. But, secondly, a person may be said to be "an authority" on something, meaning that his views or utterances are entitled to be believed (including, to complicate matters, beliefs about the right and wrong way of doing things).[20]

The distinction made by Friedman is echoed by Gary Young who argues that these two forms constitute a sub-species of a third type of authority, one he calls "on-authority."[21] Young suggests that the overarching form of authority relates to a response elicited *on the authority of* a party. Young's categorisation, however, shifts the focus away from the *subject* of authority—the locus—and moves to consider the *object*—the response to authority. Thus he views authority in terms of the receptive position of authority, rather than in the locus of such authority. In doing so, Young's "on-authority" could be understood as a consideration of what it means to be "under" authority, whether that be authority expressed by office or by influence. Rather than providing a third categorisation for the locus of authority, what Young effectively offers is an umbrella term for all ways in which the locus of authority may act. In doing so, he removes any reference to the genre of authority expressed by the subject, and considers authority exclusively as something received by the object. By so doing,

---

20. Friedman, "Concept of Authority," 57.
21. Young, "Authority," 581.

"on-authority" relates solely to the subject and in no way to the object—or locus—of authority, and thus it makes no sense to consider it as a locus for authority at all. Rather than, as Young suggests, fulfilling a role as an umbrella form of the locus of authority, "on-authority" constitutes a variation of what it means to be "under" authority.

The Locus of Authority

The locus of authority, therefore, can be regarded as being expressed in Friedman's two understandings of a party being "in" authority and being "an" authority. In both senses, authority is conveyed by a party, yet the party possessing authority holds this differently depending upon the type of authority concerned. It is "in" authority that regulates how actions are conducted, while "an" authority may influence action or belief. The distinctive nature of these understandings is subtle but recognisable. The location of authority as originating from a party "in" authority provides a formalised and potentially prescriptive form of authority, while authority originating from a party who is "an" authority provides a moral and descriptive form of authority.

Being "in Authority"

The locus of authority associated with a formalised approach is most closely recognised in the form of authority described by Friedman as "in authority." With this locus, authority is held in an office or status within a given context. It is by holding such an office or status that "in authority" is conferred upon a party. A teacher is "in authority" in the classroom where she is teaching, or in the playground when she is on a schedule to do so. However, outside the classroom or the school, a teacher is not formally classified as a person "in authority" except perhaps by those over whom they are "in authority" within the school. Without the context indicators (such as within a classroom), a teacher may be unrecognisable to the population as holding such authority. The same could be said of a police officer out of uniform or a Church Minister without a clerical collar.[22]

22. It is to be recognised that not all Church Ministers wear a clerical collar. The point made here emphasises the significance of contextual indicators that mark out an officer as holding that office; a clerical collar, like a police officer's uniform, does so explicitly.

The role of being "in authority," therefore, is based on the extent of the context in which it applies. For example, a teacher "in authority" in one school does not, as a result of that alone, have authority in another school. However, a teacher's status may ensure that they are considered "an authority" when elsewhere.

Friedman suggests that "in authority" "occurs whenever men cannot agree on what is to be done, so that, to avoid chaos, there must be agreement about who is to decide what is to be done."[23] This places the need for formalised authority derived in such a manner to be a fundamental part of the social structure. Thus, just as Austin argued for the place of authority as a method for providing human flourishing, Friedman's argument places the need for authority as an inevitable part of society. This instinctive need to provide an authority figure within society draws parallels between the concept of authority and the provision of leadership. Leaders are, *de facto*, "in authority" while those "in authority" are, whether this is recognised or not, leaders. These two roles cannot be logically separated. No other purpose makes logical sense.

However, while the recognition of those "in authority" is dependent upon the context, the context formulates how the party "in authority" is to be authorised or recognised. A teacher may be appointed and authorised by the governors of a school to be "in authority." In this case, the source of authority resides with the governing body who are the authorising body and are in a position both to place a party in authority and, in necessary circumstances, to remove such authority.

Therefore, because authority is formally appointed by an authorising body, who may take steps to ensure their authorisation is given to those qualified to occupy a position of authority, in placing a party "in authority" the legitimacy of the authority is located in the act of appointment itself. The credentials by which authority is recognised is, therefore, not dependent upon a subjective reading of the officer, but objective by nature of the office.

Those who are "in authority" are therefore in a formal position whereby authority is prescribed by nature of the office or status. This authority is one that can be defined with a job description or constitution and has boundaries to what it may affect formally, with authority effectively delegated from those who formulate these descriptions or constitutions. While "in authority" is a formalised locus of authority,

---

23. Friedman, "Concept of Authority," 77.

whose position is not questioned per se, nevertheless those who are "in authority" may possess methods to secure compliance to their authority if such is necessary.

Such methods of compliance are what separate "in authority" from the moral or descriptive "an authority" as it brings with it the weight of an authorising body. Although Platonic authority may disapprove of such measures, preferring instead for a consensual relationship between the parties, the pragmatism associated with being "in authority" dictates that formalised authority requires appropriate measures to secure—or compel—obedience.

Being "an Authority"

In distinction to being "in authority," a party who is deemed to be "an authority" has not achieved such a status through formal appointment, but may be regarded as such as a result of other achievements or qualifications. Friedman suggests that such an authority "is thought to have special knowledge, wisdom, or insight or to be the recipient of a revelation or unique experience not available to other men."[24] Those regarded as "an authority" cannot be considered such through a *de facto* recognition of office or status, but are considered such in an optional manner, "because of certain special personal characteristics that set him apart from other men."[25] Whereas "in authority" is formally prescribed with its defined jurisdiction, those parties regarded as "an authority" have no such role to fulfil while their authority may extend across a wider sphere.

Therefore, based on Friedmann's argument, the existence of "an authority" presupposes two things. First, that there must be inequality between individuals that allows for such authority to be present. The nature of being "an authority" necessitates superior knowledge which must indicate that one person is more wise, knowledgeable, experienced, qualified or has received particular revelation or insight. This is unlike "in authority" where equality between individuals may prevail while one person is chosen to lead.

The second presupposition, which draws on the work of Alasdair MacIntyre, suggests that it is only possible to concede to "an authority" if it is epistemologically feasible to recognise an authority on a topic. This

24. Friedman, "Concept of Authority," 80.
25. Friedman, "Concept of Authority," 81.

requires a framework that acknowledges that there is something on which someone may be "an authority." MacIntyre's example is that an authority on playing chess is only feasible because there are prior agreed rules to play the game, and thus it is only possible to be "an authority" in the game because the game has pre-agreed rules. The framework in which an individual may be regarded as "an authority," therefore, is dependent upon the recognition that there is some epistemological way in which "an authority" might provide authority on a topic or field.

Because it relies upon an inequality of special knowledge or wisdom, or on the unique acknowledgement that authority is feasible, "an authority" is fundamentally different to "in authority":

> In the latter case, a person claims that his decisions should be deferred to because he has authority; if he does not have authority, there is no reason to defer to him. By contrast, in the case of being "an authority," the person claims he should have authority because of his special capacities: if people do not acknowledge his authority, it remains the case that they ought to, since his special knowledge does not cease just because he lacks acknowledgement.[26]

While "in authority" may be regarded as procedural, drawing on office or status, "an authority" has a role in providing for the formation of a belief "and not merely external conformity." In this way, "an authority" is responsible for providing "a statement to be believed" rather than a prescriptive pronouncement to be followed.[27] It is in the acknowledgement of "an authority" (or, indeed, the refusal to acknowledge a supposed authority) where it becomes possible to defer to one individual in the pursuit of a belief. Charismatic authority, as Weber describes, to which this form of authority most readily relates, is therefore about convicting or compelling another of a belief and not about ensuring action. Thus acknowledgement of "an authority" is reliant on the recipient's belief that such authority is to be believed. Only on such occasions does "an authority" exist.

The different forms of authority, explored here as "in" and "an" authority, demonstrate the formal and informal nature of authority and the ways in which such authority and influence can be seen to have a common locus. These two forms, therefore, provide two different types

---

26. Friedman, "Concept of Authority," 81.
27. Friedman, "Concept of Authority," 81.

of authority that can be understood to have authoritative effect and thus ensure obedience, albeit through different means. However, the distinctions in these forms can only be seen in the way in which obedience is affected and not in the results themselves.

Another Side of Authority

As mentioned previously, authority may be defined in simple terms as a way of securing obedience. Although scholars are keen to emphasise that such authority must be without violence or coercion, these distinctions are not apparent in popular discourse on authority. Frank Furedi, in his analysis of the Jimmy Savile scandal which first made the news in 2012, outlines the difficulty which arises when talking about authority within contemporary culture:

> Unmasking authority has become a fashionable enterprise that resonates with popular culture. Those who hold positions of responsibility and power—politicians, parents, teachers, priests, doctors, nursery workers—are regularly "exposed" for abusing their authority. The fact that the word "authority" is associated so readily with the act of abuse is symptomatic of Western society's disenchantment with the so-called authority figure.[28]

The corruption of authority, and its "unmasking," produces a difficulty for the concept of authority. If such understandings were to be all pervasive, authority would be recognised universally as a damaged concept. In some ways, Furedi suggests that such a point has already been reached while Austin judges that it is "the common assumption in Western societies today that we can and should live with as little authority as possible."[29] This, however, is to acknowledge the fallibility of authority without considering its purpose. Austin emphasises the need for authority in order for human flourishing. It is the need for leadership to direct and to provide flourishing that supplies the purpose for authority in society. He argues: "Without authority, people cannot act in concert except in the least complex of situations, and in particular we would fail to achieve such complex projects as require the sustained, coordinated effort of humans over time. So human society requires authority."[30]

28. Furedi, *Moral Crusades*, 86.
29. Austin, *Up with Authority*, 124.
30. Austin, *Up with Authority*, 125.

It is, therefore, in providing for the social flourishing of communities that authority, flawed, fallible and liable to err as it may be, becomes necessary.

On one side of authority, however, is coercion. To coerce a party into compliance or obedience tends to cause such compliance against their will. In the cases of force or violence such compliance is clearly not voluntary. In terms of violent coercion, this includes not only physical force applied to the person or the person's possessions, but also psychological abuse which might occur, for example, through bullying or the theft of intellectual property.

When force is used to coerce, authority ceases to be characterised by voluntary consent and is replaced by involuntary coercion. Such a use, therefore, contravenes any sense of equality between parties. Reformer Martin Luther turns to Augustine to argue that "no one can or ought to be forced to believe anything against his will."[31] Such a position is similarly argued by John Locke insofar as it would be contrary to human nature to consent to something that would cause damage to property: "no rational creature can be supposed to change [their] condition with an intention to be worse."[32] The result, therefore, is that coercion whereby an individual's physical or mental wellbeing is taken away cannot be consensual. In a summary of wrong use, Arthur Ripstein outlines how property, contract and status can be used in ways that are not in keeping with the voluntary nature of consent:

> The wrong in property is that of interfering with another's ability to set and pursue such ends as he has set for himself. The wrong in contract is failing to advance another's end in a way that you have given him a right to have it advanced. The wrong in status is using another person to advance my ends. In so doing, I deprive that person of the freedom to set his or her own ends.[33]

Therefore, the reduction of freedom afforded through the use of coercion means that flourishing is no longer possible. While alternative interpretations of authority may be based on other premises, when focused on securing flourishing it is not logically possible, therefore, that coercion expresses authority.

---

31. Luther, *On Secular Authority*, 26.
32. Locke, "Second Treatise," 156 (§131).
33. Ripstein, "Authority and Coercion," 19.

A non-forcible coercion, however, is not destructive and can be regarded as persuasion. When being persuaded of a point, the parties consider the authority to be "an authority" and are therefore responding to the authority as a knowledgeable influence. This voluntary acceptance may therefore occur as a result of the parties' consent to concur with the authority. Such a position advocates the voluntary contract entered into through the nature of social and relational interaction and is grounded in the Lockean idea that people would consent only to improve their position, not to reduce it. As participants in the contract, however, parties are not equal; in cases of persuasion the influence of one party over the other is greater. In terms of a voluntary contract, the role of the authority places an inequality in the relationship. It is this inequality which must be treated with care if persuasion is to result in a truly voluntary assent to authority.

While coercion is most often recognised as a failing of authority, it is possible to consider persuasion as a valid component of the consensual relationship. In terms of persuasion, when obedience is secured by consent, it is possible to recognise this as an influence in the functioning of authority. However in the case of any use of coercion whereby the person's freedom has been contravened or removed, the voluntary and flourishing properties of authority are similarly displaced. The paradoxical challenge of coercion is recognised by Timo Airaksinen who argues against the legitimacy of coercion in authority: "It simply should not be practiced as it implies threats, violence and bondage. Still its total rejection implies a utopian anarchist theory without a real-life basis."[34] Therefore, it is clear that while authority is most legitimately demonstrated through securing obedience by non-coercive means, persuasion has its place in understanding the concept of authority as to disregard it is to remove any "real-life basis" to authority's influence.

While coercion is focused on the ability of the subject of the authority to secure obedience, trust is a factor that rests much more with the object and on the reception of the authority. Trust is a complicating factor in any relationship and invites parties to make judgments based on factors that are not always tangible. However, it is a party's trust in an authoritative figure that may influence the extent to which obedience may be secured.

---

34. Airaksinen, "Coercion, Deterrence, and Authority," 115.

While authority does not depend upon any specific relational characteristic, trust can be understood in terms of two aspects: competence and motivation.[35] While relationships exist where these two aspects are absent, trust is dependent upon the assessment of these two factors. The apparent competence of an individual, Council, or organisation rests largely on social factors such as the experience of past behaviour and the broad level of ability and training those involved can demonstrate. It is a largely quantifiable assessment of a party's trustworthiness.

Like competency, motivation is a complex matter, complicated by the challenge to discover and assess the evidence on which to base any reasoned conclusions about motivation. Motivation is a characteristic that is less clearly defined by external factors (such as evidence of formal qualifications or a resumé) while it is open to being influenced by outsiders such as peers, organisations, advertising and so on.

Whereas competence is largely assessed quantitatively, motivation is based on personal values, beliefs and aspirations and is thus largely qualitative. Those with similar values and beliefs may therefore be understood to be more trustworthy because of common motivations and aspirations, while those who inhabit a different belief or social system may arouse more scepticism. Being formed of so many facets the question of trustworthiness, therefore, is not one that is easily answered.[36]

Trust, therefore, may affect the way in which authority is regarded and the extent to which it may affect obedience. In terms of those "in authority" trust does not have a direct bearing on its ability to operate. If doubt about the actions of someone "in authority" creeps in, the only possible avenues to follow are mutiny or desertion. Trust is unlikely to nuance a response to those "in authority." However, trust has a greater impact on those regarded as "an authority." In these cases, if the authority is unable to convince of their trustworthiness, they are unlikely to affect belief of those they are influencing. In such cases, they will no longer be

---

35. Cook et al., *Cooperation without Trust?*, 21–22.

36. A number of studies have considered trust and trustworthiness, including: Bachmann, "At the Crossroads"; Dekker, "Political Trust"; Dietz, "Going Back to the Source"; Furedi, *Culture of Fear*; Marty, *Building Cultures of Trust*; Parry, "Distrust and Consensus"; Reed, "Organization"; Seligman, *The Problem of Trust*; Tan and Lim, "Trust in Coworkers"; Woolthuis et al., "Trust, Contract and Relationship Development."

Other studies explore the effects of religion on trustworthiness, including: Proctor, "Religion as Trust in Authority"; Welch et al., "Trust in God"; Wisneski et al., "Religiosity and Trust."

regarded as "an authority." A lack of trust may, therefore, adversely affect the extent to which an authority is considered capable of securing obedience, while increased trust may enable compliance.

In light of these further considerations, it may be possible to refine the definition of authority suggested previously. Rather than being simply *that which can secure obedience*, it is clear that it is pertinent to consider the voluntary nature of compliance. This considers the effect of persuasion as a factor that is permitted within a consensual relationship, yet prevents the legitimation of coercive force or violence as part of an understanding of authority. True authority, therefore, has to be secured voluntarily.

The exploration of trust further demonstrates that authority is trustworthy when it is competent to secure obedience. This places upon both parties the need to demonstrate their competence if authority is to be secured. Awareness of a party's credentials, be that position or experience, can inform parties of the competence of the party holding authority and therefore aid obedience. It is possible to secure obedience if it is clear that a person holds authority. It becomes necessary, therefore, in order to facilitate obedience, that authority must also be clearly visible.

These two additions, therefore, add both clarity to the presence of authority and the voluntary nature of its obedience to create a suggested definition:

> True authority is that which can, *through explicit means,* secure *voluntary* obedience.

Thus, voluntary obedience becomes the outcome of true authority. Although securing obedience may be perceived as counter to such voluntary compliance, the voluntary nature of authority provides a freedom of choice to accept the authority being explicitly expressed. It is, therefore, the consensual acceptance of authority, in line with the subject's will, that provides the voluntary obedience. Thus, where obedience is achieved against the consent of the subject, true authority ceases to exist. The acceptance of true authority is, therefore, characterised through the influence of either "in" authority (where compliance is secured) or "an" authority (where authority is accepted as a result of reason or epistemological recognition).

Authority in Theology and the Church

The exploration of the concept of authority until this point has paid no attention to distinctive qualities concerning authority which pertain to a theological or ecclesial framework. Yet doctrine and ecclesiology offer two distinct yet interlinked contexts in which to examine authority: concept and practice. Focus on the Church offers a practical exploration of authority as it is expressed in the life of the community of believers. In this way, authority in the Church, while informed by the underlying theology of the Church and based on specified sources, concerns both what Gordon Arthur describes as executive authority, namely the authority employed by the Church to make decisions, and also that of non-executive authority, described as the teaching authority (or influence) of the Church.[37] These two forms of authority categorise the Church's ability to manage its own life (to be "in authority") while speaking to its members and others about the Christian teachings the Church has agreed (certainly as "an authority" in people's lives, but potentially seen also as "in authority" in the lives of others).

It is through its decision-making and its teaching that the empirically realised authority of the Church can be explored. Authority, therefore, is an important part of the way in which the Church is present in the world and indicates much about how the Church can be seen as a body in the life of the world. Authority is an ecclesiological question, open to ecumenical and contextual variations.

Such variations were apparent in an ecumenical consultation convened by the Faith and Order Commission of the World Council of Churches held in Moscow in 2011. The differences in ecclesiological understandings across the ecumenical spectrum were demonstrated through the varied use of authoritative sources for different traditions, including such diversity as the Holy Spirit, the Church congregation, reason, hierarchy, liturgical texts, and the Magisterium. In her "Editor's Introduction" to a volume produced after the consultation, Tamara Grdzelidze states that "it became clear that each source contributes in a very specific way to the church's authority, and these specific ways of contributing define their roles for various traditions."[38] The understanding of authority, therefore, is seen differently in the particularities of different Church communions, traditions and polities, each emphasising nuanced

---

37. Arthur, *Law, Liberty and Church*, 5–6.
38. Grdzelidze, "Editor's Introduction," xii.

differences in their understanding of "in" and "an" authority. As authority is understood differently in the various Churches, the way in which authority is realised in the Churches informs the different ecclesiological understandings, structures and ministries. It could therefore be argued that a central issue resulting in the existence and continuation of the vast variation of Churches is that of a difference in understanding of authority. This makes authority a key consideration in ecumenical ecclesiology.

However, while authority in the Church is concerned with the practical outworking of theological principles, it is the more conceptual understanding of authority in a theological sense in doctrine that provides a basis for ecclesiology. It is the purpose of authority in theology that focuses again on compelling obedience. P. T. Forsyth, the early twentieth-century Congregational theologian, remarks that authority "is not a passivity but a receptivity, a loyalty, an obedience."[39] He continues:

> For religion is an obedience before it is a liberty; and its first requisite is an authority; and for authority the first need is a real objective which is at once the source of our life, the home of our soul, and the God of our worship.[40]

Authority in theology, therefore, is concerned most notably with the source of that authority. Forsyth remarks that "authority which has its source in ourselves is no authority."[41] Theology, therefore, is concerned with an authority that is located not in earthly people or institutions but located finally in the authority of the triune God. This authority, revealed by the mediator of Jesus Christ, the Word, is the location of the final authority in theology. Forsyth states: "The final authority is a gracious God in salvation—miraculous, because if we could explain this act He would cease to be an authority, and the authority would then be the explanatory principle."[42]

This is echoed too by Grdzelidze, writing in response to the World Council of Churches consultation, by considering that the "ultimate authority in the church is Jesus Christ and his ministry."[43] Thus, for Forsyth, the location of authority, ecclesiological speaking, is to be found in event and person, not in the prescribed texts of creeds, ecumenical Councils,

---

39. Forsyth, *Principle of Authority*, 174.
40. Forsyth, *Principle of Authority*, 211.
41. Forsyth, *Principle of Authority*, 299.
42. Forsyth, *Principle of Authority*, 302.
43. Grdzelidze, "Editor's Introduction," xii.

catechisms, confessions, tracts or systematic expositions. Therefore, such assertions require recognition that authority is not available directly but draws on a number of sources and interprets them for the context.

Regarding Authority

The concept of authority involves a multiplicity of understandings which are contextually driven. Where Arendt sought to understand the post-war German context in light of Fascism, her context required an understanding of authority that was directed towards an understanding of a free state. Austin's exploration, focused on the importance of human flourishing, highlights the community benefits that come from the successful use of authority. A functional description of authority works only where the functions authority provides are needed and demonstrable, and yet portrays authority as a negative force in the world, against a Platonic ideal of social cohesion, freedom and equality.

Such difficulties with authority make it a challenging aspect to study as an understanding of it conceptually is so dependent upon contextual indicators. The same is true in considering the concept of authority within theological discourse. The Church's understanding of its context—its theology and its socio-historical background—influences the way in which the Church can begin to understand the place of authority in its life.

As can be seen in this complex discussion of authority, the impact of authority in the life of United and Reformed Churches has a number of considerations. If the premise of authority itself is that of securing obedience, then questions quickly arise as to the purpose of such obedience. On the face of it, Austin's understanding of authority as fulfilling the purpose of human flourishing satisfies all possible explanations. However, in the context of a Church, the flourishing which is sought is achieved in obedience to God, for it is God who seeks to "secure voluntary obedience."

In being voluntarily achieved, therefore, obedience to God is as a result neither of force nor compulsion, but is a result of the miracle of salvation. Through event and action, the believer can be convicted and assured of God's authority and, in doing so, obedience is secured.

As a source for the Church, the authority of God is fundamental and unquestionable. However, in the outworking of the life of the Church, the quest of ecclesiology is to offer the same freedom, equality and flourishing within the life of the Church that God offers to each believer. It remains, therefore, the task of the Church to ensure that in seeking obedience to the institution, it too is seeking to, "through explicit means, secure voluntary obedience." In the freedom and equality of the Church, particularly one with a United and Reformed polity, such authority is paramount.

2

A United and Reformed Church

THE FORMATION OF THE United Reformed Church (URC) was a momentous act that marked the first time since the Reformation that two Churches of different traditions had united in England.[1] In bringing together two different forms of Church governance, each infused with different understandings of mission, ministry and membership, the union provided a crucible in which the diverse and historically grounded perceptions and experiences of authority were tested and refined. The staunch Independency of early Congregationalism was to be cast together with the formulated Conciliarity of Presbyterianism.

Yet, however momentous the union was in historical terms, the resultant denomination was not to become uniform, but was to develop its own sense of uniformity. The inherited understandings of authority from the different Reformed traditions, together with aspirations for the new Church's authority, would enrich and restrict the denomination's understanding of mission, ecclesiology and, ultimately, identity. It may be astonishing that such a union was possible, but questions of authority have never been far from the denomination's story.

In his short publication, *Getting the name right*, published by the URC, Keith Forecast explored what it meant for the URC's self-understanding to be regarded as United and Reformed.[2] At its most basic, this understanding is grounded in an awareness of what it means to be Christians living out the Gospel, seeing "its formation and growth as a

---

1. Introductions to the URC can be found in Slack, *URC*; Taylor, *Tell Me*; URC History Society, *URC*. See also McIntosh, *Elders Meeting*; Robson, *Church Meeting*.
2. Forecast, *Getting the Name Right*, 23–44.

part of what God is doing to make his people one" (§A.8). It is a *United* denomination, formed through the historical action of union of several Churches. It is a *Reformed* denomination, which grounds its theological outlook and polity on the ideas generated during the sixteenth-century Magisterial Reformation and among subsequent Calvinistic traditions. It is a *Church*, a body of believers in the present seeking to live out the Christian gospel in the world. It seeks to give concrete expression to these ideas through adherence to its foundational document, the *Basis of Union*. These aspects each characterise the way in which the URC is to be understood and gives a framework through which it can be described.

The URC's *Basis of Union* states both that the URC "as a united church will take, wherever possible and with all speed, further steps towards the unity of all God's people" (§A.8) and also "reserves its right and declares its readiness at any time to alter, add to, modify or supersede [the] Basis so that its life may accord more nearly with the mind of Christ" (§A.9). The provisionality of the denomination's structure is, therefore, grounded in the understanding that the Church remains open to consider the way in which Christ calls the Church and to follow when this changes. It is through recognising that the denomination is to be provisional in its polity, while committed to the call to be united, that the eschatological nature of the Church is demonstrated. Thus, the URC recognises that its ecclesiology is not yet perfected and one which cannot be until The Church is fully and organically united. A Church that is united while continuing to seek unity, and structured but provisionally so, is the result.

History: The Story of Becoming United

David Cornick's influential history of the URC, *Under God's Good Hand*, was written when the denomination was twenty-five years old. Cornick traced the separate history of the three traditions in chronological order and discussed the social and ecclesiastical developments which accounted for the emergence of the URC's antecedent denominations. To be a historian of the URC, Cornick noted, is "to consider not one denomination but three, as well as the united church itself."[3] Although he comprehensively explored the antecedent traditions, Cornick's book did

---

3. Cornick, *Under God's Good Hand*, 1. Cornick wrote prior to the union with the Congregational Union of Scotland.

little to address the contemporary realisation of the URC or to explore in depth the union and the resulting Church, recognising that "history [was] too close and little serious research [had] been undertaken on the contemporary United Reformed Church."[4] A further twenty-five years on, at the marking of the URC's Golden Jubilee, the passage of time provides a useful and necessary perspective from which to review the union.

The word *United* in the denomination's title reflects the historical background which led to its formation and a reflection of the wider pursuit by denominations in the United Kingdom to work towards greater organic union. The origins of the movement towards Church union are rooted in the early part of the twentieth century. Conversations to explore closer collaboration between the Congregational Union of England and Wales (CUEW) and the Presbyterian Church of England (PCE) in the 1930s and 1940s had not produced any firm commitment to union of the two traditions although the Free Churches had become closer during the nineteenth century, usually united to fight for their rights against a State which continued to exclude them in various ways and manifested locally in Free Church Councils and nationally in the Free Church Federal Council.[5] During the twentieth century, the Free Churches gradually became less hostile to the privileges of the Established Church. And yet, despite the formation of the British Council of Churches in 1942, the wider ecumenical scene in Britain after the Second World War had reached what David Cornick describes as an "ecumenical impasse" centred on the question of episcopal ordination.[6] In 1946, Geoffrey Fisher, at that time Archbishop of Canterbury, preached the university sermon in Cambridge, and called upon the Free Churches to "take episcopacy into their system," and thus open up ways of closer intercommunion.[7] For Fisher, the primary stumbling block for mutual recognition of ministry revolved around the perceived invalidity of a ministry which was deemed to fall outside the so-called apostolic succession due to the lack of episcopal ordination. Fisher's sermon intended that paths be opened for the sharing, and maybe later the uniting, of the Churches in England.

---

4. Cornick, *Under God's Good Hand*, 183.

5. Personal recollections of the process towards union are recorded notably by Arthur Macarthur and John Huxtable. See Huxtable, *As It Seemed*; Macarthur, *Setting Up Signs*; Macarthur, "Formation of the URC."

6. Cornick, *Under God's Good Hand*, 168.

7. Rawlinson and Micklem, *Church Relations in England*, 11.

The Archbishop's invitation was pursued. Conversations between representatives of the Archbishop of Canterbury and representatives of the Evangelical Free Churches in England examined the challenges on both sides of the discussion, ranging from issues of ordination and re-ordination, to women's ministry (at that time accepted among many of the Free Churches but not permitted in the Church of England).[8] The Church of Scotland was minded to pursue Fisher's call for a modified form of episcopacy, and there was interest in some quarters of the PCE to form a partnership with their Scottish cousins. The plan was "to take bishops-in-presbytery into the Scottish system" where "[t]hey would be ordained by Anglican bishops and act as permanent Moderators of presbyteries."[9] As a result of PCE interest in the Scottish scheme, the Congregational-Presbyterian conversations in England suffered. However, the Church of Scotland later rejected the scheme and neither the Church of England nor the English Presbyterians had the opportunity to test the proposals.[10]

In 1959, Howard Stanley, then the General Secretary of the CUEW, announced in an Address to the May Assembly the work of a project entitled "The Next Ten Years." Consisting of eight Commissions established by the Union's Council the previous year, "The Next Ten Years" sought to grapple with the issues Stanley had observed of disunity, despairing, complaining and "no sure sense of purpose or mission" within the CUEW.[11]

Of the Commissions that were subsequently established, two of them created significant ripples throughout English and Welsh Congregationalism and impacted directly on the discussions which would eventually lead to the establishment of the URC. Commission II was mandated with the task of generating a *Statement of Faith*. English Congregationalists had produced declarations previously. In forming the CUEW in May 1832, a "summary . . . much more compendious [than the Savoy Declaration of 1658] and more appropriate to the present need" was circulated to congregations and in the following year it was "accepted as the Declaration of the Congregational Body, with the distinct understanding, that it is not intended as a test or creed for subscription."[12] In

---

8. Rawlinson and Micklem, *Church Relations in England*, 35–41.

9. Cornick, *Under God's Good Hand*, 169.

10. Cornick, *Under God's Good Hand*, 169; see also Macarthur, "Formation of the URC," 7.

11. Stanley, *Next Ten Years*, 4.

12. Walker, *Creeds of Congregationalism*, 546.

1960, the Constitution of the CUEW referred to the simple doctrinal confession of faith as "To serve and bear witness to the Kingdom of God by confessing and proclaiming Almighty God as Creator, Sustainer and Father of all, Jesus Christ His Son as Lord and Saviour, and the Holy Spirit as the living power of God."[13] During the process which eventually led to the birth of the URC, efforts to create a more comprehensive statement were met with requests to maintain the simple confession of faith and not to apply further doctrinal conditions upon Congregational membership. Yet in the creation of a *Declaration of Faith* it was asserted that "its formulation is not imposed upon any as a definition of what must be held; but . . . as an acceptable statement of truths which each church member is summoned to make his own in his own way."[14] Thus, the Commission, the Congregational Council, and the denomination as a whole navigated the many criticisms of subscribing to a confessional statement and in 1967 published the agreed *Declaration of Faith*.

In his Address to the Assembly in 1959, subsequently published for wider circulation, Stanley made sure that the delegates were aware of the nostalgia he had encountered in his travels, where there was

> a stubborn refusal to accept the present times as normal, as if the clock would somehow, sometime be put back and morning coats and spats re-appear, and it would again be the done thing to go on Sunday to the church,—all this needed to be shed and replaced by a realistic facing of a new challenging, contemporary situation, the eyes of the church focussed to discern the signs of these new times, and its ears attuned, not to some echoes of a day for ever passed, but to the voice of the living Spirit of God.[15]

In this context, Commission I was mandated with addressing the contemporary challenges to Congregational polity. The Commission soon invited the Union to consider adopting a change that would give a stronger sense of denominational identity. Stanley wrote in the *Congregational Monthly* in 1961 to advocate change and to give an opportunity for a wider consultation. He stated the Commission's premise: "The Commission is united in the view that the member churches of the Union should be invited to enter a covenanted relationship with one another," before going on to elaborate that "it is necessary for

---

13. *CUEW Constitution*, 3(i), in CYB (1960) 27.
14. CCEW, *Declaration of Faith*, 4.
15. Stanley, *Next Ten Years*, 4–5.

Congregational churches to covenant with one another for the purpose of their distinctive Churchmanship and to express in some corporate form their 'belonging together' which is so plainly a fact of their experience."[16] While the concept of the Local Church as a body of believers gathered in one place and covenanted together to live the Christian life and bear witness to the gospel was familiar to Congregationalists, this proposal invited Local Churches, rather than individual Christians, to enter into a covenant with each another to form a wider body, and therefore to extend the commitment of "belonging together" that covenant itself enshrined.

To complement the circulation of the report around the Union, the Commission produced *Some Questions and Answers*, a short document addressing some of the topics that were raised in considering the Commission's proposal. In addition to addressing concerns about centralisation the Commission stated that the object of the proposal was "not directly to bring Church union nearer, but it is in the mind of the Commission that the proposed covenanted relationship might remove some difficulties which are at present in the way."[17] When the proposal was brought to the CUEW Assembly in May 1962 for a decision to be made on the way forward, Stanley reported that eighty-two Churches had previously expressed themselves against the proposals while 656 Churches had expressed in favour (eighty-nine had requested further detail).[18] The vote on the recommendation passed with less than a dozen votes against and a Draft Constitution Committee was formed—of which a number of members would later be involved in the Joint Committee negotiating the formation of the URC.[19] On completion of the Committee's work, the proposed constitution was circulated to Local Churches for indications of response. The minutes of the Assembly in 1966 record that 1761 Local Churches (representing 80 percent of Local Church members) were in favour, while forty-two Local Churches (representing 1.2 percent of the Local Church membership) were against (fifty-six had deferred decisions and twenty-four were in correspondence with the Union). With the approval of the CUEW Assembly (with 1776 votes in favour

---

16. Stanley, "Message," 20.
17. CUEW, *Some Questions and Answers*, A.8.
18. CYB (1962) 89.
19. CYB (1962) 90.

and forty-two votes against), the Congregational Church in England and Wales (CCEW) was inaugurated at the Assembly in May 1966.[20]

Throughout the process to form the CCEW, the approach adopted by the Union sought to reflect the accepted process of authority within the CUEW. The involvement of the Assembly to form the Commissions and to steer the relevant committees resulted in proposals being put to Local Churches for consideration. Although the Assembly was permitted to produce such proposals, the engagement and response of the Local Churches were the characterising features of the Congregational approach to authority. The authority in Congregationalism, therefore, relied not on central proposals, however well informed and devised, but upon the concurrence of the Local Churches.

Meanwhile, with separate proposals involving conversation with the Church of England and the Congregationalists, the PCE needed clarity in its direction. Standing in a car park after a 1959 conference in Rugby to discuss their options, Arthur Macarthur (then Convenor of the PCE's Inter-Church Relations Committee) recalled a "decisive" conversation where Tim Healey, the PCE's General Secretary, informed him of an approach from the CUEW "to ask if the time had not come for a renewal of direct conversation."[21] A number of conversations followed between PCE and CUEW officers before a proposal to pursue formal conversations was put to the two respective Assemblies in 1963. Following the approval of both Assemblies, the Joint Committee first met in November 1963.

The Congregational-Presbyterian Joint Committee

The membership of the Joint Committee consisted of a panel of representatives from both the CUEW and the PCE, totalling thirty-four in number. When John Huxtable became General Secretary of the CUEW in 1964, John Marsh took his place as Joint Chairman of the Committee (Huxtable remained on the committee *ex officio*) while on the Presbyterian side, Frank McConnell took over as Joint Chairman when Alec Neil was taken ill and subsequently died. Martin Cressey, a young Presbyterian minister serving in Coventry, was appointed Secretary of the Joint Committee. A number of key individuals from both denominations became members of the Committee, representing a broad spectrum

20. CYB (1966) 88.
21. Macarthur, "Formation of the URC," 8.

of expertise. Most notable among the participants were the Revds J. A. Figures (Lancashire County Union), A. L. Macarthur (by that time PCE General Secretary), A. G. MacLeod (Principal of Westminster College), and H. S. Stanley (previously CUEW General Secretary).

A number of other members played important roles during the process of the Committee, including the Revd. Ronald Bocking (key in drawing up Synod and District boundaries), Sir Harold Banwell (responsible for legal arrangements) and the PCE's Legal Adviser Norman Pooler. The Revd. Kenneth Slack was notable among the participants as the only member to sit on the Joint Committee first as a Presbyterian and later as a Congregational minister, changing his denominational service during the time of the talks.[22] Due to ill health, Hubert Cunliffe-Jones, the Associate Principal of Northern College (an independent Theological College training Congregational Ministers) and Professor of Theology in the University of Manchester, was unable to participate for long in the work of the Committee, yet left his legacy to the group in the first draft of "A statement of convictions on which a united Church, both catholic and reformed, might be built"—a document that Arthur Macarthur asserted "laid the foundation of the whole enterprise."[23]

Norman Pooler, the PCE Legal Advisor, sat on the Joint Committee throughout its life and, together with Philip Simpson (CUEW/CCEW Legal Advisor), took a leading role in drawing together the legal framework for the proposed union. There was awareness among the denominational legal experts of the complex legal disputes that occurred after the formation of the United Free Church of Scotland from the union of the United Presbyterian Church of Scotland and the majority of the Free Church of Scotland in 1900. A minority of congregations of the Free Church of Scotland rejected the union and they asserted that in altering the Church's principles the majority had departed from doctrine and thus forfeited their claim on the assets of the Free Church of Scotland. On appeal of a Session Court, the House of Lords (General Assembly of the Free Church of Scotland v. Lord Overtoun [1904] AC 515) ruled in favour of those who did not join the union, regarding the minority as "the true Free Church," resulting in the transfer of assets that were "disproportionately great for the number of members of the true Free Church."[24]

---

22. Coates, "Slack, Kenneth," 207.
23. Macarthur, "Formation of the URC," 9, 15.
24. Paton, "Opinion," §§7–8.

For obvious reasons, this was a situation the Joint Committee sought to avoid. The easiest way to ensure that such a situation could not arise was to transfer all property automatically and to place this within a legal framework that would not be open to subsequent legal challenge. Pooler's presentation of this plan to the Joint Committee in December 1968 elicited enthusiastic applause.[25] Within this approach, merger of the two denominations would not be sufficient as the "two ways of being the Church were too diverse for patchwork"; both denominations had to vote to cease and a new denomination needed to be voted into existence.[26] To ensure that the property of the two denominations would be legally recognised as belonging to the URC and establish a method for disposal of assets, Pooler and Simpson advised the Joint Committee that an Act of Parliament would be necessary. The Bill subsequently placed before Parliament ensured that doctrine and structure remained the responsibility of the denomination while the legal trusts were consolidated from their respective Congregational and Presbyterian trustees and combined as URC assets. While the use of legislation was to ensure that the legal trusts were appropriately apportioned, the effect of the URC Acts in 1972, 1981, and 2000 has been to restrict the authority of the denomination to make certain amendments to the URC's structure without the need for further legislation.

After the establishment of the Joint Committee, an informal approach to explore possibilities of union was made from the Union Committee of the Churches of Christ.[27] The Churches of Christ represented another aspect of British nonconformity with distinctive qualities of "weekly communion and believer's baptism by immersion."[28] After the 1964 Faith and Order Conference in Nottingham, the Churches of Christ made informal approaches to the Congregational-Presbyterian Joint Committee and the Baptist Union. In 1966 the Union Committee of the Churches of Christ was formally authorised by its Association's Annual Conference to continue exploring possibilities of union with

---

25. Pooler, *Proposed Legal Arrangements*, 4; Also: "It earned the only spontaneous applause that I recall during those nine years" (Macarthur, "Formation of the URC," 14; echoed in Macarthur, *Setting Up Signs*, 104–5). And: "Mr. Norman Pooler made a speech of such considerable consequence that, as far as I can recall, it was the only one delivered to that Joint Committee which was applauded" (Huxtable, *As it Seemed*, 58).

26. Macarthur, "Formation of the URC," 14–15.

27. Thompson, *Let Sects and Parties Fall*, 190.

28. Thompson, *Let Sects and Parties Fall*, 9.

other Churches. David M. Thompson's history of the Churches of Christ recollects that the Congregational-Presbyterian Joint Committee "readily invited Churches of Christ to send observers" and that these observers "rapidly discovered that their comments on the draft plan of union were very seriously considered."[29]

During the 1960s, the Congregational-Presbyterian Joint Committee worked to draw together a number of proposals which were discussed in committee and sub-committee, and then, when in a form possible for wider comment and discussion, submitted to the respective Assemblies for information, discussion and, ultimately, decision. This "scrutiny of all concerned" became part of the process and "the Committee did its utmost to draw the churches into the conversation at every point."[30] The Assemblies of both denominations were given opportunity to discuss and referred for consideration at local level the *Statement of Convictions* (1965), a draft *Constitution* (1967), an interim report (1968) and a *Scheme for Union* (1969). Sub-committees worked on the detailed sections of the *Scheme*: Group A on the doctrinal statements of the new denomination; Group B on the conciliar shape and functions; Group C on the "common life of Provinces, Districts and Local Churches and . . . how they might be served by offices and officers";[31] and Group D looked at legal, financial and property issues (although this group sub-divided at a later stage to take these issues separately). The URC's *Manual* as it came to be constituted, representing the *Basis* (A), *Structure* (B), and *Rules of Procedure* (C), can be seen, therefore, to map on to the corresponding work and responsibilities of the respective groups.[32]

Although the Joint Committee itself had conducted the lion's share of the work, the Assemblies of both denominations had to make the decision to move towards union. While Presbyterian polity allowed the PCE Assembly's decision to be binding on all Churches (without the need for a local vote), the consent of the Congregational Church's Assembly would refer the matter to local Churches to make the decision for themselves.

---

29. Thompson, *Let Sects and Parties Fall*, 190. The three Churches of Christ observers noted in the minutes for the Joint Committee's December 1968 meeting (but with apologies recorded for that meeting) were Revds. W. W. Hendry, P. Morgan, and Mr. D. Thompson.

30. Macarthur, "Formation of the URC," 10.

31. Macarthur, "Formation of the URC," 10.

32. The most up-to-date version of the Manual is found on the URC website (see URC, "The Manual").

As a reflection of their polity, it had been agreed by the Joint Committee that local Congregational Churches would require a 75 percent approval of their membership to join the URC, while local Presbyterian Churches could vote to leave the union if they voted against by greater than 75 percent of their membership.

The crucial votes came at the 1971 Assemblies. Meeting on the same day, the Assemblies both gave the required majorities: the CCEW Assembly gave 89 percent consent (1888 to 233), while the PCE Assembly consented by 79 percent (434 to 115). 1668 local Congregational Church meetings agreed to join (representing 82.2 percent of the total Congregational membership) while 597 Churches did not. Only two Presbyterian Churches, Guernsey and Jersey, voted to opt out of the union.[33]

Plans were made for both Assemblies to meet together as Uniting Assemblies in October 1972 when, in line with the requirements of the *Scheme of Union*, a declaration would be made by "each of the Uniting Assemblies voting first separately and then as one body."[34]

On 5 October 1972, it took the three thousand assembled Congregationalists and Presbyterians seven minutes to resolve to become the United Reformed Church.[35] The newly formed denomination would be defined and governed by the content of the agreed *Basis of Union*.

The approach employed in forming the URC, therefore, reflected the understanding of authority and the processes for decision-making used by the two antecedent denominations. In the CCEW, although denominational agreement was required, it was the Local Churches who were each to vote in favour of the proposals. A Local Church could dissent from the decision of the CCEW Assembly simply by taking no action. This emphasised the authority of the Local Church in matters relating to its mission. The PCE, however, placed authority on the decision of the General Assembly and required that Local Churches should vote overwhelmingly (in this case by more than three-quarters) to dissent from the Assembly's decision.

These two alternative, if not seemingly contradictory, approaches to authority reflect, therefore, the differing mentalities to decision-making that the URC inherited from its antecedent denominations. It was the

---

33. Cornick, *Under God's Good Hand*, 175.
34. URC, *Manual*, 5.
35. *Reform* (November 1972) 8 (Colin Evans).

formation of the *Basis* with such approaches in mind that led to both being possible within the URC's polity. Where dissent is to be made easily achievable while allowing for individual consent, a "Congregational" understanding of authority can be considered appropriate while in cases where denomination-wide acceptance is to be achieved, a "Presbyterian" understanding can be applied.

Further Unions

After 1972, the *United* aspect of the denomination continued to develop. Ongoing conversations with the Churches of Christ resulted in *Proposals for Unification with the United Reformed Church* being published in 1976. These proposals required the Churches of Christ to move from their Congregational polity and accept the URC's conciliar structure and required both denominations to accept "a dual baptismal policy with due recognition of conscientious objection provided that both modes of baptism were available in each congregation" in addition to the creation of an auxiliary ministry "for those in secular employment."[36] In considering the introduction of these new policies on baptism and on auxiliary ministry, these proposals reflected the URC's provisionality to its own polity whereby changes, even at an early stage of the denomination's life, could be considered in pursuit of the direction the Church felt called to take. The introduction of such a baptismal policy with the recognition of "conscientious objection" would further place into the URC's polity the right of individuals to dissent from a denominational policy, even though the denomination itself would subscribe to it.

The process for uniting with the Churches of Christ echoed the previous union by requiring two thirds of Churches to agree, each doing so by three quarters of the membership.[37] While the proposals were accepted by the URC's General Assembly in 1977, the Churches of Christ were unable to secure similar approval. Meanwhile, the Charity Commissioners had been consulted by the Churches of Christ about how legally to transact the union and the Commissioners had "advised that provision be made for the dissolution of the Association."[38] When the 1978 Annual Conference met, the Council presented a resolution that

36. Cornick, *Under God's Good Hand*, 182.
37. Cornick, *Under God's Good Hand*, 182.
38. Thompson, "Dissolution," 110.

confirmed the intention to work towards union with the URC, invited Churches which had not obtained 75 percent vote in favour "to reconsider their position in light of the majority vote of the churches," reporting such change by November that year, and authorised the Central Council either to work with the URC to bring about union or to enact the dissolution procedure.[39]

By the November deadline, there was still insufficient support among the Churches and therefore the Annual Conference of 1979 set the date of dissolution to be the 31 March 1980. Fifty-four Churches in favour of union with the URC formed the Re-formed Association of the Churches of Christ while the remaining twenty-one chose not to join. It was this body, "a new legal entity," that came into union with the URC in 1981. As a result, for the first time the URC had a presence in Scotland, making the URC a Church in three nations, though these Churches belonged to the Northern Synod, the vast majority of whose Churches were in the north-east of England.

A further series of conversations between the URC and the Congregational Union of Scotland led to union between the two denominations in 2000. Two changes in URC terminology came about as a result of this union. First, the terms "Provincial" or "Provincial Synod" were replaced with "Synod," these being "National Synods" in respect to Scotland and Wales. This was in part the result of recent political developments and the introduction of devolved Parliaments and Assemblies. The second was to use the term "Areas" instead of "Districts" in the Synod of Scotland. With these minor amendments, the *Structure* remained largely unchanged between the URC's formation and the beginning of the twenty-first century.

In three decades, the formation and expansion of an ecumenical vision had resulted in the development of a denomination that sought to manifest the essential unity of all Christians in Christ in the world by commitment to be together and "to pray and work for such visible unity in the whole church of Christ as Christ wills and in the way he wills, in order that people and nations may be led more and more to glorify the Father in heaven" (§A.Sch.D.v1.9). The provisionality of the URC's polity demonstrated through this time the need to adapt and make changes that reflected the move towards this ecumenical vision. This was incorporated through the adoption of a dual baptismal policy, auxiliary

---

39. Thompson, "Dissolution," 111.

(now known as Non Stipendiary) ministry and by the introduction of a National Synod of Scotland. While the denomination's understanding of authority had been largely defined at its formation, the union with the Churches of Christ incorporated a baptismal policy that allowed for conscientious objection and individual dissent to the denomination's policy. The development of the URC's understanding of authority thus ensured a polity in which unity, not uniformity, could be provided. While these unions offered small but important changes to the denomination's polity, it was entry into a fourth decade that brought about significant changes to the URC's polity and structure.

Polity: The Reformed Shape of the URC

The URC's polity is grounded in an understanding of Reformed churchmanship inspired and characterised by the understandings of Church order demonstrated by its antecedent Congregational and Presbyterian polities. As a conciliar Church, the URC at formation in 1972 recognised four Councils—the General Assembly, the Provincial Synod, the District Council, and the Local Church (consisting jointly of the Church Meeting and the Elders' Meeting). These Councils ensured links between the different spheres of the Church's life and connected Local Churches together into the denomination.

Much of what can be said about the URC's polity in the twenty-first century could have been said about it at the denomination's inception. The *Structure* of the denomination has been largely unaltered during the URC's lifetime, a fact attributed by one of the denomination's architects, Ronald Bocking, to the freedom of Councils "to determine the pattern that best suited their particular area."[40] Writing at the time of the denomination's twenty-fifth anniversary in 1997, he added: "This basic flexibility has served the church well over the years and has meant that the pattern for the life of the United Church worked out by the Joint Committee has needed very little constitutional change."[41]

However, by the beginning of the twenty-first century, problems created by declining and ageing membership and the fact that further union appeared unlikely had accentuated concerns within the denomination about the URC's identity. The temporary nature of the URC's existence,

40. Bocking, "Background, Formation, and After," 16.
41. Bocking, "Background, Formation, and After," 16.

focused on being a catalyst for the formation of a united Church, had previously been considered a primary strength of the denomination, because "this structure, elegant and sensible though it was, was but a stepping stone towards a greater united church in England and Wales. It was not intended to last forever."[42] Indeed, Martin Camroux regards the URC's ecumenical vision as the sole characteristic of the denomination adopted at its inception, claiming that "[t]here was little need to define a role or identity for the United Reformed Church because the Church would only be in existence for a short time."[43] He further explains the denomination's predicament through an exploration of the URC's ecumenical vision:

> The URC had been founded on a model of ecumenism which was already becoming irrelevant when the church adopted it. Beginning with no sense of purpose beyond the ecumenical it had largely failed to develop an identity. Its intellectual life had withered and its understanding of the Reformed tradition was unsure.[44]

The result was that, while the URC's structure had served well for thirty years, the challenges of denominational decline and an identity crisis led to serious discussions to make difficult decisions. In 2002, the denomination established a group to "urgently and radically re-think the Church's priorities, programmes and processes."[45] The substantive report of this *Catch the Vision* Steering Group came to the General Assembly in 2005. The report summarised the future priorities of the denomination in four categories: new ways of being Church and deeper engagement in mission; a slimmer, more rigorous organisation; renewed ecumenical commitment; a new spirituality for the twenty-first century.[46] Each of these categories invited the URC to consider its identity and to look towards positive expressions of Church at the beginning of the new millennium.

What proved to be the greatest influence of the Catch the Vision (CTV) process was the result of the second area of the report's work—namely an attempt to address the organisational structure of the URC.

---

42. URC, *CTV*, 17 (§68).
43. Camroux, "Origins of the URC," 45.
44. Camroux, "Where Do We Go from Here?," 220.
45. MC, Minute 02/97; quoted in GA Record (2004) 50.
46. URC, *CTV*, 3–9.

The report asserted that the URC's polity owed much to the provisionality included in the original drafting of the *Basis*. It emphasised "the centrality of taking counsel together, not the number of councils" used to facilitate its common life.[47] It further claimed that the denomination was "still a conciliar people," and asserted that there was "widespread agreement that our present pattern of councils hinders rather than enables our wishes to seek God's will together, enjoy fellowship in Christ and express our belonging to each other."[48] The report sought to address this hindrance.

The CTV process had a significant impact on the URC's life by abolishing District Councils (one of the Councils of the Church), establishing a biennial General Assembly and giving more authority to Mission Council. Although the claim was this maintained conciliarity, it certainly impacted significantly on authority and, arguably, did not facilitate the hoped for renewal in Church life.

As a consequence, a report produced for the General Assembly in 2018 proposed a number of changes to the post-CTV operation of the denomination, focusing on the costs involved in maintaining the existing centralised governance structures. Resolutions were brought to General Assembly in 2018 and to Mission Council in March and November 2019 to progress a number of consequential structural changes. The resolutions included returning to a smaller, annual General Assembly and an annual meeting of Mission Council—to be known once again as Assembly Executive—between meetings of Assembly, and required that Assembly Executive members from Synods had been members of the preceding General Assembly. These changes also returned the denomination to the appointment of a single General Assembly Moderator (Minister, CRCW, Elder, or lay) to serve for a year alongside the annual General Assembly, with the Moderator taking up their year of service at the end of an Assembly rather than at the start. This means Moderators chair the General Assembly at the end of their year of service rather than as their first task. Additionally, the changes removed the rotation of General Assembly venues around the denomination, fixing instead on a single location (the Hayes Conference Centre, Swanwick, Derbyshire), with a single meeting of the Assembly Executive between meetings of General Assembly. General Assembly and Mission Council approved these

---

47. URC, *CTV*, 12 (§36).
48. URC, *CTV*, 12 (§37).

changes, and annual General Assemblies took place from 2020, with an annually appointed Moderator elected in 2021, to serve from 2022.

The CTV period (2006–2021) can be thus characterised within the denomination as a period of a biennial General Assembly, together with the associated implications for Moderatorial terms of office and Mission Council authority. Subsequent changes, implemented from 2021, reversed some of the CTV changes and refocused the conciliar governance on an annual General Assembly, and a consolidated Executive.

A Reformed Structure

Maintaining conciliarity as an honoured principle of being a *Reformed Church*, the URC's structure includes local and denominational and is established in such a way as to provide for flexibility in the local and regional contextualisation of the denomination. As a result, the provisions within the *Structure* ensure that responsibilities and functions are allocated to specific conciliar bodies but that the contextual outworking of these functions are not prescribed. This allows for the different geography and demography around the denomination to be catered for in the application of the *Structure*.

This flexibility, as discussed previously, has been part of the URC's strength. Yet, as Bocking noted about the early years of the denomination: "Some found it hard to discern their freedom and there were soon cries largely because of a failure to recognise that where there seemed to be some overlap of responsibilities between District and Province [Synod] that was simply to allow for local decision."[49]

With such freedom, the arrangements for the distribution of responsibilities can take place within the locality of the relevant conciliar bodies. Such "local decision" on the application of conciliar functions and responsibilities demonstrates the claim that "no denominational bureaucracy is ever sacrosanct"[50] and also illustrates the complexity of the URC's polity. Conciliar responsibilities may be exercised in different ways in different contexts. Therefore, while the *Structure* outlines the responsibilities and functions of the conciliar bodies, the approach to overseeing those responsibilities may differ from Synod to Synod and Local Church to Local Church. The emphasis of a given locality, therefore, may

49. Bocking, "Background, Formation, and After," 16.
50. Bocking, "Background, Formation, and After," 16.

subtly alter the location of a decision and a view of delegated authority to make such a decision. Therefore, while this summary examines the general principles of the conciliar structure, differences in how the responsibilities are fulfilled between conciliar bodies may result in the same issue being dealt with differently across the denomination. Thus while the conciliar structure is based on general principles, these differences may result in a delegated authority provided to a different Council and therefore result in a shift in the locus of authority.

As outlined previously, the base element of the URC is the Local Church, understood as Christians who "associate in a locality for worship witness and service" (§B.1.(1)(a)). The Local Church, therefore, is the place in which people are gathered together in worship and witness and where the URC finds the basis for its denominational existence. The *Structure*, therefore, places an emphasis on the Local, stating that "the proper functioning of the local church is so fundamental to the life of the [URC]" (§B.1.(1)(a)).

It is the fundamental role of the Local Church in the life of the URC that places it at the beginning of any consideration of the URC's polity. The Local Church is the primary expression of the One, Holy, Catholic and Apostolic Church (§A.25). As the localised expression of the URC, it is where URC membership is held, and where the members of the denomination meet together as a Church Meeting "at least once a quarter" to "have opportunity through discussion, responsible decision and care for one another, to strengthen each other's faith and to foster the life, work and mission of the Church" (§B.2.(1)). Through the actions and decisions of the Church Meeting, therefore, the Local Church is empowered in its responsibilities towards the outworking of its expression of the URC in the locality. The *Structure* lists the functions of the Church Meeting as "Concerning the outgoing of the Church" and "Concerning the nurture of the fellowship" (§B.2.(1)), in addition to those things that "may be necessary in pursuance of its responsibility for the common life of the Church" (§B.2.(1)(xiv)). In regard to the "outgoing of the Church," it lists furthering the Church's mission, developing ecumenical relationships, supporting the wider Church "at home and abroad," addressing public questions relating to the Christian faith, and raising concerns with the wider Councils of the denomination (§§B.2.(1)(i–vi)). For nurturing the fellowship the *Structure* lists the calling of a minister or the consideration of a ministerial candidate, the election of elders, the maintaining of the membership standards and roll, the adoption of accounts and the maintenance of buildings, and the receiving of reports and proposals from the wider Councils of the URC (§§B.2.(1)(vii–xiii)).

The Elders' Meeting is formed of elders elected from the membership of the Local Church and "shall exercise oversight of the spiritual life of the local church" (§B.2.(2)). It is the responsibility of the Elders' Meeting to "serve the local church" and to "represent the whole Church to the local" (§B.2.(2)). Like Ministers, Elders are set apart for office by being ordained (which makes them eligible for election in any URC congregation at any subsequent stage). Elders serve the Local Church on terms arranged locally, but may or may not be for a fixed term (§B.2.(1)(viii)). The functions of the Elders' Meeting include fostering a concern in the Local Church for the work of the Church in the community, provision of public worship, pastoral care for the congregation, maintenance of the membership roll in consultation with the Church Meeting, recommending arrangements for the maintenance of property, bringing concerns from the Church Meeting to the wider Councils of the URC, and anything else that may be necessary for the furthering of the Church (§§B.2.(2)(i–xii)). The functions of the Elders' Meeting dovetail with those of the Church Meeting, with a consultative or recommendation role in one or both directions, and this ensures that there is a flexibility in the approach afforded to each Local Church in the way in which its responsibilities are exercised.

Concerning wider Councils of the URC, the Church Meeting and Elders' Meeting take part at different stages of the engagement with the conciliar bodies. The *Structure* indicates that Church Meeting receives business from the wider Councils for discussion and action while the Elders' Meeting is responsible for preparing and making any response. This ensures that it is the Church Meeting, as the formal conciliar body, that engages with the other Councils of the Church while the Elders' Meeting "serve the local church" by securing any required response. While this does not prevent the Elders' Meeting from engaging with the Councils of the Church, or making recommendations to the Church Meeting, the source of the response is intended to be the meeting of the membership in the Church Meeting and not its elected Eldership.

Although District Councils were abolished as a conciliar body through the CTV process (2005), the inclusion of them in the URC Acts has resulted in them remaining formally part of the *Structure*. In their original form, District Councils were a conciliar body located between the Local Church and the Synod and were concerned with the life of the

URC within the area. However since CTV, although they are defined as a separate conciliar entity there is "a single district council" in each Synod making this Council coterminous with the Synod (§B.1.(2)(a)). Its purpose and function is not, therefore, comparable with the District Councils instigated in the URC's formation. Its membership includes the Synod Moderator, and representatives chosen by the Synod (§§B.2.(3)(a–e)) and there is an expectation that the District Council should meet once per year unless notified by the secretary (§B.2.(3)). The functions are "those matters which are the responsibility of the district council under the United Reformed Church Acts of 1972, 1981 and 2000 (including the Schedules to those Acts)" (§B.2.(3)(i)) along with any other matters delegated to it by the General Assembly (§B.2.(3)(ii)). The responsibilities of the District Council, therefore, are predominantly restricted to the handling of property matters, most notably the disposal of property in line with the requirements of the URC Acts.

Between the Local Church and the denomination's General Assembly one Council exists. This is the Synod. There are eleven Synods covering England and National Synods in Scotland and Wales, totalling thirteen Synods. The term "Synod" has three connotations within the life of the URC: the representative conciliar meeting (the "Synod Meeting" usually occurs twice per year); the geographical area covered defining the region (or nation); or the governance and administration which functions from the Synod office. The term "Synod," therefore, can be used interchangeably to represent each of these meanings.

The role of the Synod is to be "representative of the local churches in that province or nation united for the purpose of dealing with matters of wider concern" (§B.2.(4)). Membership of the Synod consists of all serving Ministers in the Synod, representatives from each of the Local Churches in the Synod, those performing roles as Synod officers or interim moderators of Local Churches in vacancy, and two young people, while retired ministers who are no longer exercising an official ministry are associate members without voting rights (§§B.2.(4)(a-j)).

The work of the Synod is wide-ranging, positioned between the functions of the Local Church to ensure the local mission of the URC and the General Assembly acting as the "central organ" of the denomination (§B.2.(6)). As a result, its functions include those which are oversight functions on behalf of Local Churches and those where the Synod acts on behalf of the General Assembly (§§B.2.(4)(A)(i–xxvi)). The Synod normally meets twice a year where policies and formal decisions are made by the Council, but the work of the Synod continues throughout the year through its Officers and Committees. The oversight functions the Synod carries out include the furtherance of the Church through the development and adoption of mission initiatives within the Synod (including Church growth and extension), grouping, joining or dissolving of Local Churches, appointment of an interim moderator in the case of a pastoral vacancy, authorisation for lay people to preside at the sacraments, building, reconstruction or disposal of property, and hearing and deciding upon appeals submitted to the Synod. Other functions relate to the role of the Synod acting on behalf of the General Assembly, notably the appointment of representatives to the General Assembly ("ministerial and lay in equal numbers" and including "at least two representatives aged 26 or under"), transmission of proposals for consideration by the General Assembly, ordination of ministers and commissioning of Church Related Community Workers (CRCWs) into service in the URC, having care for the Local Churches of the Synod and the process for assessing candidates for ministry, invoking the Disciplinary or Incapacity procedure towards a minister or CRCW, and to consider the resignation of ministers and CRCWs. In these two ways, therefore, the Synod sits between the Local Church and the Denomination, offering functions on behalf of the oversight of the Local Church and acting on behalf of the General Assembly.

The Synod further embodies the relationship between the Denominational and the Local through the role of Synod Moderator. This role, appointed by the General Assembly and responsible to it, is performed by a minister of Word and Sacraments who is "separated from any local pastoral charge" and is to "preside over the meetings of the synod and exercise a pastoral office towards the ministers, CRCWs and churches within the province or nation" (§B.2.(4)). The appointment to the office of Synod Moderator (rather than to a second order of ministry) is for set period (currently seven years) with possible extension (for a further five years) (§C.7.2.1 and §C.7.2.2). In being linked to the General Assembly and the Synod in this way, the Moderator is both part of, and set apart from, the Synod, responsible to the General Assembly but with functions deeply embedded into the Synod's life. These functions include facilitating and encouraging the work of the Synod, suggesting and introducing prospective ministers to vacant pastorates, and presiding at the ordination, commissioning and induction of ministers and CRCWs. In each case, the Synod Moderator acts as an officer of the General Assembly representing the Synod and is therefore acting on behalf of one or other

Council. This duality ensures that within the Synod the Moderator represents the General Assembly, and that when the Synod Moderators meet together (as they do monthly "for the better discharge of their duties") they represent the Synod to the denomination.[51]

As each Local Church utilises the Synod's functions differently depending upon context, Synods are free to organise their own structures in order to fulfil their functions according to the *Basis* (§B.2.(4)). Each Synod maintains its own structures and procedures for its operation, to some degree making each one independent from the others. This leads to multiple ways of carrying out the functions required of Synods. Most notable among these has been the emergence of smaller groupings within Synod boundaries, in some places approximating to former District Council boundaries, and the delegation of Synod functions to these groups. This increases the diversity of approach to fulfilling the functions of the Synod, most notably regarding oversight of the Local Church where a sub-group of the Synod is better-positioned to carry out such oversight. In some parts of the denomination, Area Committees fulfil roles approximating to the pre-CTV District Councils, incorporating the pastoral functions of the Synod.

The General Assembly encompasses the entirety of the denomination within its conciliar role. As with Synod, the term "General Assembly" can relate to the conciliar body of representatives (which now meets every year), but also can refer to the work of the denomination in three-nations continued between meetings of the Assembly by Officers and Committees. It is the role of the General Assembly, therefore, to "embody the unity of the [URC] and act as the central organ of its life and the final authority, under the Word of God and the promised guidance of the Holy Spirit, in all matters of doctrine and order and in all other concerns of its common life" (§B.2.(6)). In this way, the General Assembly fulfils a role as final authority within the denomination alongside being responsible for the policy and practice of the denomination (§§B.2.(6)(i–xxviii)).

The functions of the General Assembly include oversight of the denomination (especially concerning the spread of the gospel, the welfare of the URC, and the wellbeing of the Church and the communities in which the Church is found), ecumenical interaction, setting standards for ministry and training, interpretation of doctrinal matters, invoking the Disciplinary or Incapacity procedure towards ministers or CRCWs

---

51. MC, Paper S2 (March 2014) 67 (§§21–23).

(particularly those in Assembly appointments), raising funds for the work of the Church, disseminating questions for discussion and decision by other Councils of the URC, and addressing questions raised by other Councils. Additionally, the General Assembly acts as the final authority in the URC, including the interpretation of the doctrinal statements of the denomination (including the *Basis*), ruling on when personal conviction is counter to the peace and unity of the Church, altering the *Basis* (or any other parts of the *Manual*) or any rules or procedures linked to the denomination, deciding upon the outcome of any appeals, and making decisions on the addition or removal of individuals from the Roll of Ministers or Roll of CRCWs. In fulfilling this large number of functions, therefore, the General Assembly acts in a capacity both with concern for the life of the denomination but also as its final authority.

With the Assembly meeting annually, a significant role is found for the Committees carrying out work on behalf of the denomination, with Committee membership consisting of lay and ordained members from around the URC. Committee membership is discussed and new members approached by the Assembly's Nominations Committee formed of a representative from each Synod. It is the responsibility of this committee to fill vacancies or denominational representation in other places. In doing so it follows the URC's policies on equal opportunities to ensure representation of often under-represented gender and ethnic groups.

Each committee includes a convenor and a staff contact at the denomination's offices in London, colloquially known as "Church House." In most cases, these are Staff Secretaries, employed by the denomination to oversee the day to day working of the department associated with the Committee's work. Both Convenors and Staff Secretaries may be lay or ordained although some roles (such as the Secretary for Ministries) require the post-holder to be a minister of Word and Sacrament.[52] In addition the other members of each committee are selected from across the denomination for their skills, expertise, or experience and with a view to maintaining gender balance and to ensure involvement from ethnic minority groups.

During the CTV period, the General Assembly was presided over by two Moderators, one minister and one elder, elected to serve office jointly for a two year period. This has since returned to be a single Moderator serving for a year. The Moderator(s) of General Assembly, together with

---

52. MC, Paper M1 (March 2014) 28 (§2a).

the General Secretary (a minister of the URC), Clerk of Assembly (an ordained or lay member duly appointed), Treasurer, and Convenor of the Business Committee constitute the Officers of the Assembly. The Officers of Assembly are *ex officio* members of most of the Assembly committees.

The General Assembly's membership includes representatives from the Synods along with Synod Moderators, Assembly Committee Convenors, student and staff representation from the URC's designated theological colleges, representatives of UK and worldwide ecumenical partners, immediate past Moderators of the General Assembly, two previous Moderators of the General Assembly (or its predecessors), three youth representatives from URC Youth, a representative of the Council for World Mission (CWM) and the Chair of the URC Trust (the legal trustees with responsibility for the charitable oversight of the URC) (§§B.2.(6)(a–n)). The Roll of Assembly is presented at the beginning of the Assembly and the membership remains for the annual period of that General Assembly. It is possible to recall Assembly between Assembly meetings; a recalled Assembly (as occurred in both 2000 and 2015) is a subsequent meeting of the preceding Assembly and the membership remains the same.

Alongside the Committee work which continues between the meetings of the Assembly, Assembly Executive (formerly Mission Council) is appointed by the General Assembly "with power to act in its name between meetings of the General Assembly and to discharge such other functions as the General Assembly may from time to time direct" (§B.2.(6)). Assembly Executive meets residentially once per year and consists of a smaller body of representatives. Synods each have four representatives including their Moderators, and Assembly Committee Convenors are also present. Along with representation from ecumenical partners, URC Youth representation, the Chair of the URC Trust, and the Officers of Assembly, Assembly Executive is a body of approximately seventy voting members. It is the responsibility of Assembly Executive to act in the name of the General Assembly, acting as an Executive Committee of the Assembly.[53] As a result of its "general delegatory powers" (§B.2.(6)(xxvii)) Assembly Executive acts for the Assembly and with its authority. Despite its place in the *Structure* of the URC and its apparently wide-ranging decision-making role, it is not an official Council of the Church but is a derivative of the conciliar function of the Assembly itself. The powers

---

53. Mission Council was instigated in 1992 and replaced what had previously been the Assembly Executive Committee.

and authority of the Assembly may be exercised either by the meeting of the General Assembly, or through a meeting of Assembly Executive. In the polity of the denomination, both of these decisions carry the same authority; namely that of the General Assembly.

Although Councils may act and fulfil their responsibilities in accordance with their remit as outlined in the *Structure*, there are opportunities for consultation between the Councils. Consultation is required to hear the views of "other councils or of local churches likely to be affected by the decision" before any decision is made (§B.4). In the case of decisions at the Assembly level to amend "the Basis, Structure and any other form or expression of the polity and doctrinal formulations of the United Reformed Church" (§B.2.(6)(xi)), a formalised process is triggered whereby changes must be sent beyond the Assembly for further conciliar approval prior to being adopted (§B.3). In most cases, these changes are referred to Synods for their view on the matter agreed by the Assembly (or Assembly Executive) but they may, in exceptional circumstances, also be referred to Local Churches for their decision. If more than a third of Synods (or Local Churches) pass resolutions that the matter is not to be proceeded with, the Assembly (or Assembly Executive acting on its behalf) will not ratify, and therefore not adopt, the change.

The Assembly's role, therefore, is one of "final authority" for the denomination. Martin Cressey remarks that it was with these words: "that the Congregationalist partners in the 1972 union had to come to terms, since they had hitherto restricted the work of such a body at national level to advice and guidance or at most to decision on matters referred to it by the local churches."[54]

Cressey further states that this came too with the recognition "of the subsidiary but real authority of all the other councils, each at its own level."[55] Therefore, this subsidiary relationship of other Councils results in the General Assembly's role as the final arbiter "in matters of dispute"[56] within the Councils of the URC. Recognising that any Council may err, the Assembly is therefore open, as the *Basis* states, to change. The penultimacy of such "final" authority, therefore, means that decisions made by the General Assembly can only be definitive until such time as the Assembly may choose to change its stance.

---

54. Cressey, "Being a Conciliar Church," 361.
55. Cressey, "Being a Conciliar Church," 361.
56. Thorogood, *No Abiding City*, 75.

In addition to the structural governance bodies as defined in the *Structure*, note must also be taken of the legal responsibility afforded to the Trusts responsible for the charitable and financial oversight of the work of the URC. These bodies fulfil statutory roles as Trustees at Synod and Assembly levels and hold responsibility (and liability) for the legal basis from which the Councils function. The reality of this is that finance and property is legally held, invested, and spent by the Trust bodies—not within the Councils, including Local Churches. While the Trustees are appointed by the Councils to act in this role on their behalf, the Trusts are legally responsible for the use of their resources, which include both finance and property and must act to the benefit of the Trust's aims. This means that they need not act in accordance with a decision of a Council where this is deemed not to be in keeping with the charitable aims or where it is contrary to policies adopted by the Trust. While this is unlikely to occur, there remains, however slight, the possibility of a conflict of priorities between the Council (the decision-making body), its finance committee (considering detail on its behalf) and the Trust (whose responsibility is legal and charitable and not recognised in the *Structure* as a decision-making body).

Although the role of the Trust bodies is to serve the charitable work of the conciliar structure, their impact on the ability of the Councils to act in their own right without further approval is not insignificant. Decisions made by a Synod or General Assembly resolution will still be subject to approval by the corresponding Trust if it affects finance or property. While it would be broadly expected that the Trust and the conciliar body would act together, this does not preclude the possibility of tensions emerging in this relationship. The URC's ecclesiological integrity, therefore, is potentially compromised by the statutory provisions affecting charitable trusts.

Since 2006, the URC has expressed itself through three spheres of conciliar governance: Local Church, Synod, and General Assembly. Each Council has "consultative, legislative and executive functions" as assigned to them in the *Structure* and possesses "such authority, under the Word of God and the promised guidance of the Holy Spirit, as shall enable it to exercise its functions and thereby to minister in that sphere of the life of the United Reformed Church with which it is concerned" (§B.1.(3)). The *Structure* gives a flexibility to the various Councils to operate in a way that is best for their context. Yet it is also within the polity of the URC that any decisions should be reached "only after the fullest attempt has been made to discover the mind of the other councils or of local churches likely to be affected by the decision" (§B.4).

However, while decisions made by a Council are carried out through a process of consultation, there is no stipulation that these decisions must be adopted by other Councils. Although decisions made by the General Assembly are "final and binding" (§B.2.5), this does not necessitate that all Councils will further subscribe to the decisions. This has become most noticeable in the ways in which denominational policy and local practice have been left to local decision. For example, the General Assembly passed an enabling resolution in 2012 allowing Local Churches who wished to conduct Civil Partnerships on their premises to be able to do so. This gave consent to those congregations that wished to take up this opportunity. Those who did not wish to offer Civil Partnerships did not need to opt-in. This recognises that within the denominational polity the Assembly may request, allow or deny Synods and Local Churches but cannot (and often would not wish to) direct how Synods and Local Churches respond.

Therefore, with minimal use of Assembly authority to impose on Synods and Local Churches, and of Synod authority to impose on Local Churches, together with an inbuilt flexibility in the polity and policies of the denomination, the URC maintains an approach to policy-making that allows for a variety of opinion and understanding and an openness to various expressions of Church, churchmanship and ministry. This is characterised by an increased number of denominational policies which are dependent upon appeals to personal conscience. This has resulted in a tendency to adopt policies which enable a plurality of perspectives. While this is largely in keeping with the negotiations carried out in the formation of the URC, such a position does suggest that the only definitive statements of URC policy and doctrine may be those enshrined in the foundational documents, and that any further adaptations of the *Basis* may lean towards enabling action for those who wish to pursue a practice while being sure not to censor those who object. It may be in this way that the URC continues to be both *United* and *Reformed* while maintaining its provisionality.

3

Theological Authority of the Word of God

A FUNDAMENTAL SOURCE OF authority in any Christian denomination will be found in God's Word to the Church, recognising that in different denominations this might mean different things. Indeed, Martin Luther stated that "Christians can be governed by nothing except the Word of God alone."[1] The URC's *Basis* states that the URC "confesses the faith of the Church catholic in one God, Father, Son and Holy Spirit" and "acknowledges the Word of God in the Old and New Testaments, discerned under the guidance of the Holy Spirit, as the supreme authority for the faith and conduct of all God's people" (§A.12). This does two things. First, it affirms the trinitarian understanding of God, Father, Son and Holy Spirit. In doing so, the denomination considers the centrality of God as "Source, Guide, and Goal" (§A.Sch.D.v2) as the primary clause in its confession and therefore the source from which all faith flows. Second, it acknowledges that the Christian Scriptures, discerned by the Holy Spirit, constitute the primary authority in the denomination regarding matters of faith. The incorporation of both a clearly expressed trinitarian formula and an acknowledgement of the role of Scripture discerned under the guidance of the Holy Spirit into the *Basis* ensures that the URC has a definite sense of the place of the Word in the life of the Church.

To examine the Word of God in light of a United and Reformed Church is to explore a fundamental understanding of ecclesial authority. The *Basis* indicates that the Word of God can be understood as consisting of both Scripture (in the Old and New Testaments) and the discernment

---

1. Luther, *On Secular Authority*, 33.

of the Holy Spirit. Together these are intended to be seen as offering a single framework from which to examine the Word of God.

However, within wider Reformed discourse a further framework may be utilised to explore such ecclesial authority. In his opening volume of *Church Dogmatics*, Swiss Reformed theologian Karl Barth expounds the idea that the Word "is one and the same whether we understand it as revelation, Bible, or proclamation."[2] While Barth's theological method may seem distant from those who through the Joint Committee formulated the URC's foundational documents, the influence of Barth on Congregationalists was recorded as early as the late 1920s.[3] In a review of C. H. Dodd's *History and the Gospel* (1939), C. J. Cadoux of Mansfield College, Oxford remarked that it was now clear that "Dodd has definite leanings in the direction of Barthianism."[4] During the 1940s, while the *Presbyter* published contributions from Basil Hall who felt that Barth's theology provided "a good challenge, a good stimulant,"[5] H. Cunliffe-Jones was stating his "dissent to those who accept Barth as the basis for all future theology."[6]

Barth's influence was not universal. Although the "so-called New Genevans . . . [who] were able to instigate a rediscovery of Reformed theology and a renewal of worship within Congregationalism"[7] were some of the advocates for Barth's theology, not all Genevans were convinced. Prominent "Genevan" Nathaniel Micklem at Mansfield College, Oxford "would never become a Barthian,"[8] while other "Genevans" such as his colleagues H. F. Lovell Cocks at the Yorkshire Independent College in Bradford, Sydney Cave, President at Cheshunt College in Cambridge, and John S. Whale at Mansfield (succeeding Cave at Cheshunt in 1933) "played an important part in the broader context of Barth reception in Britain."[9] An example of the influence of these Congregational Barthians can be seen in the widespread use of texts such as J. S. Whale's *Christian Doctrine* in theological education.

2. Barth, *CD* 1/1:120 (§4.4).
3. Morgan, *Barth Reception*, 73–84.
4. Cadoux, Review of *History*, 590.
5. Hall, "Presbyterian Church," 32.
6. Cunliffe-Jones, Review of *Reformation*, 25.
7. Pope, "New Genevans," 641.
8. Morgan, *Barth Reception*, 83.
9. Morgan, *Barth Reception*, 84.

Unsurprisingly, during the development of the CCEW's *Declaration of Faith* in the 1960s, a number of those involved in the process of drafting the text claimed to be influenced by Barth. In a book entitled *Christian Confidence*, published in order to give a more detailed theological account of the *Declaration*'s clauses, the convenor of the Commission responsible, W. A. Whitehouse, indicates a Barthian influence on the *Declaration* and among those involved: "Readers whose delight it is to detect sources and influences will notice here a debt to Karl Barth."[10] D. Densil Morgan suggests that Whitehouse "had ensured that Barth's theology would characterise English Congregationalism's doctrinal stance as it entered into organic union with the Presbyterian Church."[11] With the *Declaration* and the *Basis* both being drawn up in the 1960s, and with the involvement of prominent individuals such as John Huxtable in drafting both, a Barthian influence in the *Basis* cannot be ruled out.

Thus, while Barth's direct influence on the URC's *Basis* is not proven, his indirect influence through a number of its architects can be seen. In the approach taken in the *Basis* to the Word of God, paired with a clearly expressed trinitarian formula, a clear echo of the threefold understanding of the Word of God Barth expounds in *Church Dogmatics* can be heard. His model, therefore, reflecting the components of the URC's understanding of the Word of God, provides a useful framework in which it is possible to explore the source of authority in terms of the threefold Word, first in terms of the revelation in Jesus Christ, secondly in the biblical Scriptures, and thirdly in terms of the source of proclamation as discerned through the Holy Spirit.

Word of God: Jesus Christ

When reading the *Basis* it is impossible to ignore its understanding of the centrality of Jesus to the life of the Church. The opening statement of the *Basis* declares:

> There is but one Church of the one God. He called Israel to be his people, and in fulfilment of the purposes then begun he called the Church into being through Jesus Christ, by the power of the Holy Spirit. (§A.1)

---

10. Whitehouse, *Making the Declaration of Faith*, 14.
11. Morgan, *Barth Reception*, 278.

The place of Jesus as the agent through which the Church, by the power of the Holy Spirit, was brought into being is therefore asserted in the *Basis*. It is from this position that the *Basis* opens up a discussion of the URC's understanding of Christology.[12] Following from this clause, the *Basis* moves on to focus on the redemption of Christ (§A.2), the on-going call of Christ to proclaim the Gospel to all people (§A.3), the apostolicity of the Church entrusted with the Gospel (§A.4), and Christ's continued mercy toward "the Church in all its failure and weakness" as a catalyst for reform and renewal (§A.6). The Christocentric nature of the *Basis*, seeking the "mind of Christ" throughout, recognises that "Jesus Christ holds his people in the fellowship of the one Body" (§A.10). In this way, the *Basis* demonstrates the denomination's understanding of and commitment to authority as sourced and located in Christ. The Congregational theologian P. T. Forsyth expounded this point succinctly: "Our ecclesiastical rights are not to be defined by our membership of a Church, but by our membership of Christ."[13]

Seeking the mind of Christ and reflecting Christ in its life is identified as the Church's primary task according to the *Basis*. This is significant when attempting to evaluate the URC's understanding of authority. Forsyth stated that "[w]e do not exercise authority, we recognise it."[14] In this way, the role of the Christian is to recognise authority as external to the self, and external to the Church, and to seek rather the authority of Christ.

Forsyth clarifies this insofar as "[t]he centre of gravity and source of authority for any Church is Christ's person and act, historic, yet immediate."[15] Such an assertion has significant ramifications for the question of authority as it highlights the recognition of Christ's "person and act" in the life of the Church. The *Basis* recognises this in the redemptive act of Jesus as historic yet dwelling in the Church today (§A.2). It is this historic yet living reality that brings Christ into the centre of the Church, and acts as the centre of gravity as Forsyth suggests.

This echoes the ecclesiological statements made by Protestant theologians two centuries earlier. John Owen wrote that the combining together of individuals into the Church "is *a voluntary act* of the obedience

---

12. An exploration of the URC's understanding of Christology can be found in Peel, *Reforming Theology*.

13. Forsyth, "Moral Authority," 73.

14. Forsyth, *Principle of Authority*, 152.

15. Forsyth, *Principle of Authority*, 257.

of faith unto the authority of Christ; nor can it be anything else."[16] This uniting together around Christ's authority into a voluntary society can also be seen in Locke who argued that "religion was personal, not private, and social"[17] and therefore "that persons joined the Church as social beings entering into fellowship with others."[18] Both of these seventeenth-century thinkers assert the centrality of society as a voluntary community in which, in Locke's terms, property (known also to mean freedom) is given up to allow for covenanting together in fellowship. By its focus on Christ, living and dwelling in the Church, the fellowship has no option but to recognise the authority of Christ.

The twentieth-century Congregationalist H. F. Lovell Cocks (a student of Forsyth) expressed concern that an institutionalised reading of the Church led to a deficiency in the understanding of the centrality of Christ. "The Church is not an estate in chancery. There is no will to execute, for Jesus is alive."[19] For Lovell Cocks, the question of the catholicity of the Church is one of being in the apostolic succession. Echoing Forsyth's belief that "[w]e are in the apostolic succession rather than in the ecclesiastic,"[20] Lovell Cocks states that "we already stand in the real apostolic succession, for it is in the contemporary Christ, the living Lord, that the Church's life across the centuries is summed up and secured."[21] This on-going apostolicity is considered by the *Basis* in terms of the proclamation of the Gospel entrusted to the apostles by Christ rather than through the episcopal ordination of those claiming direct descent from the apostles. Forsyth's understanding of the apostolic succession is centred on the role of the first century apostles to represent Christ "more than they did the Church. They stood for Christ to the Church and not for the Church to Christ."[22] This place of the living Christ as the cornerstone to the Church's Gospel means that, in the words of Lovell Cocks, "[t]here are no executors, for there is nothing for them to do."[23] The Church is founded not on a dead source, but rather is forever "renewed

---

16. Owen, *True Nature*, 37.
17. Sell, *John Locke*, 337n105.
18. Sell, *John Locke*, 171.
19. Cocks, "Foundation in Christ," 52.
20. Forsyth, *Principle of Authority*, 127.
21. Cocks, "Foundation in Christ," 53.
22. Forsyth, *Principle of Authority*, 135.
23. Cocks, "Foundation in Christ," 52.

and reformed" (§A.6), receiving its life continually from the living Christ in its midst.

The living Christ's authority in the Church extends to the personal and the moral. Forsyth's writings on authority address the question of the personal nature of authority on Christian people. Such authority, writes Forsyth, "acts on wills" and "must have moral quality,"[24] because "this Christ is the authority to our soul as directly as He is to the Church."[25] The Christ who holds personal authority over us does so through "God in His gracious relationship to man."[26] It is through this relationship, argues R. A. Wilson, that authority "has two centres, the believing individual and God."[27]

It is this relationship, through which the "Christ interpreted by faith"[28] acts upon the soul, where authority may be demonstrated to be "not magisterial but moral."[29] The importance of freedom upon the believer is, therefore, significant as it is not to be imposed or used to coerce, for "[a]lthough everything is done in Christ's name, infallibility is neither claimed nor conceded . . . [and] we may not coerce one another in Christ's name."[30]

It is this freedom to be convicted of Christ's authority that underlies the URC's understanding and application of conciliar government. Congregational theologians meeting halfway through the twentieth century asserted the belief "that the mind of Christ for His people is given to Councils" while being clear that within such a system it cannot be claimed "that our interpretation of His Will is infallible."[31] Thus, while Christ is finally authoritative, it is not always certain that Christ has been heard properly or that Christ has said all there is to be said. Forsyth expressed this in terms of looking towards "an Elector, His choice, His historic gift, and His Holy Spirit in His Church" and warned that "no majority vote can guarantee His presence or His will."[32] Recognising that for some "the authority of the institution is itself the vision," Presbyterian theologian

24. Forsyth, *Principle of Authority*, 308.
25. Forsyth, *Principle of Authority*, 317.
26. Wilson, "Religious Authority," 63.
27. Wilson, "Religious Authority," 63.
28. Wilson, "Religious Authority," 63.
29. Cocks, "Foundation in Christ," 55.
30. Cocks, "Foundation in Christ," 55.
31. International Congregational Council, "Message to the Churches," 160.
32. Forsyth, *Principle of Authority*, 234.

John Oman echoed the views of Congregationalists by suggesting that the Church as a "means to the freedom of personal discernment and consecration" is "at best an imperfect and passing means."[33] Such views are also reflected in the *Basis* whereby it affirms an openness to "accord more nearly with the mind of Christ" when it has become clear that this has been interpreted anew (§A.9).

However, it is through the redemptive act of Christ that the Church sources its clearest authority in its task to proclaim the Gospel to the world. Forsyth expressed the belief that "[t]he world can only be converted by a Church which believes that in Christ the world has already been won."[34] In relation to the Church, which "Christ continues to entrust . . . with the Gospel" (§A.4), such assurances place Christ's redeeming work as both historic and living authority to the Church. In examining Oman's work, Wilson expresses his argument that it is impossible for the Church to exist without Christ. Quoting Oman's statement that the Church is "the supreme manifestation of her Lord," Wilson ponders "how, if His present embodiment is the Church, we can return to Him without intermediary."[35] Yet Forsyth is certain that "the Word alone gives final value to the Church's polity, propaganda, philanthropy, and sacraments"[36] and that "[t]o renounce the Word is, in principle, to dissolve the Church."[37] It is through the centrality of Christ's life as a source of authority that the Church "determines with which authority she would be clothed."[38] Forsyth is certain that such a mandate is required:

> The Church is not a mere religious assembly which could remove God, the historic existence of Christ, or the finality of Redemption from its belief, so long as it did all with the note of charity, and abolished Christ in the "spirit of Christ". A nation may survive regicide, but a Church cannot.[39]

Therefore, it can be suggested that Christ himself is the fundamental authority in the Church according to the Nonconformist traditions and that these traditions are reflected in the *Basis*.

---

33. Oman, *Honest Religion*, 167.
34. Forsyth, *Principle of Authority*, 342.
35. Wilson, "Religious Authority," 194.
36. Forsyth, *Principle of Authority*, 249.
37. Forsyth, *Principle of Authority*, 252.
38. Oman, *Vision and Authority*, 158.
39. Forsyth, *Principle of Authority*, 236.

Word of God: Holy Scripture

An authority centred in the person of Christ is affirmed in the assertion that "revelation is given in a person, not simply in his words, but in himself."[40] Yet the Church relies upon the revelation of Christ through the witness of Scripture to form the basis for its life and mission. The words of Scripture, therefore, become the method by which Christ's authority can be experienced in the Church rather than through any first-hand transmission. In living out the Gospel, the Church relies upon the revelation of Christ as found in Scripture. In the *Basis*, the URC "believes that, in the ministry of the Word, through preaching and the study of the Scriptures, God makes known in each age his saving love, his will for his people and his purpose for the world" (§A.13). The continued revelation of Christ is therefore to be maintained by the study of the Scriptures and preaching. Within the URC's understanding Scripture constitutes the source from which the revelation of Christ can be seen and experienced. Christ's witness to the world is through the text of Scripture.[41]

However, Scripture's status is derivative of the authority of Christ discerned within it. The *Basis* asserts that the URC "acknowledges the Word of God in the Old and New Testaments, discerned under the guidance of the Holy Spirit, as the supreme authority for the faith and conduct of all God's people" (§A.12). As one commentator has written, "the use of the phrase 'the Word of God in' explicitly recognises that the Scriptures are not *per se* the Word of God, but that the Word of God is contained in them."[42] In this way, combining the biblical text with the process of discernment demonstrates the way in which the Word of God is associated with, but not confined to, the words of Scripture. The influence of discernment of the Spirit is explored in the next section. However, the place of Scripture as the "supreme authority" warrants further examination distinct from that of the Spirit's influence. While Riglin's assertion—that the *Basis* refers to the broader significance of "the Word of God in"— makes the biblical text alone insufficient for the URC's understanding of the Word, the Bible retains its significance as an authority.

To identify Scripture as the sole authoritative source in the life of the URC requires a significant degree of expansion upon the text of the

---

40. Huxtable, *Bible Says*, 78.

41. An exploration of the URC's understanding of the Bible can be found in Campbell, *Being Biblical*.

42. Riglin, "Animating Grace," 28. Emphasis original.

Basis. Reference to the Scriptures, explicitly named as the Old and New Testaments, occurs in only two paragraphs of the *Basis*. These same paragraphs are additionally referred to in the ministerial ordination promises (Schedule C) and in the *Statement concerning the nature, faith and order of the URC* (Schedule D). The repetition of the acknowledgment that the Word in the Bible is the supreme authority for faith and conduct of God's people suggests that it constitutes a core belief of the URC. But with what justification does Scripture hold such a supreme authority when this constitutes the *Basis's* only explicit reference to it? Should such authority be more explicit in the life of the denomination and its *Basis*? These areas deserve further exploration.

The Reformed maxim of *sola scriptura*—Scripture alone—has been a key belief for Churches within the Protestant tradition.[43] The purpose of such a maxim was to dispense with the hold of Church authority and to assert that the Christian message can be read in Scripture by anyone without subjecting them to the doctrines and practices of the Roman Catholic Church. In doing so, "the Protestant Reformation replaces the authority of the Church with the authority of the Bible."[44] This, notes Wilson, led to the "tremendous confidence in the authority of Scripture" that formed the basis of "the reconstruction of dogmatic systems as rigid as any medieval theological construction."[45] While Reformed theology is grounded in such confidence, the renewal of ecclesiological and doctrinal orthodoxy was being carried out by a newly inspired generation. The work of Luther and Calvin on the continent and their influence on Knox in Scotland and further afield fed into the development of these Reformed ideas in Britain.

The impact of Reformation ideas on the URC's antecedent traditions can be seen. In both the Presbyterian and Congregational traditions, the seventeenth-century statements of faith, which the URC "accepts with thanksgiving" and "recognises as its own particular heritage" (§A.18), demonstrate a strong influence of Reformation thought. In both the Westminster Confession ("Presbyterian", 1647) and the Savoy Declaration ("Congregational", 1658) the supremacy of Scripture, and explicitly the content of the biblical canon, is clearly stated. However, the definition of the contents of Scripture is not the sole scriptural reference

---

43. A modern look at the effect of *Sola Scriptura* from within the URC tradition can be found in Peel, *Sola Scriptura*.

44. Wilson, "Religious Authority," 23.

45. Wilson, "Religious Authority," 26.

in the Westminster Confession. When the Confession was published and given to Parliament for debate, the printed copies soon became annotated with scriptural references. The copy of the Confession owned by Francis Bacon, the Member of Parliament for Ipswich is now held by the URC History Society at Westminster College, Cambridge. This copy contains his copious biblical annotations, grounding the Confession in a scriptural framework. A subsequent publication of the Confession included these scriptural references highlighting the claim that doctrine and ecclesiology are drawn from Scripture alone.

The contemporary URC's *Basis*, however, is not constituted in such a scripturally formulaic manner. Work on an alternative Confession of Faith (explored more fully later) produced accompanying notes where scriptural justification was provided.[46] However, a corresponding version, to give commentary on the *Basis* as a whole, appears never to have been produced.

The lack of biblical reference within the *Basis* does raise a question concerning the extent to which Scripture forms the supreme authority for the denomination. Were Scripture to hold such a place, could it be reasonably expected that all the *Basis*'s clauses would be justified by including the appropriate biblical reference, and that the centrality of Scripture would be continually affirmed in the text?

But an alternative approach is possible. British theologians in the early twentieth century were involved in discussions about a number of issues in theological and biblical scholarship. One such issue involved the historical critical approach some late nineteenth century scholars had taken, resulting in literalist readings of the biblical text. In his book, *The Bible Says*, John Huxtable refers to the 1861 book by J. W. Burgon, *Inspiration and Interpretation*, as an example of Conservative Evangelical biblical fundamentalism. Huxtable quotes Burgon as saying "The Bible is none other than the Word of God, not some part of it more, some part of it less, but all alike the utterance of him that sitteth upon the throne, faultless, unerring, supreme" and Huxtable subsequently notes that "the same fascinated awe for the written Word is still characteristic of their [Biblical Literalists] thinking."[47] The response of Forsyth and Oman to this literalism, however, was to approach Scripture in terms of "the gospel

---

46. GA Reports (1996) 101–2.
47. Huxtable, *Bible Says*, 61–62.

behind and within the gospels"⁴⁸ with Oman recognising that "the Word of God is something that even the Bible serves."⁴⁹ They were both certain that literalist approaches failed to encompass the fullness that Scripture has to offer and that the gospel required a more complex reading of the text to become present.⁵⁰

Thus the witness of Scripture was not to be of an infallible and inerrant text, but of a text that contained the gospel. For Oman, Scripture possesses authority but only because it bears witness to the gospel, not because its text may stand up to a literalist interpretation.⁵¹ It was, for Oman, the experience of the gospel within the text of Scripture that gave it the authority of a witness. This echoes Forsyth who asserted that "[n]othing, truly, can be final authority which is not experienced, but the experience is not the authority."⁵² In reading the Scriptures, both authors were adamant about the place of the gospel within the text, asserting this to be that of a witness to the final authority in Christ.

If the role of Scripture is to be understood in terms advocated by Oman and Forsyth as a witness to revelation and not as a literalist collection of proof-texts, then the *Basis* may be regarded as the outworking of such an understanding. Here, the message of the gospel need not be stated with chapter and verse because the message to Christ's Church is to be understood through exegesis of the Scriptures revealing the gospel message. The call to unity, justice, conscience and love, implicit within the *Basis*, therefore echoes gospel themes. An approach that transcends literal readings seems to have imbued the *Basis* with an inherent reading of Scripture that moves away from the need for direct reference to the biblical text. As a result, Riglin notes that "[t]his has led some to suggest . . . that the United Reformed Church is essentially a liberal church, in the sense that it is clearly not fundamentalist, literalist, or even 'conservative' in its use of holy scripture."⁵³

Nevertheless, the lack of specific biblical references within the *Basis* cannot be read as a lack of scriptural significance within the URC's

---

48. Cornick, "P. T. Forsyth," 155.

49. Bevans, "Prophet's Eye," 126; see also Bevans, *John Oman*, 41–62; Oman, *Concerning the Ministry*, 228–43.

50. An exploration of Forsyth's understanding of Scripture can be found in Paddison, *Scripture*, 5–32.

51. Wilson, "Religious Authority," 80.

52. Forsyth, *Principle of Authority*, 50.

53. Riglin, "Animating Grace," 152.

constitutional documents. Instead, the presence of the gospel can be seen to be intrinsically woven into the fabric of the *Basis*. Whereas a nineteenth century example of a Constitutional document may well have exhibited a degree of literalism and proof-texting, the theologians of the twentieth century involved in developing the URC's *Basis* adopted an approach whereby Scripture was treated holistically as a revelation of the gospel.

Yet while a more holistic approach may be taken to the *Basis*, this leaves unanswered the justification of Scripture as the supreme authority for God's people. Although explicit reference to Scripture is absent in the *Basis*, the gospel inherent within the *Basis* effectively saturates the text with Scripture. It is because Scripture bears unique witness to the good news of God's work in the Old and New Testaments that the Bible is supremely authoritative to Christians. Without such unique witness to the gospel, the Bible could not be claimed to hold such supremacy in the life of the Church.

Thus it has to be demonstrated that while claiming a supreme authority in Scripture, the *Basis* derives such authority through appreciation of the witness to God's work as recorded in the Bible. Where the gospel is witnessed to, there is found the authority of God.

Word of God: Discernment of the Spirit

An examination of the three-fold Word of God requires exploration of the pneumatological action of discernment as demonstrated in the *Basis*. It has already been seen that Scripture has a living nature whereby the biblical text reflects the gospel of God's work in the revelation of Christ. Although this has been explored separately from any pneumatological implications, the presence and act of the Holy Spirit can be understood to be the agent of such living transmission. It is, therefore, by the power of the Holy Spirit (§A.1), under the guidance of the Holy Spirit (§A.6 & §A.12), in the freedom of the Spirit (§A.10), and in receiving and expressing the renewing life of the Holy Spirit (§A.11) that the "glorious Gospel is made effective so that through faith we receive the forgiveness of sins, newness of life as children of God and strength in this present world to do his will" (§A.17).

The Spirit can thus be understood as an agent of the living transmission of the gospel, participating in the enlivening of the Word in the Church. Colin Gunton, himself a URC minister, expresses concerns that "because a *logical* link has been claimed between Spirit and institution" the Church sometimes "made too confident claims to be possessed of divine authority."[54] Yet, the presence of the Spirit in the life of the community facilitates the relationship between the finite and the infinite. The role of the Church, notes Gunton, is "to be the kind of reality at a finite level that God is in eternity."[55] This, he argues, could be achieved because the "action of the Spirit is to anticipate, in the present and by means of the finite and contingent, the things of the age to come."[56] The Spirit makes present the existence of "a church then and now and to be."[57]

As Wilson notes in his discussion of Oman's work, this connection between the two realms, through the presence of the Spirit, transmits to the Bible the promise "not of an infallible, but of a living transmission."[58] This promise can, therefore, extend also to the living transmission of Christ in the Church, for, as Wilson states, "the only Christ we can know is the Christ interpreted by faith."[59] Such an interpretation relies upon the Church as the community of faith through which the Spirit's work can be recognised. Oman is certain that without the presence of the Spirit in the Church it would be little more than "the most corrupt of human institutions."[60] He asserts that the sure "evidence of the spiritual gifts which have adorned the lives of the humble and faithful souls" is demonstrated only as a result of "the continuous presence of the Spirit."[61] It is, notes Oman, where "the institution is only a means to the freedom of personal discernment and consecration, and all imposed order at best an imperfect and passing means" that the Church is focused on the future eschatological fulfilment.[62]

It is through the relationship between God and Humanity that the role of the Spirit can be most clearly recognised. Wilson notes Oman's "emphasis upon individual insight" and how this "expresses [Oman's] conviction that authority resides in a certain relationship between God

---

54. Gunton, *Trinitarian Theology*, 67.
55. Gunton, *Trinitarian Theology*, 80.
56. Gunton, *Trinitarian Theology*, 67.
57. Gunton, *Trinitarian Theology*, 82.
58. Wilson, "Religious Authority," 65. Wilson cites from Oman, *Vision and Authority*, 128.
59. Wilson, "Religious Authority," 65.
60. Oman, *Vision and Authority*, 137.
61. Oman, *Vision and Authority*, 136.
62. Oman, *Honest Religion*, 167.

and the believing person."[63] Building on the sure evidence of spiritual gifts among God's people, Oman further states that the place of personal conviction is not to be left unchecked by others:

> To accept our brother's conclusions, without ourselves attempting to reach them, is not to honour either God or our brother by our meekness, but to dishonour both by our slackness; and to believe that our brother wishes us to be convinced by him and not by the truth is to believe him also capable of dishonouring God.[64]

The personal relationship with God, therefore, establishes a powerful connection between the finite and infinite, mediated by the Spirit through the Church. Forsyth considers this authoritative relationship as between the individual and "our new Creator," and considers this to be a "final authority"—all other authorities, "either a Church or a Book," being "the products of such communion with God."[65] Thus, through the relationship with God transmitted by the Spirit the believer—personally and corporately—finds the authority that is being sought.

Such thinking is, to some extent, reflected in the *Basis* which holds personal conviction in high regard in terms of the principles upon which the URC is founded. Yet, similar to Oman, such conviction may not remain unchecked. "The United Reformed Church . . . upholds the rights of personal conviction. It shall be for the church, in safeguarding the substance of the faith and maintaining the unity of the fellowship, to determine when these rights are asserted to the injury of its unity and peace" (§A.Sch.D.v1.7). Thus it is the communal act of the Church in discerning the Spirit's conviction for the individual and the community that enables both to give honour to God, for to do otherwise is "to dishonour both by our slackness."[66]

Discernment within the community is a matter of practical significance in the life of the Church. When the Church comes together "the members have opportunity through discussion, responsible decision and care for one another, to strengthen each other's faith and to foster the life, work and mission of the Church" (§B.2.(1)). In pursuing these aims, Church meetings are constituted in prayer and are open to hearing the

---

63. Wilson, "Religious Authority," 89.
64. Oman, *Vision and Authority*, 190.
65. Forsyth, *Principle of Authority*.
66. Oman, *Vision and Authority*, 190.

Spirit. It is, therefore, the role of the Church, in meeting, to listen for the Spirit and to seek to discern the voice of God in the community. This approach makes Church meetings distinctive from meetings elsewhere. The intention of such meetings is to make "responsible decision" in the life of the community and for the mission of the Church, directed by the voice of the Spirit.

Although all functions of the Church Meeting require discernment of the Spirit's guidance, discernment is most significant when considering the call of individuals into roles of membership (§B.2.(1)(ix)), eldership (§B.2.(1)(viii)), and ministry (§B.2.(1)(vii) and §B.2.(1)(x)). It is for the Church to decide whether these personal convictions are in line with the beliefs of the community and discern whether the Church can concur with such convictions. In all cases, it is for the Church to discern how these personal convictions may affect the unity and peace of the whole Church. Yet, while such testing acts to discern the direction for the Church, such discernment leads the Church to make decisions that affect the lives of individuals. While other functions place legal requirements upon the Church (such as in the adoption of financial reports (§B.2.(1)(xi)) the process of discerning someone's call and personal conviction invites the Church to discern the Spirit most profoundly.

However, questions about the nature of Church Meetings were raised during the late 1960s when local Congregational Churches were invited by the Assembly of the CCEW to vote on the proposed Scheme of Union. The CCEW's Minister Secretary, John Huxtable, received vast quantities of correspondence questioning the type of meeting being requested. One piece of correspondence, found in the URC Archive, suggested that the insistence upon calling a "Special" Church Meeting to decide upon union would be indicative of "the kind of domination over the local Church that might be expected in the [United] Reformed Church." In a typical response, Huxtable expressed the view that Congregational Churches would have a "Special" meeting to decide upon the calling of a Minister and that "the decision that churches are being asked to make is of that order of importance."

More frequent correspondence suggests that many Churches were concerned about the involvement of their full membership in the vote on the Scheme. A typical letter would ask Huxtable to explain why only those present at the meeting could vote and whether various members unable to be present could have absentee votes. A similar letter was received from Cambridge University Presbyterian-Congregational Society

(Prongsoc) members indicating that their membership resided at various Congregations away from Cambridge and that their vote would therefore remain unrecorded either from their "Home" Church or from their "Worshipping" Church. The response from Huxtable in each case drew upon the nature of the discerning and living Spirit alive in the gathering of the community. Such a response would read: "There are various legal reasons for this but even more important there is our own theological understanding that in the phrase church meeting, meeting is as important a word as church. It is difficult to see how folk who cannot be there can be said to meet."

Thus while the discernment of the Spirit requires a commitment to participate in meeting together, and to do so within an environment of worship, the extent to which the Spirit can be heard remains a significant factor in decision-making. Forsyth questions "How large must a deciding majority of such religious atoms be to be the Word of the Spirit?"[67] In an attempt to answer a similar question, since 2007, the URC has adopted a Consensus model of decision-making for use during both the General Assembly and, where applicable in Synods. The Consensus decision-making process moves away from "for" and "against," it invites participants to listen to one another, indicate how they are feeling about the issue being discussed, and, when moving towards a decision, asks whether they will be willing to agree with the majority if they have previously indicated otherwise. It follows a three-tiered process of seeking information for clarification, discussing the matter, and finally moving towards a decision to conclude the discussion. Such a model is grounded in seeking to preserve the unity and peace of the denomination and has sought to ensure that decisions are consensual rather than the result of simple majority vote. After a challenging General Assembly in 2014, the denomination's magazine *Reform* published a number of letters calling for the adaptation or removal of the Consensus process from the Assembly's Standing Orders, with one correspondent suggesting that the process appeared to be open to manipulation by a minority.[68] These Assembly debates will be more fully considered later. However, whatever the practical situation in the debate, Consensus has created a level of disapproval among some within the denomination and this method for seeking agreement through discernment of the Spirit is not without its critics.

67. Forsyth, *Principle of Authority*, 244.
68. *Reform* (September 2014) 10 (Peter Brain).

In theory, and to some degree, the Consensus decision-making process eliminates Forsyth's concern for what constitutes an appropriate majority, because it invites all those participating to concur even if their inclination was against the majority. The openness, however, in the meeting to listen to one another, participate in the discussion and to seek the will of God gives rise to the opportunity to discern the voice of the Spirit in the community.

In noting that the URC "has never clarified how such 'discerning' is effectively achieved in practice,"[69] Riglin further asserts that the URC has "a clear pneumatology—a belief that divine animation is necessary" to bring forth a living transmission.[70] It is the living transmission that gives Christ anew to the Church; "it is only through the Spirit that the human actions of Jesus become ever and again the acts of God."[71] Thus discernment of the Spirit demonstrates the authority by which God's living transmission is made manifest and the Church proclaims the Word of God.

Call to Unity

In addition to the threefold Word of God, United Churches place as a fundamental biblical imperative the command of Jesus to be one. The concluding paragraph of the *Statement concerning the nature, faith and order of the URC*, in a version created for liturgical use (§A.Sch.D.v2), makes a bold statement, declaring:

> We affirm our intention
> to go on praying and working,
> with all our fellow Christians,
> for the visible unity of the Church
> in the way Christ chooses.

As a statement consented to by ministers and elders at their ordination and induction, this reasserts the significance of "the visible unity of the Church" in the life of the denomination. Unity is not a matter of

---

69. Riglin, "Animating Grace," 9.
70. Riglin, "Animating Grace," 11.
71. Gunton, *Trinitarian Theology*, 67; also "In other words, the Christian life, in terms of faith and belief, sanctification and morality, and in terms of regeneration itself, is dependent on the Sovereign act of God in Christ made known in human lives by the Spirit" (Pope, "Nonconformists and Holy Spirit," 231).

theoretical importance but is to be kept as an important influence on the URC's life and a significant part of its nature.

United denominations fundamentally consider that their very existence accords with this. In the case of the URC, the uniting of the vast majority of Churches belonging to the CCEW and PCE into the URC in 1972 demonstrates the place of unity as a catalyst in the denomination's life. According to the *Basis* the URC "sees its formation and growth as a part of what God is doing to make his people one" (§A.8). However, not only is this part of the process of God's work, the formation of the URC was "in obedience to the call to repent of what has been amiss in the past and to be reconciled." The inclusion of the Churches of Christ in the union discussions in the 1960s and the prospect, subsequently realised, of the inclusion of some of their congregations in the union, affirmed the place of unity as an aspect of the URC's nature and self-understanding. Although "visible unity" has, since 1972, become manifest only by the unions in 1981 with the Churches of Christ and in 2000 with the Congregational Union of Scotland, the nature of the URC remains to seek this unity. The status of organic unity as a *raison d'être* of the denomination has caused criticism from some, such as Martin Camroux, who suggest that the URC's aspirations for unity are "increasingly archaic" and "held primarily by an aging cohort"[72] while "[t]he reality of failure is visibly demonstrated by the hopelessness of the task which the United Reformed Church set itself when it sought to break the ecumenical log-jam."[73]

While such commentary may suggest the quest for organic unity has suffered an "ecumenical retreat,"[74] the commitment to visible unity, based on the theological conviction that the Church's essential unity should be manifest on earth, is a fundamental principle embodied in the *Basis*. With its place embedded in the *Basis*, it therefore exercises authority in the denomination's life and decision-making. In this way, the imperative for unity has acted as an authority on the denomination, distinct from that of other biblical mandates, as seen in the way in which organic unity is specified as the primary reason for the URC's initial formation. Central to the URC's self-understanding is that "failure and weakness of the Church have in particular been manifested in division" and that this

---

72. Camroux, "Ecumenical Church Renewal," 158.
73. Camroux, "Ecumenical Church Renewal," 148.
74. Camroux, "Ecumenical Church Renewal," 148.

is responded to through "obedience to the call to repent." It is this emphasis on the place of unity in the *Basis* that evidences the imperative for organic unity as a source of authority for the denomination.

Unity is therefore significant for the URC; its name places a focus on the united nature of the denomination, the mandate for which was perceived to be biblical. John Huxtable suggested that in terms of the numerous discussions towards Church unity throughout the twentieth century "none of them singly nor all of them together would have been so lastingly powerful had it not been obvious that the strongest motive for such a concern was to be found in the Bible itself."[75] Huxtable was, undeniably, a key player in the English ecumenical scene of the second half of the twentieth century. He was involved in the CUEW's Commission I, established by Howard Stanley's *Next Ten Years* project, to explore Christian unity. When Huxtable succeeded Stanley as Minister Secretary of the CUEW he found himself involved in the Joint Committee seeking to form the URC and fielding extensive queries, questions and criticisms of the proposed Scheme for Union. After the formation of the URC and having served as its first Moderator of General Assembly and Joint General Secretary, Huxtable moved in January 1974 to become the Executive Officer of the newly formed Church Unity Commission.[76] Work among the ecumenical players had led to the production of *Ten Propositions for Unity*, and an extended scheme, the *Covenant for Unity*, which suggested an approach by which unity among the Churches in England could be achieved. In his role as Executive Officer, it was Huxtable's job to advocate these among the Churches. Huxtable retired from public service in 1978 when the Churches Council for Covenanting first met, taking on the mantle of the Church Unity Commission.[77]

Huxtable's legacy as a key architect of the formation of the URC, however, has been criticised, most recently by Congregational minister and historian Alan Argent. In his book, *The Transformation of Congregationalism 1900–2000*, Argent leaves little doubt that he believes Huxtable sought union against the best interests of the Congregational Church, dealing with Huxtable's influence on the URC's formation in a chapter entitled "Vision and Destruction: The Ascendancy of John

---

75. Huxtable, *Christian Unity*, 11.

76. Huxtable, *As it Seemed*, 65.

77. Huxtable, *As it Seemed*, 70,

Huxtable."[78] Yet in the Congregational Lectures delivered in 1965, Huxtable stated, in light of biblical evidence "the cumulative effect of which I find entirely unavoidable: the vocation of the people of God implies and demands unity. This is why disunity is sinful, which is in the end the proper adjective to describe anything which, for whatever reason, is other than God's intention for it."[79] Huxtable's approach, echoed in the *Basis* that he was so key in producing, is to repent, be reconciled, and to be formed and grow "as a part of what God is doing to make his people one" (§A.8). He wrote: "it is through such purgation that Christians of this and that communion will be drawn together in the fires of repentance and reform. Unity imposes on us a deeper exercise than clever ecclesiastic joinery."[80]

However, despite being an advocate of the URC's formation, Huxtable suggested that the Christian objective of unity "is at once clear and blurred: it is unity; but we are not sure what that is and how it can be given visible expression."[81] It may be argued that the *Basis*, therefore, gives this vision that is "clear and blurred," calling, as it does, for "further steps towards the unity of all God's people" (§A.8). The intention of the *Basis* to make such unity "visible" is reflected in the *Statement concerning the nature, faith and order* quoted earlier. However, this "visible" aspect of unity is not otherwise easily observed in the *Basis*. Instead, the *Basis* refers to "one Church of the one God" (§A.1), the sharing "in the life of the Church in all ages and in the communion of saints [who] have fellowship with the Church triumphant" (§A.16), and being made as "one Body of Christ" (§A.17). Thus, drawing on Huxtable's assertion that it is the vocation of all Christians to demand unity, while the *Basis* is clear that unity is an imperative, it leaves in flexible terms how best to make it manifest. This may be a consequence not only of the ecumenical scene of the 1960s, but of the failed efforts to secure visible unity by means of the Covenant for Unity.

With visible unity as a future hope for the URC, it is possible to consider briefly how this hope demonstrates an eschatological perspective for the denomination. In his use of Craig C. Hill, John Bradbury outlines a model for the eschatological realisation of the Church by

---

78. Argent, *Transformation of Congregationalism*, 462–94.
79. Huxtable, *Christian Unity*, 14–15.
80. Huxtable, *Christian Unity*, 16.
81. Huxtable, *Christian Unity*, 28.

exploring Hill's consideration of "future" and "strongly realised" eschatological visions of the authority of the Church.[82] Hill claims that a future orientated eschatology leads to Churches that are "more stable and institutionalised," whereas for those with a realised eschatology "[a]uthority is more charismatic, and structure tends to be flatter."[83] Bradbury notes, therefore, that a future eschatological orientation is focused on the cross with resurrection awaiting, whereas a realised eschatological orientation is focused instead on the body that has already been resurrected.[84]

With this future/present juxtaposition, it is possible to note how this understanding may relate to the URC's understanding of unity as an authority. While the scriptural mandate to be one was taken as an authoritative approach to the formation of the denomination, the move away from such ecumenical programmes, especially during the 1990s, posed significant questions to the URC's denominational identity which can be especially understood in terms of its eschatological orientation.

In Hill's terms, it could be argued that, while visible unity remains a future orientated act, awaiting its completion, the URC's identity has regarded its position as being a "strongly realised" eschatological vision. Using Hill's analysis, the URC's polity relates to an ecclesiology that is "flatter, with fewer levels and intermediaries" while a claim of stability and institutionalisation would be more difficult to assert. If stability is to be measured in terms of longstanding structures, policies and practices, the URC has applied itself more readily to frequent change than to stability and to a preference for local and particular unity than any sense of denominational or generalised union. When the denomination was formed, the establishing of formal structures and procedures in the Manual, along with the consolidation of structures from both traditions, arguably contained "considerable structure and locate[s] authority in recognised offices and traditions"[85] and in doing so established a structure that contained what could be perceived to be a Kingdom shaped ecclesiological vision.

The reality of contemporary union being characterised in Local Ecumenical Partnerships (LEPs) and in Local Sharing Agreements has removed from the denomination the authority to direct such moves and

---

82. Hill, *In God's Time*, 189, cited in Bradbury, *Perpetually Reforming*, 160.
83. Hill, *In God's Time*, 189.
84. Bradbury, *Perpetually Reforming*, 160.
85. Hill, *In God's Time*, 189.

instead makes simple, realisable gains rather than aiming for institutional union. Thus progression towards a flatter polity with fewer levels and "belief that God gives us the power now to transform life in the present"[86] suggests that the URC inhabits a strongly realised eschatology rather than aiming for the future hope of visible unity. Such a position would be in line with the diminished hope for visible unity of the Churches in England.

It must be recognised that such realised eschatological vision of the URC's polity may appear counterintuitive to a denomination that maintains the right to change as an essential tenet of its *Basis*. However, it may be argued that the achievement of union in 1972 (and to a lesser extent the union in 1981) gave the denomination a sense of completion, bringing to an end a process begun many years previously. Although the *Basis* commits the denomination to further union and to change, if necessary, in better reflecting how God calls the Church to be, a sense of completion in achieving the goal of union does suggest that, at least to some extent, the URC regarded itself to be eschatologically realised.

The need to emphasise that the URC has not become complete, therefore, suggests that it was necessary to reiterate the incompleteness rather than allow it to be regarded as eschatologically realised. In response to a letter in *Reform* calling for a more detailed rule book for the denomination, Jeff Davison from Canada warned that "the larger and more beautiful the structure, the greater the danger it becomes an end in itself"[87] echoing the aspirations of John Huxtable in his sermon at the URC's inaugural worship in Westminster Abbey on the 5 October 1972: "We hope that we have but begun."

Therefore, it can be claimed that while the URC has held on to unity as an authority and *raison d'être* for its life, the ecumenical scene since the collapse of the *Covenant* and the complete absence of long term goals for denominational unity has led to the practical erosion of any future hope for unity and thus its virtual elimination as an authority in practical terms.

Although in practical terms the prospect of unity is diminished, unity retains a conceptual source of authority for the URC. This is true whereby the Church's peace and unity—including the commitment to stay together—retains a strong hold on the life of the denomination,

---

86. Bradbury, *Perpetually Reforming*, 160.
87. *Reform* (April 1978) 27 (Jeff Davison).

especially when it considers contentious matters. Yet, due to the lack of practical results, the authority of unity has diminished its effectiveness. In such an environment, authority may be affected as this, Hill suggests, "easily leads to an overestimation of the innocence of insiders and the culpability of outsiders" and "does not promote tolerance and empathy and may well encourage sectarianism."[88] Therefore, the potential for those outside a given context (Local Church, Synod, Denomination) to be perceived as culpable and not deserving of empathy and tolerance, while there is innocence of those inside the context, is possible; this undoubtedly has the potential to affect the practical effectiveness of conciliar authority.

In light of the centrality of unity in the denomination's ethos, the diminution of the future orientated realisation of organic unity questions the authority unity has in the life of the Church. Although a number of consultations continue to take place in the formation of LEPs and within regional and national ecumenical bodies, with the lack of full denominational unity on the horizon at present, the authority associated with unity is largely regarded as historical rather than current. While the future hope of wider organic unity must remain part of the denomination's life, the altered environment has eroded the authority unity once held in the URC.

Word Spoken and Word Heard

It seems that the place of the Word of God is fundamental to an understanding of ecclesial authority. It is also clear that any understanding of ecclesial authority would be lacking without the centrality of Christ in the Christian Church. Together within the threefold Word of God, alongside Scripture and Spirit, a significant grounding for ecclesial authority can be located.

For the Church, the authority of the Word of God is based on the premise that this is not merely "an" authority among many, but this is "in" authority. The underlying basis for ecclesiology is found only within discernment of the Word of God. Yet this is given context through the voices through which the spoken Word is heard. The Word is spoken to each ecclesial community, yet it is the hearer of such Word that acts to constitute, form and organise a Church.

---

88. Hill, *In God's Time*, 193.

In reflecting on the principles underpinning the URC's hearing of the Word, it's been possible to explore the authority this has in a United and Reformed context. Yet while the Word of God is "in" authority for an ecclesial community, the Word—its principles and its fundamental understandings—may not necessarily be regarded as such within its members. The place of such authority as Church authority, may permeate among its members, but its interpretation, weight and significance, may not necessarily be taken on by all those involved. The process of hearing, discerning and following, therefore, rests not only with the ecclesial community but with its individual and constituent members. In United and Reformed Churches, the authority of the Word of God and the fundamental place of Unity may be considered universal constants, but how this is lived out in by individuals within the ecclesial community, in its empirically realised ecclesiology, worship and mission, may not always represent the authority afforded to the Word of God by the ecclesial community.

4

Authority Rooted in Identity

IF SEVENTEENTH-CENTURY ENGLISH CLERIC John Donne is to be believed, none of us are an island. We have an interlinked association with wider society, with those around us and those before us. This historical perspective draws us into a succession of community on which we build and from which we are reliant. The history that forms us and grounds us in the now, however much we seek to escape it, is part of our being and constitutes the source of our experience and knowledge. The permeating presence of history in our current experience feeds our need for permanence and reliability, and the security and authority that comes with it.

However, the sources we acknowledge as part of this history are not all made equal. Some sources are ancient, tried and tested over many generations, while others relate to more recent centuries. These sources are deeply rooted in ancient tradition and significant movements in the global socio-political landscape. Yet some sources are formed by recent history, influenced by social trends and technological developments. They can be influenced by the developments of business and industry or influenced by the global impact of war or pandemic. When we address the place of all such sources, we are drawn into the question of permanence and reliability, considering not only history but revelation. We assess reliability alongside permanence, drawing out the need to not only appreciate the authority but understand the significance of what we experience.

No occurrence takes place in a vacuum separated from history. The influences on the present are informed and shaped by the history which forms an identity. Such identity creates a framework in which to read history and to understand the narrative of the Church's story in contradistinction to other—often prevailing—forces.

Confessing Identity

Confession is one of the key aspects of faith. In professing a given type of faith system, the Church or believer give definition to the understanding of theology that they expound. In stating a faith, the Church creates for itself an authority in matters of doctrine in which aspects of the Christian faith and the Church's ecclesiology are defined.

It has been part of the Church's witness to formulate confessions and state creeds throughout its history. These stretch back to the early centuries including the Apostles' and Nicene Creeds. During the Reformation, Presbyterians in England produced the Westminster Confession (1647) and Congregationalists produced the Savoy Declaration (1658). At later times, Thomas Campbell's Declaration and Address (1809) was looked to by the Churches of Christ in Great Britain and Ireland "as an expression of their essential concerns."[1] In each case, the intention remained "as stating the Gospel and seeking to make its implications clear" (§A.18).

The existence of such statements is, as Geoffrey Nuttall notes, a paradox drawing on both an eagerness to "bear witness to the Christian faith" while also being hesitant in attitude to statements that impose a fixed, intellectual exposition of doctrine that is a man-made construct.[2] During the seventeenth century, these statements, creeds or covenants were regarded by some, such as John Goodwin, as "an unchristian Usurpation upon the Consciences of Men" and had "no imaginable Use."[3] However, Nuttall suggests such positions "are exceptional" while "most of the Congregational churches had a written covenant."[4] The Church "covenant" enabled local congregations to affirm their unity around a common confession of their faith, where "place is found for witness to God's glory and also for the upbuilding of the church."[5] The production of the Westminster Confession and Savoy Declaration both demonstrate the role such statements had for their authors as a sign of Nonconformist

---

1. Thompson, *Stating the Gospel*, 119.
2. Nuttall, *Congregationalists*, 111–24.
3. Nuttall, *Visible Saints*, 78.
4. Nuttall, *Visible Saints*, 78.
5. Nuttall, *Congregationalists*, 119.

witness as well as presenting respectively Presbyterian and Independent polity in the hope that these would form the basis of a national Church settlement.

Thus the URC's *Basis of Union* contains a Confession of Faith (§A.17) that "at the date of formation confesses its faith." As such, its expression and conceptual understanding was considered to be grounded contextually. Through recognition that expression and understanding develops and changes, it acknowledged the possibility that the Confession should be changed as well. Since 1997, an alternative Confession of Faith has been contained in the following paragraph in gender-inclusive language. Thompson's book, *Stating the Gospel*, includes the full text of doctrinal statements considered to belong to the URC's particular heritage; the entire *Basis of Union* is published alongside the Westminster Confession, Savoy Declaration, and Campbell's Declaration. Although making clear in his introduction to the book that the Confession is found in paragraph seventeen, Thompson regards the full text of the *Basis* to be confessional in status.

The right to change and to make new statements and declarations is enshrined in the *Basis*. The denomination's Doctrine, Prayer and Worship Committee adopted this approach in the mid-1990s. When formed by the merger of the Doctrine and Prayer Committee with the Worship Committee in 1994, the committee's work included "to lead the Church in its continual study of theology, enabling it to reflect upon and express the doctrines of the United Reformed Church."[6] It therefore responded to the request to consider writing a Statement of Faith in inclusive language. The *Basis* was amended in 1990 to remove gendered language when referring to human beings, but the Confession in paragraph seventeen had been explicitly excluded from this re-drafting because of the contentious nature of the debate about language for God.[7] The Assembly's remit to its Doctrine, Prayer and Worship Committee was to regard its work as supplementary to the existing statement rather than to supersede it.

A proposed form of words for such a Confession came to the General Assembly in 1995, drafted by the hymn writer and URC minister Alan Gaunt.[8] While not endorsing those words, Assembly encouraged the Doctrine, Prayer and Worship committee to produce a revised

---

6. GA Reports (1995) 58.
7. GA Record (1990) 31.
8. GA Reports (1995) 59.

Confession for the 1996 Assembly. When the revised Confession was presented to the Assembly in 1996 the Committee stated that "the revision tries to take account of the views expressed" both through the discussions at the 1995 Assembly and through correspondence received from several members of the Assembly.[9] The version produced replicated the pattern of the existing Confession in the *Basis* yet sought to offer it as "more readily usable in worship." Furthermore, the Committee believed that there was no change being proposed that would alter the substance of the faith in the previous Confession that formed part of the denomination's foundational documents.[10]

The debate on the alternative version of the statement in paragraph seventeen was "long and careful" chaired by former Assembly Moderator, Revd. Malcolm Hanson.[11] Although a number of amendments to the text were tabled during the debate, none of the suggested amendments received a majority in favour.[12] When the Assembly came to decide whether to make the addition to the *Basis*, it received the requisite two-thirds majority for constitutional changes. Because the change was to amend the *Basis*, the matter was sent to Synods to seek their concurrence with the proposed change. If fewer than two-thirds of the Synods had concurred the addition would not have been put before the next Assembly for ratification. However, when it returned to the Assembly for ratification in 1997, although four synods had voted against this addition to the *Basis*, the support of eight synods was enough to bring the change to the Assembly.[13] This provision, occasionally known as the "Barrier Act," is more fully examined later. Requiring a simple majority vote, the Assembly ratified the change and the alternative version of the statement was added to the end of paragraph eighteen and the denomination made an addition to its Confession of Faith.

Alongside the paragraphs that explicitly refer to a Confession of Faith, the *Basis* contains the *Statement concerning the nature, faith and*

9. GA Reports (1996) 100.

10. GA Reports (1996) 100.

11. GA Record (1996) 29–30. The Moderator of General Assembly in 1996 was Dr. (now the Revd. Professor) David M. Thompson who was presenting the work from the Doctrine, Prayer and Worship Committee as its Convenor. Malcolm Hanson was Moderator of General Assembly 1991–2.

12. GA Record (1996) 30.

13. There were twelve Synods at this point as it predated the union with the Congregational Union of Scotland.

order of the URC. This statement is, unlike the Confession of faith, to be "read aloud at ordination and induction services" of both Elders and Ministers. This Statement is included as Schedule D of the *Basis of Union*. As with the Confession, the Statement exists in two forms. The first version was included in the 1972 *Basis of Union*. However, within a short period of time, the denomination's magazine, *Reform*, began to publish letters from URC members that expressed displeasure with the form the Statement took when used in worship. The second version, in a preliminary form penned by the hymn writer and URC minister Dr. Brian Wren, first appeared in *Reform* in February 1977.[14] Its adoption in an amended form by the Assembly in 1981 and publication in the denomination's 1991 hymnbook *Rejoice and Sing* made a liturgically appropriate Statement more readily available for congregational use. It is interesting to note that the 1972 Confession of Faith as found in paragraph seventeen was not published in the hymnbook, even though the Apostles' and Nicene Creeds were published alongside the *Statement concerning the nature, faith and order of the URC*. The *Companion to Rejoice and Sing* notes that the Statement "is probably unique among historic Creeds, in that it includes a recognition of the possibility of its own amendment."[15]

The inclusion of the Schedule D statement in *Rejoice and Sing*, therefore, has led to this statement being easily accessible to the ordinary Church member while the Confession remains in the *Manual*. The practical effect of this is that the Statement is available for use while the Confession is not as easily available for the denomination's members. Arthur Macarthur's lament that "much of what we did to give [the URC] shape is now words in a Manual little read and often regarded as history" seems to apply well to this case.[16]

However, although confession may be part of the life of the Church, this does not necessarily make it an authority. Instead, it is necessary to consider its role in the Church's life. Schedule E of the *Basis* stipulates the criteria that Ministers of the URC are expected to adhere to in order to maintain their ministerial status. The second paragraph (§A.Sch.E.2) reads: "Ministers must conduct themselves and exercise all aspects of their ministries in a manner which is compatible with . . . the affirmation

---

14. *Reform* (February 1977) 7.
15. URC, *Companion to Rejoice and Sing*, 910.
16. Macarthur, *Setting Up Signs*, 115.

made by ministers at ordination and induction . . . and the Statement concerning the nature, faith and order."

This paragraph thus establishes a cyclical relationship between the various component aspects of the *Basis*. The Schedule E commitments ensure that ministers abide by the ordination promises in Schedule C and the *Statement concerning the nature, faith and order* in Schedule D. Not to do so is therefore an act subject to discipline. However, both Schedule E and Schedule C assert the importance of the Statement in Schedule D. The question posed to the minister is "will you undertake to exercise your ministry in accordance with the statement concerning the nature, faith and order of the United Reformed Church?" (§A.Sch.C.v1.9). This asks ministers at ordination and induction to confirm their recognition of the statement and to assent to its content. In exercising ministry in accordance with the Schedule D Statement, ministers agree that the *Basis* embodies "the essential notes of the Church catholic and reformed" (§A. Sch.D.v1.5) and affirms that "We conduct our life together according to the Basis of Union" (§A.Sch.D.v2). By affirming this ministers acknowledge the *Basis* in its entirety as authoritative in the life of the Church.

Yet, through the use of the Statement read aloud, the congregation too assent to its content. Although the intent of those in the congregation cannot be presumed, the affirmation of the Statement by the ministers and elders present confirms its place as a key component in their own ordination and subsequent inductions. In reading aloud the Schedule D Statement in public acts of ordination and induction the Statement and thus the *Basis* are renewed as an authoritative text maintained by the denomination.

The *Basis*, therefore, develops cyclical, interconnected relationships between its various sections, linking one to another. It is thus through this interconnectedness that the Confession of Faith and the Statement are given their authoritative status. While it would appear that the Schedule D Statement holds a stronger place as a confessional text, its content draws together all the components of the *Basis* and incorporates fully the understanding of the trinitarian faith, the nature of a united and ecumenically minded Church, and the place of ministry within the provisional denominational structure. The Statement dovetails together these disparate aspects by incorporating the two Confessions alongside the wider text of the *Basis* as part of the entire confessional statement of the URC. While this echoes Thompson's treatment of the *Basis* as an entire Confession, it does nothing to release the *Basis* from being largely hidden in the Manual.

Establishing Separation

The historical identity which forms the root network sustaining the URC is one of English Nonconformity, forged in the English Reformation, inspired by Congregationalism and the Continental Reformed movements. This identity is deeply rooted in the history of Britain, with the many challenges, chances and conclusions that British politics has manifest, informing understandings of what it means both to be Reformed and to be United.

It is, perhaps, given this history rooted in the English Reformation, that the identity of the URC is one that has a distinctive reticence towards the involvement of the State in the life of the Church. Such a view is seen internationally, where Christian Churches are not intrinsically linked with the State and not only sit apart from political establishments but also actively promote the freedom from State interference. This is visible across the globe, with freedom from religion inscribed in the First Amendment to the American Constitution, while nations on all continents exclude established religion.

While many Christian denominations around the world are in countries where state establishment of religion does not exist, in the British context, the URC is in an environment where an established Church does. This makes the URC's context specific while offering a commonality of nonconformist witness around the world.

The insistence in the *Basis* that "Christ gives his Church a government distinct from the government of the state" (§A.Sch.D.v2) outlines in bold language how the URC understands the Church's relationship to civil government. There are, of course, disclaimers to such a statement, recognising that concerning "obedience to God the Church is not subordinate to the state, but must serve the Lord Jesus Christ" while "Civil authorities are called to serve God's will of justice and peace for all humankind" (§A.Sch.D.v2). This denies to the state the right to interfere in ecclesial matters or in matters of faith and conscience, but gives to the state its divine vocation of securing peace and justice.

To outline the relationship between the state and the Churches in England would result in a lengthy and complex historical, political and ecclesiological narrative. Such narratives are well documented in a number of sources and depict the life of the Church in England as it moved from Catholicism under Rome to the multi-denominational, multi-religious environment of the twentieth and twenty-first centuries.[17] However, alongside that well-rehearsed narrative there lies another story relating the understanding of authority as it progressed through the generations from the early English Dissenters to those who formulated the URC's *Basis* in the 1960s.

It is almost impossible to describe the concept of a Reformed Church within the English context without relating it to the relationship between Church and state, growing as they do from the Reformation movements against the Established Church. This juxtaposition results in the words of "Dissent" and "Nonconformity" being used to describe how alternative strands of churchmanship have developed alongside the state sponsored Church of England. In this sense, the title of "Supreme Head" (taken by Henry VIII) or "Supreme Governor" (taken by his daughter Elizabeth) of the Church of England was challenging to those who sought greater reform of the Church who believed that it is Jesus who is the Church's "only Ruler and Head" (§A.Sch.D.v2). The execution of Charles I in 1649 created a challenge for those who had placed store in the role of the monarch as the Supreme Governor of the Church of England as it fundamentally questioned the ecclesiological role of the monarch. The remainder of the seventeenth century brought about some of the most turbulent political wrangling and the most challenging political philosophy, reflecting struggles not only in the political sphere but also in the ecclesial world.

Authority in society is reflected in political as well as theological texts of this time. Drawing on English political philosophy, it is possible to consider the ways in which English political thought was viewed during the seventeenth century and the interconnectedness between the political and the ecclesial during this period. Two texts notable for their engagement with political and theological thought within the context of the English Reformation thus provide useful insight into the topic of authority in an English, Reformed perspective. Thomas Hobbes's *Leviathan* (first published in 1651) and John Locke's *Two Treatises of Government* (first published in 1690) cover the challenges to the political realm through the confusions of civil war, regicide, commonwealth, restoration,

---

17. Examples of such include Cornick, *Under God's Good Hand*; Haight, *Christian Community*; Nuttall and Chadwick, *Uniformity to Unity*; Pope, *Companion to Nonconformity*.

and the wide-ranging implications of the Glorious Revolution of 1688. Both authors address their task with passion, and in doing so provide political and philosophical justification for the context in which they lived.

Hobbes takes the question of sovereignty and makes the case that where there is no defined sovereign there is the possibility for disagreement among the people and a consequent inability to maintain peace. While he is happy to contend that sovereignty may be Monarchical, Democratic or Aristocratic,[18] he is clearly influenced by the actions that led to Civil War and, ultimately, the death of the King. His sometimes fiercely Royalist polemic gives little space for the view that an assembly of gathered representatives can govern. He writes that the difference between Monarchy and Democracy "consisteth not in the difference of power; but in the difference of convenience, or aptitude to produce the peace, and security of the people; for which end they were instituted"[19] and goes on to stipulate that "a monarch cannot disagree with himself, out of envy, or interest; but an assembly may; and that to such a height, as may produce a civil war."[20] For Hobbes, this central place of a monarch ensures that a centralised sovereign authority is established. Furthermore, it seems inconceivable to him that within a society there can be deviation "from the views established by the sovereign"[21] for this simply does not imply a united, peaceful society.

Hobbes offers a further critique of the assembly model because, he asserts, assemblies are as open "to be seduced by orators, as a monarch by flatterers."[22] What he suggests is that the popular view of the monarch was of one who had taken counsel from those whom he chose rather than listen to the widest representation from the widest constituency. Yet his accusatory tone suggests that his view of parliamentary democracy in the mid seventeenth century was one of partisan oratory swaying the assembly in a direction Hobbes believed to be damaging. However, in spite of what could be considered conservative concerns about democratic government, he draws a further point concerning injustice within the assembly system, stating that "[f]or to accuse, requires less eloquence (such is man's nature) than to excuse; and condemnation, than absolution more

18. Hobbes, *Leviathan*, 123 (XIX.§1).
19. Hobbes, *Leviathan*, 124 (XIX.§4).
20. Hobbes, *Leviathan*, 125 (XIX.§7).
21. Tralau, "Hobbes Contra Liberty," 74.
22. Hobbes, *Leviathan*, 125 (XIX.§8).

resembles justice."[23] Ultimately, while Hobbes argues that an assembly can be fickle in hearing condemnation from less eloquent speakers, he places this alongside the possibility that a monarch may be swayed by flattery. Both systems are, in Hobbes's view, flawed.

Whereas Hobbes was writing during the upheavals of the end of the civil wars and the execution of the King and while England was designated a Commonwealth under Cromwell, Locke was writing at a time in which the monarchy had been restored and the ascent of William and Mary to the throne in 1688 following the so-called "Glorious Revolution." The context in which he wrote his *Treatises on Government* clearly impacted on his understanding of civil government and thus the relationship between monarch, government and the governed. It acts as much as an explanation of why Civil War and Regicide occurred as it does a treatise for future government. In this way Locke offers a theory for how government should be understood in light of the tumultuous seventeenth century, with a mind towards how government within the post-Revolution state should be constituted.

Locke's understanding of civil authority is formed by his understanding of consent required to join society. The natural position for Locke is for humans to exist in a "State of Nature" whereby individuals possess the property that is theirs. In such a position, possession of property is contestable and open to dispute, each party seeking to safeguard their personal property. In this way, Locke understands both wealth and personal freedom in terms of property. In moving from this state into a society, one is assumed to give up autonomy by denying one's own freedom and consenting to release it in the service of the wider community.[24]

Locke's fundamental understanding of society, therefore, concerns the giving up of personal freedom in order consensually to enter into society with others. In doing so, individual persons move from being "free, equal, and independent" to being "a community, for their comfortable, safe, and peaceable living one amongst another . . . wherein the majority have the right to act and conclude the rest."[25] Later thinkers, such as Rousseau, also echoed these perspectives: "[I]n order that each citizen shall be at the same time perfectly independent of all his fellow citizens

---

23. Hobbes, *Leviathan*, 126 (XIX.§8).
24. Locke, "Second Treatise," 141 (§95).
25. Locke, "Second Treatise," 141 (§95).

and excessively dependent on the republic."[26] This places the benefits of government to be above that of independent co-existence. The presence of government given a majority of the right to act for all places the communal above the individual.

These two authors therefore offer subtly different interpretations. In Hobbes, the move from the "State of Nature" symbolises a move from individuals fighting for their freedom coming together into a unified, peaceable society. It indicates the need no longer to contest the property each seeks to possess, but allows each to live peaceably with their property. Furthermore it does not advocate government as a worthy end in itself. However, Locke believes that it is justice which is best served as part of the consensual society. This is summarised early in the *Second Treatise* where he writes "therefore God hath certainly appointed government to restrain the partiality and violence of men."[27] Government is therefore required by Locke to ensure that human bias in acting as law maker and law executor does not result in injustice, either towards the self or towards others.[28] This restraint of "partiality and violence of men" means that in giving up personal freedom to become a member of a society, the reciprocity offered in return is that of an authoritative body capable of securing justice for all.

Locke's understanding of society is very much a communal experience whereby, in spite of personal property being available for its owner's use, the collective body shares among its own people the resources from its own collective wealth. Where Hobbes's approach to consent strongly suggests a "safety in numbers" mentality whereby consent is a way of looking after the self,[29] Locke considers living as society to be the best way to ensure that all are looked after; "all human life, not just one's own, must be preserved."[30] This approach "conveys a specifically political authority, and it conveys that authority to clearly identified individuals" by ensuring that specific freedoms are given to those assigned the duty to govern.[31]

26. Rousseau, *Social Contract*, 62.

27. Locke, "Second Treatise," 105 (§13).

28. The three reasons Locke gives are outlined in three sections seen in Locke, "Second Treatise," 155 (§§124–6).

29. Seen in Hobbes, *Leviathan*, 82–106 (XIII–XV).

30. "Hobbes proceeds from the assumption that each person will seek to preserve only himself" (Forster, *Locke's Politics*, 241).

31. Forster, *Locke's Politics*, 250.

Because of this interdependency upon one another and the interconnectedness of one another's freedoms, rebellion is not undertaken lightly. This rests on the recognition that while individual consent is offered to join society, one of the freedoms is the right to have individual opinion valued in all cases, "[f]or in making the original compact you tacitly consented to be bound by the decision of the majority."[32] It is believed, therefore, that to maintain such strength in a consensual government, Locke's understanding of democracy relies upon the assumption that members of any given society share a common moral theory from which decision-making may be drawn. This eliminates the possibility of extreme disagreements among the *polis* leading to rebellion. Such common moral theory may be drawn from sharing a common religion.[33]

Both Locke and Hobbes consider the ways in which compliance may be assured. For Hobbes, the establishment of a covenant immediately creates "a power capable of enforcing the covenant."[34] This places the consenting covenant as the defining factor in generating an authoritative body with the power to impose sanctions. For Locke, authority is the force which draws individuals to consent to be members of a common society. In this way, a monarch, as a focus for the community around which members consent to join, is able to draw individuals into society. As the focal point for drawing in members to the community, the sovereign is also perceived to be the only means possible of causing submission and compliance.[35] Therefore, the role of a sovereign monarch provides an authoritative focus within the society.

Thus, Hobbes and Locke provide a discussion of the relationship between the sovereign monarch and the common society formed through consensual agreement. Such a discussion produces a political philosophy which considers how authority has been established and where it has been located in society. In doing so, both Hobbes and Locke provide a commentary on differing understandings of authority through an important period in the development of nonconformist thought in England.

Therefore, nonconformists do not always accept the focus of authority on a sovereign monarch enthusiastically and the relationship between nonconformity and the state is important in examining the Church's

---

32. Thomas, *Locke on Government*, 28.
33. Forster, *Locke's Politics*, 258.
34. Copleston, *Hobbes to Hume*, 40.
35. Forster, *Locke's Politics*, 249.

understanding of authority. The inclusion of an Address to the Throne in the agenda of the URC's General Assembly adds a perplexing element in the overall commitment to separation. It seems that two aspects need to be considered: the relationship of Dissent to the monarchy and the place of Addresses to the Throne; and why it is legitimate for the URC to present such Addresses.

The sixteenth and seventeenth centuries saw significant encroachment by the monarch on the religious freedoms of those who wished to dissent. While the young Edward VI advocated churchmanship akin to a Presbyterian system of governance, later monarchs were unwilling or unable to bring this to fruition. Attempts by Charles I to impose a new form of Church in Scotland were a contributing factor to the unrest that led to the first Civil War. While the Protectorate offered a degree of freedom, which was further asserted in the *Declaration of Breda* in 1660,[36] the Restoration brought with it the Act of Uniformity (1662) and the imposition of the Prayer Book and the Thirty-nine Articles as doctrinal, liturgical and ecclesiological standards for religion in England.[37] It was not until the Revolution settlement of William and Mary that the so-called Act of Toleration (1689) granted greater freedoms to Nonconformists including the removal of barriers which had hitherto prevented the legal existence of a Nonconformist witness.

Yet one of the key components of the relationship between Dissenters and the Monarchy is grounded in the simple maxim that Dissent does not equate to disloyalty, although it may be perceived as such. Early Dissent was grounded on the premise that it was not the State *per se* which was the target of nonconformist anxieties, but rather the State's fervent and invalid interference in the Church and in matters of conscience. In August 1639, the General Assembly of the "presbyterian" Church of Scotland asserted its "testimony of our fidelity to God and loyaltie to our King"[38] while the General Assembly in 1648 wished the King "a righteous and peaceable reign" in "declaring their duty and loyalty to his majesty."[39] The text of the *Solemn League and Covenant*, produced during the Civil War, invited Covenanters "to preserve and defend the King's Majesty's person

---

36. Kenyon, *Stuart Constitution*, 331–32; see also Gardiner, *Puritan Revolution*, 465–67.

37. The effect of the Act of Uniformity on the creation of the first Nonconformists is explored in Nuttall and Chadwick, *Uniformity to Unity*, 149–87.

38. Church of Scotland, *Acts of the General Assembly*, 42.

39. Church of Scotland, *Laws of the Church of Scotland*, 288.

and authority . . . that the world may bear witness with our consciences of our loyalty, and that we have no thoughts or intentions to diminish his Majesty's *just* power and greatness."[40] William of Orange gave "a distinct assurance . . . that all loyal Dissenters should be free from religious persecution" as long as these "Dissenters" were Protestant and trinitarian.[41] In 1691, concerning their "Demeanour towards the Civil Magistrate," an agreement between Congregational and Presbyterian Ministers "in and about London" asserted "That we ought to yield unto them not only *subjection in the Lord*, but *support*, according to our station and abilities."[42] Just a few years later loyalty was explicitly directed towards William after an unsuccessful assassination attempt in 1696. A covenant was drawn up by Parliament "affirming their loyalty to him" and this was subscribed to around the country where "[p]eople flocked to the meeting-houses to append their names . . . and then sent them up to London."[43]

In the early part of the eighteenth century, two bodies—the Protestant Dissenting Deputies, and the General Body of Protestant Dissenting Ministers—based within ten (and later twelve) miles of London came into being. These bodies were actively involved in bringing the political concerns of nonconformists to the attention of government. The Deputies, selected from Dissenters within the London area, represented Presbyterian, Independent and Baptist traditions and were particularly influential in the late-eighteenth and early-nineteenth century movements to repeal the Test and Corporation Acts, as well as being involved in a number of other discussions with the government. Referencing the minutes of the *Committees for Repeal of the Test and Corporation Acts*, Davis outlines that the work of the Deputies and the Ministers from Dissenting traditions were significant in the repeal process.[44] This "extraparliamentary campaign," Davis suggests, gives an indication of how these bodies operated internally while also demonstrating their approach to "broaden the definition of religious toleration."[45] This, he argues, also illustrates how a geographically restricted pressure group can affect the national stage and, he believes, provides "an early model of reform tactics

40. Drysdale, *Presbyterians in England*, 290. Article 3. Emphasis original.
41. Drysdale, *Presbyterians in England*, 425.
42. Anonymous, *Heads of Agreement*, 14.
43. Jones, *Congregationalism*, 118.
44. Davis, *Committees*, vii.
45. Davis, *Committees*, vii.

that was widely used in later campaigns."[46] With their work also covering the educational reforms of the later nineteenth century, the success of the Deputies resulted in the easing of a number of state restrictions affecting nonconformists.

While most of their work was focused on redressing the position of nonconformists within the state through engagement with the political establishment in parliament, these Dissenters were "accustomed from the time of the Revolution to appear at Court . . . to pay their respects."[47] In 1688 an Address was presented to William of Orange by about ninety ministers introduced to him representing the General Body of Ministers, while for the accession of Queen Anne in 1702 "they adopted the more sensible plan of sending a small deputation,"[48] led by influential Dissenter Daniel Williams.[49] This right of approach has been maintained by the Deputies through subsequent centuries; in recent years this act has been directed by the Free Church Federal Council and, latterly, the Free Churches Group.

However, disagreement between Dissenters is, to an extent, inevitable and the Deputies have been no exception. During the eighteenth century, the Presbyterians, constituting the predominant group among the Deputies, took the lead in presenting addresses to the monarch. This caused some resentment among the other denominations and when this came to a head over who would present the Address on the accession of William VI and Queen Adelaide in July 1830, the Presbyterians agreed that presentation would in future be rotated around all three denominations.[50] After it became legally permissible to hold Unitarian views in 1813 it became possible for the Presbyterian ministers and congregations who had become Unitarian to be classified as such. As a result a number, now Unitarian, ministers seceded from the Deputies in the 1830s and established themselves as "The Presbyterian Divines of London and Westminster."[51] This body declared themselves part of the succession of earlier Presbyterians and therefore assumed the right, which was subsequently endorsed, also to present Addresses to the monarch.

46. Davis, *Committees*, vii.
47. Manning, *Protestant Dissenting Deputies*, 453.
48. Manning, *Protestant Dissenting Deputies*, 453.
49. Jones, *Congregationalism*, 118.
50. Manning, *Protestant Dissenting Deputies*, 60–70.
51. Manning, *Protestant Dissenting Deputies*, 81.

Therefore, it can be seen that while Nonconformists regarded themselves as distinct from the Church of England, their loyalty to the monarch, as citizens of the State, confirms the assertion that Dissent is not to be equated with disloyalty. Through his assurance that loyal dissenters should be free of religious persecution, William of Orange opened the door to the presentation of addresses, and in receiving a significant number of ministers upon his arrival in 1688 and subsequently, a precedent of approach to the throne was established.

Although this examination considers the relationship of Dissent to the monarchy, historically demonstrated through the Dissenting Deputies, it leaves unanswered the question of the denominational role of the URC in presenting an Address to the Throne. Given that this Address is a key place in the denomination's life whereby a direct link is recognised between the Church and the State, the presentation of such an Address has importance in understanding something about the way in which the URC relates to civil government and particularly the Monarch. However, to understand its role in the contemporary URC as an indicator of the role of authority, some further historical exploration is required in order to discover where it had developed as a practice in the traditions that made up the URC and why it has maintained its place in the denomination's life.

Loyal Addresses to the Throne were included from the earliest synods of the Presbyterian Church in England. When the Presbyterian Church of England was formed by the union in 1876 of the Presbyterian Church in England and the United Presbyterian Church, the Synod resolved "to draw up a loyal address to the Crown, embodying a statement of the principles of the Presbyterian Church of England"[52] and this was to be "presented to Her Majesty through the Secretary of State for the Home Department."[53] Until 1906 such addresses remained occasional occurrences, marking particular events in the life of the Monarchy; in moments of celebration, such as Queen Victoria's gold and diamond jubilees, addresses of celebration were sent, while in moments of sadness, such as at the death of Queen Victoria, addresses of sympathy were sent.

In 1906 the Loyal Address to the Throne began to become part of the PCE's annual Synod. This was cemented in 1908 by the inclusion of the Loyal Address to the Throne in the business timetable of the Synod

---

52. PCE Minutes (1876) 31.
53. PCE Minutes (1876) 34.

formally stated in its Standing Orders.[54] Unlike other changes made to the Standing Orders between 1907 and 1908, there is no mention made of this addition to the Standing Orders in the report of the PCE's General Purposes Committee or through resolution in the Minutes of the 1907 or 1908 Synod. Its inclusion in the business timetable, therefore, appears to follow the practice of 1906 and 1907, but the change appears not ever to have been formally adopted by the PCE Synod. The inclusion of this practice in the PCE's Standing Orders in 1908, apparently without formal resolution of the Synod itself, thus led to the continuation of this practice through the remainder of the twentieth-century and into the life of the URC.

While this traces the regular inclusion of the Address to the Throne, the rationale behind the PCE's right and purpose in addressing the monarch is still uncertain. Occasional Addresses were also made by the CUEW, following the pattern of the pre-1906 PCE practice. An example of which was the message sent to "Her Majesty the Queen" from the 1962 Assembly in the tercentenary of the Great Ejectment: "Though the deep convictions of our fathers led them to dissent from the Act of Uniformity, and though we ourselves still dissent from many of its provisions, we, like them, seek constantly to be faithful servants of your Majesty and loyal citizens of this realm."[55]

A review of the URC practice "of presenting a Loyal Address to the Throne" was carried out in 1995. The review asserted the dissenting witness towards the State "which is a Monarchy," and affirmed that "because we recognise the State as itself under Christ, there is a ground for comment critical or condemnatory upon the actions of the Queen's Ministers." Of the changes made, the word "Loyal" was dropped from use and, instead of "signifying assent by the singing of The National Anthem," it had been "agreed that it would be presented towards the end of the Assembly and that its adoption would be by means of a vote."[56]

It may be regarded that the loss of "Loyal" from the title of the Address at the URC General Assembly is a significant departure from the historical purpose of the Address to the Throne. By removing loyalty as the key indicator of the Address, its ability to assert that Dissent does not equate to disloyalty is somewhat diminished. It may be argued that such

54. PCE Minutes (1908) 552.
55. CYB (1962) 88.
56. GA Reports (1995) 33 (§5.1).

a change reflects more accurately the change in the status of Dissenters in the eyes of the State. Whereas "Dissenter" was the name given to those who refused to assent to statutes such as the Act of Uniformity, the overriding of such legislation through subsequent Acts removes equivalent constraints on Nonconformists. However, other key components—such as recognising that both Church and State are Monarchical governments yet headed by different monarchs—take a more prominent role in the Address. These, therefore, affirm more positively the focus for a nonconformist view of Christ's kingship over matters affecting the life of the Church and directs authority away from the state and into the sphere of the Church.

The Address to the Throne, however, is not the only consideration in the relationship between the Church and State. Charity Law, set by the state, also affects the role of Trust bodies. Such legislation, along with legislation including Health & Safety, employment and child protection, features in the life of the Church. Although "Trust law has, in fact, been the driver for greater statutory involvement in Free Church life through the twentieth century,"[57] Thompson argues that the current legislative framework "has increasingly occupied the time and money of local congregations, regardless of polity, raising new questions of the ability of small congregations to cope with these official requirements."[58]

When the Covid-19 pandemic struck the UK in 2020, the restrictions put in place by the Government caused the closure of places of worship, including throughout Ramadan and Easter. When restrictions were eased, it became possible for places of worship to be opened for, initially, private prayer, and subsequently for congregational worship led within strict Covid-19 restrictions. Throughout the pandemic, restrictions imposed by the State had been questioned among the population, and when further closures were imposed in November 2020 during a second lockdown, some Church leaders expressed concerns with the State's approach. The Roman Catholic Archbishop of Westminster, the Anglican Archbishops of Canterbury and York, together with a number of other faith leaders, wrote to the Prime Minister to request the continued opening of places of worship for congregational worship.[59] Additionally, some other Church Leaders, led by Pentecostal leader Ade Omooba and

57. Thompson, "Nonconformists and Polity," 108.
58. Thompson, "Nonconformists and Polity," 109.
59. Nichols et al., "Faith Communities Letter."

supported by former Bishop of Rochester Michael Nazir-Ali, sought a legal challenge to the cessation of public worship.[60]

However, while the URC has been wary of unnecessary State involvement in the life of the Church, this second lockdown did not provoke the same response from the URC. Instead, the Moderators of the General Assembly, Revd. Clare Downing and Mr. Peter Pay issued a statement encouraging Churches to follow the guidance "rather than forensically examining the latest guidance wondering how far a rule can be pushed or where we might find a loophole to exploit."[61] It was this guidance from the Government, the Moderators asserted, which was living out the requirement of civil authority "to serve God's will of justice and peace for all humankind" (§A.Sch.D.v2) and was entirely in keeping with the *Basis* and its understanding of the role of the State. In these circumstances, rather than restrict the freedoms of the Church the action of the Government was to be serving the will of God to provide peace and justice to all. While much of the UK Government's actions during the pandemic had been subject to question, the imposition of regulations that resulted in the suspension of worship were regulations that could, with a heavy heart, be acceptable to the wider URC, recognising that such actions were not themselves restrictions of freedom to worship, but were for the health and wellbeing of all people.

Yet, although the State affects the authority of the Church (demonstrated in the statutory provisions affecting Church life), the authority of the State cannot be unquestionably accepted. While Locke attempted to show that legitimate political authority exists, scholarly scepticism of this thesis has concluded that "not all reasons, or even all moral reasons, for obeying governments are reasons for accepting that they have legitimate authority."[62]

Thus in recognising that government is not always in possession of legitimate authority, a double-edged understanding of the relationship of Church to the State can be explored. First, the State, in matters affecting its own sphere, is to be regarded as possessing authority. There is little doubt that Nonconformist witness has sought to demonstrate loyalty to the State. In its *Basis* the URC states that "In things that affect obedience to God the Church is not subordinate to the state" and thus affirms, by

60. Wyatt, "Church Legal Challenge," para. 4, 10.
61. URC, "Moderators on Lockdown," para. 8.
62. Thomas, *Locke on Government*, 14.

implication if not explicitly, that civil government does have an authority in matters that affect wider society (§A.Sch.D.v2). Locke's exploration of government as appointed by God while society is formed to create a consenting body capable of governing, therefore, acknowledges that both the state apparatus and the Church are subject to the authority of God. In matters affecting wider society, therefore, the government has responsibilities which are not those of the Church. Although these should be "always subject to the rule of God," the *Basis* does not advocate disagreement with civil government for simply being civil, but rather recognises, as the early Nonconformists did, that the Church is best kept under the rule of Christ than under a state government (§A.Sch.D.v1). The *Basis* maintains, therefore, that should the state require disobedience to God's will, the Church maintains its right to dissent.

The second conclusion is that although the state may be obeyed on moral or other grounds, it does not follow that the state is always and entirely legitimate in that authority. The engagement of the Dissenting Deputies in the life of the British government in the repeal of the Test and Corporation Acts shows that disagreement with government is possible and that, when further scrutinised, government can be shown to have erred. Civil authorities, however, "ought to respect the rights of conscience and of religious belief," insists the URC's *Basis*, and thus be open to serve the fullness of God's will (§A.Sch.D.v1). The emphasis within the *Basis* insisting that the Church is to "serve the Lord Jesus Christ, its only Ruler and Head" gives a moral framework from which the Church may draw, and sets up the possibility that it may disagree with the state on moral or other grounds (§A.Sch.D.v2). The place of the state's authority on these matters, the *Basis* posits, is not always or entirely legitimate and, therefore, like the Church's decisions, remains provisional.

Thus, the URC upholds its conviction that Church and civil government remain separate but are, under God, united in the work of bringing "justice and peace for all humankind" (§A.Sch.D.v2).

Reforming Identity

A Reformed identity, however, is grounded in the idea of re-forming ideas and being open to the possibilities of change. Although identity may be rooted in history, the understanding of Reformed identity is wrapped up in the idea of renewal, drawing on solid authorities (typically the Word of God), yet developing new understandings and revising old ideas. A Reformed identity, therefore, is not historically fixed, but is rooted in authority.

Throughout the life of Christianity, the Church's journey has not followed a single path and division among Christians led to the separation of some Christian communities from others. Whether considering the division of the Church into East and West in 1054 or the separation of the Church of England from Roman Catholicism in 1534, disagreements on matters of doctrine and polity have led Christians through the centuries to form new groups of believers. In the Protestant traditions, Luther's *Ninety-five Theses*, nailed to the Schlosskirche in Wittenberg in 1517, and Calvin's *Institutes of the Christian Religion*, first published in Latin in 1536, resulted in new statements about the way in which the Church should be structured and how the Christian faith should be understood.

Similar movements occurred too within English Nonconformity. The approach of the "Separatists" advocated further reform of the Church in England. However, when this seemed distant they "withdrew from the Church of England on the grounds that it remained—in all of its essentials—an unreformed, false institution still linked with Rome," and finally established Congregational polity with subscription to an oath.[63]

These Reformation movements held to the idea that, centred on the Word of God in Scripture, there was a need always to be open to the on-going renewal of the Church. The Latin maxim *Ecclesia Reformata, Semper Reformanda* encapsulates the need for this on-going reformation to be reformation of the Church. Neither Luther nor Calvin, nor later examples such as Wesley, desired the division that their reforms subsequently caused. Yet these men and others believed in the need to bring the Church constantly under the authority of God's Word discerned by the Holy Spirit in gaining further insight into God's will for the Church.

Following in these reformation footsteps, the URC stands by this understanding of being ready to make changes to its *Basis* "so that its life may accord more nearly with the mind of Christ" (§A.9). This assertion recognises the nature of the Church as incomplete and open to the possibility of new expressions of the faith. In this way, the ultimate nature of the Church, realised only at the eschaton, remains a future possibility. Therefore, in view of the future eschatological realisation in the new heaven and new earth, any ecclesiastical polity can only be penultimate in nature.

63. Christianson, "Reformers," 474.

The clearest illustration of change concerns confessional statements. Openness to the Spirit creates a necessity "to continually re-frame confessional statements" while seeking to develop ways "to state the 'truth' in a timeless fashion."[64] Tension between seeking the "correct doctrinal formulation" and maintaining the "provisionality of confessional texts" creates texts that are longstanding yet clear in their openness to change. The Westminster Confession states that "[a]ll synods or councils since the apostles' times, whether general or particular, may err, and many have erred; therefore they are not to be made the rule of faith or practice but to be used as a help in both."[65] Presbyterian minister W. M. Macphail, whose ministry also included offices as General Secretary of the PCE and Clerk of Synod, claimed that the Church's approach to confessions not only gave freedom to "amend and improve" but that the Church was "bound" to do so, "as to make it a more accurate expression of the Church's growing understanding of the Divine revelation enshrined, once for all, in the Scriptures."[66] He cites the case of the Huguenot Reformed Church of France which maintained its confession's subordinate nature by subjecting it to annual review and thus emphasised the claim made in the Westminster Confession that all Councils may err and that their decisions, in matters of standards, are open to change.[67]

The possibility that a Council may err is an important consideration in the discussion of a Church's practice of authority. How can a Council's decision hold authority if it may yet be overridden by claims of further change or reform? If all ecclesial statements, confessions and polities are provisional, what role is there for the Councils in making authoritative statements? These questions reflect the more basic matter of the penultimate nature of the Church and how a Church may maintain its authoritative status if it is itself open constantly to the possibility of reformation.

From the earlier discussion concerning the eschatological understanding of the URC's approach to unity, it can be seen that the process of Reformation was, in many ways, indicative of the quest to make the earthly Church attune more nearly with the great Church. Three insights drawn from Reformed thinkers may, therefore, prove useful in the discussion of authority.

---

64. Bradbury, *Perpetually Reforming*, 85.
65. *Westminster Confession Chapter xxxi.4*, in Thompson, *Stating the Gospel*, 42–43.
66. Macphail, *Presbyterian Church*, 39.
67. Macphail, *Presbyterian Church*, 41.

The first insight reminds us that what we know about God remains incomplete until God is revealed fully and completely to us. Forsyth wrote that "[e]very statement about God is challengeable till God states Himself, in His own way, by His own Son, His own Spirit, His own Word, His own Church, to our soul, which He remakes in the process."[68] The learning experience of the Christian occurs, in Forsyth's terms, when the soul is changed by God's address to it. In such a case, this brings about the renewal of our perceptions of God as more is learnt about God, Jesus, the Spirit and the Word. The reality of God is experienced in our lives. Our knowledge of God, therefore, is not *a priori*, but is continually remade by experience of Christian discipleship and through pursuit of a closer understanding of God's nature.

Second, we are reminded that reform over time makes things that seemed impossible or unobtainable part of daily life. "Many (it is said) of the views now called legitimate were at first treated by the Church as dangerous heresy. How do you know what seems fatal to faith to-day will not be a blessing to faith to-morrow?"[69] Forsyth highlights the need to be aware of what is to be achieved. Bradbury draws also on this idea when he notes that "[t]he church is not simply the sum of its historical parts, it is also formed by a future open to God."[70] While the historical legacy of the Church forms its present reality, both Bradbury and Forsyth are suggesting that in any given time and place the Church possesses a future orientated aspect. The reality of the Church today is that it also points towards the future fulfilment in Christ. It is such a direction, towards the ultimate, that endorses the view that it is in Christ's authority that the Church may source and locate its own authority.

The final insight to offer here concerning the Church's penultimacy is that there remains a need that a Church must consist of a structured body. In a section addressing the value of Church structure, Wilson remarks that "[i]t is well to remember that the One who forbade his followers to be anxious for the morrow had no praise for the man who started to build without being able to finish."[71] The possibility of "structureless groups of like-minded persons"[72] as an alternative to the flawed polity

---

68. Forsyth, *Principle of Authority*, 20.
69. Forsyth, *Principle of Authority*, 218.
70. Bradbury, *Perpetually Reforming*, 114.
71. Wilson, "Religious Authority," 93.
72. Wilson, "Religious Authority," 92.

of the Church suggests that there is still a need for communities to share together in Christian community and witness. This necessity to join in community requires some planning to take place. There is no way for the Church to reach its fulfilment, this suggests, if it does not, in some ways, first make steps towards it.

Insights such as these have provided sufficient justification for a provisional approach to doctrine and order, but they have also affirmed the purpose of striving towards a renewed understanding of the nature of God and the Church.

The URC's *Basis* provides for "its temporary and incomplete nature" and holds to an understanding of "the need for perpetual reformation."[73] In recognising that future possibilities "may accord more nearly with the mind of Christ" (§A.9), the *Basis* maintains the readiness to make changes as an authority in the life of the Church. While derivative of the need for provisionality, the right to change the *Basis* stands as an authoritative declaration to facilitate the renewal of the Church. It gives permission, if not duty, to be open to the pursuit of truth in the life of the denomination in response to the realities of the world and the impact of the Gospel on the Church by the leading of the Spirit.

Identity and Memory

Although the URC's identity draws on the importance of the separation from State involvement and the Reformed understanding of provisionality, the topic of identity relies also on the memory of its internal activity and process. Where memory and identity are lacking, it has been seen that the contemporary URC struggles to understand the authority it possesses and how, where and to what extent this is to be applied. In such cases, a lack of memory can appear as a threat to the denomination's authority: "Assembly [was] really hampered by only happening every two years and by being such a different group each time. So we suffer for a lack of institutional memory. You're asking 'How could authority work better?' It would work better if we remembered what we'd said last time and very often we don't remember."

This threat to the authority of the denomination highlights the ways in which those who are able to bridge the divide between the present and the past are granted an authoritative platform: "There are certain people

---

73. Bradbury, *Perpetually Reforming*, 85.

who become authoritative among us, personal authority, because they can remind us and they can teach us what we said last time. That's a very important function."

This personal authority, derived from being able to recall previous discussions, however, is not without its difficulties. The influence that such knowledge can have on the life of the Church includes bringing with it the threat of power rather than authority: "The people who know stuff do tend to get powerful; it's not the same as authority: knowledge is power in the URC." The knowledge and memory reasons for authority are founded on the understanding that such individuals are not formally recognised as holding office, but are "an" authority because they are "thought to have special knowledge, wisdom, or insight."[74] Therefore, and in such a way, as examined previously, "an" authority is based on an inequality between individuals and is therefore evidenced in relationships in which one is given greater status than another.

While knowledge and memory of the denomination offers one aspect of authority, concerns arise about how knowledge of the Bible and questions of faith could affect an individual's authority. In one Church, a Church Secretary considers an individual's biblical knowledge as a key part of their authority and favours them as an authoritative influence in the denomination as one who speaks with authority:

> But somebody who has a greater knowledge of the Bible, that person in my mind, I'd say, "Yes" because of that knowledge—but it doesn't mean that they are right in their interpretation—I feel [they] would have that bit more authority, and if they were dispensing this knowledge, this biblical knowledge in a way that I see fit, the proper teachings of love and peace and so on, then I think, that's how I would place that person so maybe if they became the Moderator of all, I might be "yes ok" I believe in his authority or her authority.

To regard the knowledge of Scripture, but not necessarily its interpretation, as an indicator of a person's authority is perhaps to offer a rather unquestioning approach to authority whereby appearance has a status equal or above substance. This opens up the possibility of hearing a variety of authorities from wider society. For some in the Church, within a postmodern context a number of authorities have fed into the life of society and not all of these necessarily have the same standing: "You can

---

74. Friedman, "Concept of Authority," 80.

find your authority elsewhere, so if you're not trusting of those who are making decisions but say 'so and so here says this' then that can be a very genuine authoritative voice coming out of a particular context or it could just be some doolally who's got more time on their hands."

However, this openness to hearing "other authoritative voices" may also be a reflection of the URC's understanding of its heritage. As one Assembly Officer asserts, in the history of the Christian story "there's a good healthy sense in the URC that our bit of it is provisional." She went on to ponder: "Is that why we hold our institutional memory with such a light hand? Cos what we decided five years ago isn't very interesting, we keep referring back to the big story—don't we—take our lead from that."

It is perhaps such openness, however, that may lead to suggestion of a lack of ecclesial identity for the URC as a result of a lack of theological knowledge: "It's really a case of us understanding the theology of what we are doing, [that through it we] will actually make better decisions and hopefully will allow people, erm to be gracious in terms of consensus decision-making and things."

Similarly, a Synod Moderator suggests that "[t]he problem is, not so much that there is a problem with our authority, there is a problem with understanding it." Thus, theological and procedural knowledge may play a part in the role of authority in the life of the denomination.

However, there are other reasons behind a lack of identity which some consider is a propensity to maintain unity over identity. The reason that the URC has no identity, they argue, is "because there's nothing you can point to that we don't say 'Ah yes but, you know, we don't really mean it, or if you don't like it you don't have to agree with it.'" In both a positive and regrettable way, this can be reflected in the way that while the denomination may struggle to have a common identity, Local Churches are able to develop their own distinctiveness and character: "It does mean 1500 potentially burgeoning, energetic, Local Churches; they can have identity, they can have profile. But the denomination as a whole isn't going to have profile very often. Except 'We averted split yet again.'"

To seek to find a profile—or identity—for the denomination rests with the need to explore the denomination's polity. A new understanding may be achieved if the denomination had a differing relationship to authority. "I think if we had a different model of authority, our identity might be clearer but it wouldn't be the identity we have, it wouldn't be us."

Thus, while there may be a diminished identity within the denomination, this might in part be due to the conciliar polity of the URC. This, it seems, comes hand-in-hand with the structure the denomination regards as an important part of its identity, even if that part of its identity prevents it from developing an alternative identity. This identity as the URC is therefore fed by its authority, its polity, its theology and the knowledge and memory members have of it. Authority is historically contingent and reflects the past as well as the present. The interplay between these aspects can become part of the tussle in a United denomination. A Church House Secretary remarks:

> But the health of our particular part of the Kingdom requires good communities doing theology that understand why we're structured the way that we are in order that then trust can flourish alongside the relationships that we have and then authority doesn't become a dirty word, which I think for too many it is. It becomes something that the Church holds and where individuals speak or act it's because they know what the Church has said or thinks or does on this one and people trust that.

The question of identity and memory within the denomination's authority transcends all of the conceptual understandings as it draws on the wide range of what it means to be a United and Reformed Church. It is the essence of what a denomination has been and what it strives to be. This places the idea of memory as a source of authority in the denomination's life.

However, the idea of memory and identity as an authoritative source does not match up especially well with reformed ideas of *semper reformanda*. In making a claim to the authority of memory, the URC has developed within its practice a form of ecclesiology that does not sit well alongside the active statement of a "right to change." While such an authority is drawn from the *Basis*, the empirically realised authority is less about the openness to make changes and more to respond to the authority that is characterised as a form of memory. This seems to be a significant difference between the URC's practice and the denomination's conceptual understanding of its authority.

While describing the source of authority to be "tradition" would be to overstate the evidence, the importance of memory as a stabilising influence on the denomination can be clearly seen. The role of individuals who have "become authoritative" because they have been able to "remind us and they can teach us what we said last time" has an important role to play in asserting the significance of memory in the life of the denomination. In the valued place of memory, the continuity, rather than the ever changing nature of the Reformed identity is given a priority.

Knowledge of the historical and ecclesiological details of the URC may give some an authoritative status, but it is the institutional lack of this knowledge that points towards a challenge to the denomination's identity. Concerns raised about a lack of identity focus on the need to assert memory and knowledge of how the denomination has got to where it finds itself. Identity is dependent not upon present reality, but on centuries of historical events and linked to the memory both of the Nonconformist witness in Britain and to the actions of the denomination throughout its lifetime.

In addressing the link between authority and identity, Martyn Percy asserts that questions of ecclesial identity are demonstrated in the relationship between the empirically realised Church ("the authentic") and authority.[75] Therefore, where Church authorities fail to "deal in 'real' issues and do not consult with 'real' Christians and their churches" any authority of the Churches are diminished.[76] It is, therefore, in connecting with the identity of "real" Christians, in their multiplicities, that the Church's authority may be found.

The consideration of the denomination in terms of a "one body, many members" paradigm does therefore suggest that the single body is best represented in terms of a multiplicity of identities. In drawing on a vast variation of different members, the various identities—whether those be from antecedent traditions or from differing recognitions of the URC's journey—form part of what it means to be a United Church. It is in being formed of the various historical traditions alongside a variety of theological positions that the identity of the denomination is developed. The recognition that there would be "1500 potentially burgeoning, energetic, Local Churches; [which] can have identity . . . but the denomination as a whole isn't going to have a profile very often" emphasises that the paradigm has a practical outworking. The one body has many separate identities, each with their own history and context. The denomination, this suggests will never be able to formulate an identity.

While denominational identity may not be expected to have a single, universal appearance, the value of memory as the source of authority in the URC does appear to be counter to the claims of a "readiness to

---

75. Percy, "Authority in Contemporary Ecclesiology," 141.
76. Percy, "Authority in Contemporary Ecclesiology," 143.

alter . . . so that its life may accord more nearly with the mind of Christ" (§A.9). When denominational memory, as an alternative to identity, is perceived to be beneficial, there is something inherently fixed about the way in which such memory is intended to be used. Where it takes a role of safeguarding a given position or history it restricts the propensity to change and in doing so creates a contradictory source of authority in the life of the Church.

If, however, memory is understood to prevent the life of the Church from being swayed with every whim of the age, then its role as "tradition" becomes authoritative. Memory becomes the holder of orthodoxy and can be placed besides Scripture as an authoritative source of denominational authority. In either interpretation, therefore, memory offers challenges to the denominational understanding of authority.

While memory—or indeed identity—is perceived to be lacking, the absence of such sources may evidence a closer link to the conceptual understanding of authority. Where memory is lacking, no "tradition" is being maintained and therefore, the Church might be understood more freely to be ready to alter its own understandings of the faith. Such absence, therefore, may not be as challenging as at first they seem. The lack of a denominational identity, but an identity consisting of the combined identities of individual Local Churches, sits more closely with the conceptual understanding whereby the right to change is held as an authoritative source in the life of the denomination.

5

Structural Authority within a United Ecclesiology

ANY EXPLORATION OF A Reformed ecclesiology will turn, at some point, to consider the relationship of conciliarity in the life of the Church. Although some nonconformist traditions will sit lightly to the idea of conciliarity, and other traditions (such as the Roman Catholic Church) will understand conciliarity within an alternative framework, the Reformed understanding of conciliar authority has remained largely static since Calvin instituted conciliar ecclesial government in Geneva.

However, many United and Uniting denominations do not maintain a purebred polity by nature of the combination of ecclesial structures through Union. This introduces a unique blend of polity whereby aspects of different ecclesiologies merge into new structures, representing the prevalent or pertinent aspects of union discussions.

As a United and Reformed Church, the URC brought together the polities of English Presbyterianism and English and Welsh Congregationalism into an ecclesiology that merged these two structures. This brought conciliarity and congregationalism together in a unique mixture of the two ecclesial traditions. Such unions create a bespoke combination that reflects the history and identity of the uniting traditions while also providing insight into the gifts United ecclesiologies bring to the exploration of Reformed polity. It can be through exploring the ways in which United denominations distil and focus Reformed and conciliar ecclesiology that the rich and valuable particularities that shape and enhance Reformed Churches and become visible. In observing how United and Reformed Churches understand conciliar authority it is possible also to understand more fully the significance of Reformed polity in the wider ecclesiological landscape.

Unlike some other forms of nonconformist ecclesiology, Reformed ecclesiology is often clearly systematised and documented. This gives a clear record of the structures in place and the procedures to be used within the denomination. Within the boundaries of the defined polity, the Church functions within clear rules and processes, with clear processes and authority structures. Where the rules and polity allow it, there is an agreed and approved approach. Yet where some flexibility would be preferrable or advantageous, Reformed polity may not always contain the ambiguity and suppleness to respond dynamically in a given context.

However, when this becomes part of a United denomination where the ecclesiologies are a combination of several polities, there becomes less certainty and ambiguity can creep into the ecclesiological structure. In examples such as the URC, this means that there is not the clarity of a purebred Reformed Church to lean upon, yet also not the unreserved flexibility to act in response to given circumstances.

The Structure of Conciliarity

In his book *Law, Liberty and Church*, Gordon Arthur suggests that the URC has "set up structures of varying flexibility that act like Canon Law."[1] He points towards the influence of the Westminster Confession and Savoy Declaration as the sources for the denomination's structure in drawing together Presbyterian and Congregational polities into the one Church.[2] While flawed in several ways, most notably in seeking to trace lines from Westminster and Savoy directly to the *Basis*, Arthur's consideration of the presbyterial and synodical emphasis in the *Basis* draws out the structural aspect of the Church's authority.

The structure of any institution is based on the presence of a formal (or occasionally, informal) constitution. The URC's *Manual*, Section B entitled *The Structure of the URC*, is the guiding constitution for the denomination. It is significant that within the *Basis* (strictly defined as Section A of the *Manual*) there is minimal indication of the ecclesiological shape of the denomination. This distinction, the former Secretary to the Joint Committee Martin Cressey used to remark, enabled the

---

1. Arthur, *Law, Liberty and Church*, 177.
2. Arthur, *Law, Liberty and Church*, 33–42.

structure of the denomination to remain almost entirely separate from the founding principles and doctrine behind the URC. The *Structure* is deeply informed by the theological principles behind the *Basis* yet is not intertwined with it. Within the practical and formulaic nature of the *Structure* the denomination defines the relationship between its conciliar bodies.

Conciliarity is fundamental aspect of the identity and polity of the URC. The importance of the Councils is strongly advocated by those working in roles beyond the Local Church. One Minister working as a staff secretary at Church House emphatically endorsed the conciliar nature of the Church:

> I've experienced the Church making decisions at Church Meeting, at Synod, at General Assembly and Mission Council, and I like the model that the appropriate Council makes the decision.

This has been similarly echoed by a number of people who value the conciliar nature of the denomination and the way in which each conciliar body takes responsibility for different aspects of the Church's life. One Synod Moderator asserted that "I think, there's a fluid interaction each with a particular sphere of interlinked responsibility." It is this interlinking that ensures that the different Councils can relate to one another and characterises the denomination's conciliarity:

> They have different spheres of responsibility and for just about everything they are equal in terms of the authority—they just have separate responsibilities. Occasionally, the Synods do something that's binding on Local Churches and occasionally the General Assembly will do something that's binding on Local Churches and Synods, within its powers, within its particular functions. But there's a very nice separation of powers in there with the default setting being that authority should be as close to the ground as possible.

In turning focus to the authority contained within the organisational structure of the URC, it is necessary at this stage to consider the role of sociological understandings of organisational authority and their influences on a contemporary discussion of ecclesial authority. First, the postmodern environment, especially as the twenty-first century unfolds, has brought with it a distinct shift in attitude towards institutional authority. The writings of Hannah Arendt, Michel Foucault and Richard

Sennett, to name a few, are indicative of the way in which postmodern philosophers have considered authority in society. The range of literature suggests that (post)modern society is concerned, at least intellectually, with the challenges posed by authority. The effect of World War, the end of Empire and the rise of technology (to mention just three influences on modern society) must all be recognised as factors in the development of new societal understandings of authority in organisations and institutions. Additionally, Onora O'Neill's 2002 Reith Lectures highlighted the amplified effects of trust and transparency in organisations when seen alongside the threats made to authority in contemporary society.[3]

However, ecclesial authority and structure is of a different order to that of secular institutions. As Daniel Jenkins wrote in 1944, "we cannot treat the form which Christ's Body has in the world as a mere matter of administrative convenience."[4] He goes on to elaborate on this from a Congregational point of view by emphasising that the Local Church "bears all the marks of the Church, so that no other body can be more fully the Church than it and so that it need not look outside itself for the source of its authority."[5] The Local Church's authority, suggests Jenkins, is therefore sourced within itself by nature of its manifestation of Christ in the world. This is possible, he notes, because "the Order of the Church is the outward expression of the Christian life of its members."[6] The Christian Gospel is made present and visible in the way in which the Church orders itself and by which it expresses the Christian convictions of its membership. It is this gospel that grounds the Church in values which make it a religious—rather than secular—organisation.

As "the outward expression of the Christian life" which contains all that is necessary to source its authority, the Church's structure holds an authoritative status.[7] The classification of the *Structure of the URC*, and also the *Rules of Procedure*, alongside the *Basis* as a "constitutional" document ensures that they help form and understand the denomination's nature. The requirement of denomination-wide approval prior to adaptation shows that these are important components in the life of the Church where changes are to hold widespread authority. In other words,

3. O'Neill, *Question of Trust*.
4. Jenkins, *Church Meeting*, 21–22.
5. Jenkins, *Church Meeting*, 22.
6. Jenkins, *Church Meeting*, 23.
7. Jenkins, *Church Meeting*, 22–23.

it acknowledges that while the one, holy, catholic and apostolic Church is manifest locally, changes need to be seen by the *whole* body as much as is possible.

The role of the Church is to reflect the Gospel not just in how it proclaims the Christian faith, but also in its nature and order. It is not therefore surprising that the *Statement concerning the nature, faith and order* brings together the structural and doctrinal, for in doing so the statement links together both the doctrinal and ecclesiological. This approach is echoed by Riglin who asserts that "matters of 'authority and order' are of the first order and not derivative."[8] Thus the role of the *Statement* in drawing together an expression of the URC's polity gives it an authoritative status within the denomination.

Through a conciliar structure the URC reflects an understanding of ecclesial governance understood by nonconformists in England over centuries. As Eric Routley notes, the doctrine of the "primary catholic authority of the Church of Rome"[9] was re-interpreted by the Reformers in such a way as to develop a doctrine of protest. He further notes that "Congregationalism in England at its inception is a clear example of a logical and consistent (if at times misguided) application of this doctrine."[10] The result was therefore to ground authority not in an Episcopal or Papal office, but that "the authority in the local church was vested not even in its minister but in all its covenanted people, and that the church was to be defined only and exclusively as the company of the converted and covenanted."[11] Drawing here on Robert Browne, the early Separatist, Routley argues that the authority of these covenanted people, therefore, "comes direct from Christ."[12] The covenanting together as a Local Church becomes, therefore, a symbol of Christ's presence and the location of Christ's authority. In the URC, as in Congregational polity, this is found in the Church Meeting.[13]

The role of the Church Meeting requires Church Members to be "giving up themselves to the Lord, and to one another by the will of God

---

8. Riglin, "Animating Grace," 188.
9. Routley, *Into a Far Country*, 133.
10. Routley, *Into a Far Country*, 133.
11. Routley, *Into a Far Country*, 135.
12. Routley, *Into a Far Country*, 135.
13. The Congregational idea of Church Meeting is also seen in the life of Baptist congregations.

in professed subjection to the ordinances of the gospel."[14] In the communal aspect of this voluntary "giving up," members are covenanting in the first instance with Christ and secondly with one another. Thus the establishment of a Christian community is reliant upon the bond made first through Christian profession, and then by the covenant with others in such a bond. In awareness of this covenantal bond, Congregational minister R. W. Dale, noted that the "presence of Christ in an assembly of Christian men is the ground of all the power and dignity of the Christian Church. Churches are founded that this presence may be realised."[15] It is right, Dale continued, that "Christian men should associate themselves with churches in order that they may share the strength and blessedness which this presence confers, and discharge the duties which it renders possible."[16] Thus it seems appropriate for Christians to covenant together in membership with Christ, whereby they can be built up in faith and brought into closer relationship with God and fellow Christians. Dale's description of the role of Church Membership is comprehensive and thorough:

> That Christian people who live near each other should worship together and pray together; that they should recognise the law of mutual dependence and the obligations of mutual service by placing themselves in each other's care, by asking one or more of their brethren to whom God has given a large knowledge of His truth to teach them, and by asking others to whom He has given practical wisdom and maturity of Christian life to watch over them—this is but the carrying out of Christ's great purpose of drawing into union with each other those who are in union with Himself, and of drawing them into closer union with Himself by their closer union with each other.[17]

This view of membership was echoed later by Daniel Jenkins who wrote that in Church Membership "we are members one of another and that we find our fulfilment, our integration and our personal freedom, the fullness of the stature of our manhood, only in the fellowship of the Body of Christ and the discipline of its common life."[18] Therefore, the role of

---

14. Savoy Declaration, *§8 Institution of the Church*, in Thompson, *Stating the Gospel*, 113.
15. Dale, *Congregational Principles*, 31.
16. Dale, *Congregational Principles*, 31.
17. Dale, *Congregational Principles*, 37–38.
18. Jenkins, *Church Meeting*, 23.

the Church member is not only to be part of a worshipping community, but also to participate in the entirety of Church life so that Christ may be realised and personal fulfilment may be found. Within Congregational—and URC—polity, this is manifest through the Church Meeting.

At the point of union, there was concern among Congregationalists that Presbyterian structure would dominate the life of the URC. Many letters to John Huxtable during the 1960s and early 1970s expressed these concerns, especially in light of perceived erosion of the "Independency" of the Church Meeting. In one such letter in the URC Archive, one correspondent opined that "I have always been very jealous of the authority of the Church meeting, but now any decision of this Meeting can be overruled by the Synod," while Huxtable's response stated that "in the Scheme of Union the Church meeting has been retained and a great deal of authority given to it." However, there was also recognition of the Church Meeting as an offering to the ecumenical movement. "I would deeply regret," wrote another correspondent in November 1971, "any proposal to surrender what I would have thought could have been our peculiar offering to the structure of the great united Church of the future." Huxtable's reply characterised the view of the Joint Committee towards the place of the Church Meeting in the Scheme of Union:

> If and when the [URC] comes into being, it will be for us as ex-Congregationalists to make as sure as possible that all that the Church Meeting symbolises is made a reality. It could well be that the ex-Presbyterians to whom it will all be new may help us to revive it. Perhaps our difficulty with it is that it is too familiar and we tend to take it for granted.

While conciliarity is considered a strength by those with wide experience of it, those with a focus almost exclusively on the Local Church seem less convinced of its benefits. In a Local Church, it may be felt that anything beyond the local distracts attention from what is perceived to be the focus of the Church's work—namely on the mission and outreach of the Local Church. With nearly thirty years of experience of URC ministry, an Assembly Officer opined that:

> I think the Structures of the denomination are invisible to Church Members unless they take a particular interest—the structures are largely invisible until they come to the point of needing money or wanting to call a Minister, or wanting to

redevelop their building—any of those things where the wider Church has a stake, a role to play.

This view can be substantiated from the perspective of the Local Church. A Church Secretary believed that "at a little Local Church, I think how we run, that's more important and more realistic" while this was echoed by an Area Minister who stated that "[m]ost Church Members relate to the Local Church and some of them are hardly aware of the existence of the Synod." A Synod Moderator believed that the local manifestation of the Church would always focus attention for many people because this is the location of their engagement: "Well, I mean, it's almost a sociological fact, in a way, that, that people tend to see the—a human fact—people tend to see the organisation that they belong to through its local incarnation and that's perfectly understandable."

The majority of members in Local Churches have little experience of the wider Councils of the URC. Although lacking this wider conciliar experience, the underlying principles of meeting, discussing and deciding as a Local Church through Elders and Church Meetings are held to be important in the identity and ethos of the entire URC. One Minister, previously working at Church House, said of Church Meeting that: "It's not about majority rule, it's about listening and being attentive to the voices of others and the voice of the Spirit. . . . Each voice, each individual Christian is important in that decision-making."

In addition to the discernment of the Spirit's voice, the overlapping membership at the local level between the Church Meeting and the Elders' Meeting facilitates a dovetailing together of the two conciliar bodies. It is in the reciprocity of these two groups that the conciliarity operates in such a way as to be seen as a strength. In talking about how the congregation saw the eldership, a Church Secretary has claimed "They see us, they hear us, we see them, we care, you know that, to genuinely try for the best, no ulterior motives; yes, so no political agenda: democracy."

The significance of the Church Meeting is not so much in the physical meeting but rather in the nature of its being (as the point made earlier about absentee voting demonstrates). Its grounding in Christ as a body of covenanted Christians focuses the Church Meeting less on the Boardroom table and more on the Communion table. Daniel Jenkins believed this strongly. He wrote that the Church Meeting "is misunderstood if it is not seen as the extension of the Communion, as the first concrete act of our sacrifice of thanksgiving to God in our daily lives for the mercy he has vouchedsafe to us in divine service."[19] So adamant was he about this relationship between the role of the Church Meeting for discerning the Spirit and the meeting around the Communion table that he argued that unless the Church Meeting "is given that place then it becomes a breeding ground for 'democratical heresies', an open door through which evils rush into the Church."[20] In juxtaposing the liturgical continuity of the Lord's Supper and the democratic secular society, Jenkins highlights the tensions that can exist between the ecclesial and the secular. Such tensions, therefore, cannot be easily ignored.

Jenkins echoes the concerns raised by many of his predecessors in the Congregational tradition. Forsyth wrote passionately about the discontinuity between the Church and democracy. "The Church is not a democracy. Its native spirit is not the spirit of democracy. Its assemblies are not public meetings where each stands on his equal right."[21] His dissatisfaction with the direction in which he had seen Church Meetings move was focused on the peculiarity of Church Meetings against those of the democratic society outside. For Forsyth, although both Church Meeting and democratic society formed community, he was convinced that the Meeting was both focused on the covenant of fellowship and centred on Christ. "Our ecclesiastical rights are not to be defined by our membership of a Church, but by our membership of Christ. The Church is a Theocracy. Its gatherings are meetings of those who own a common worship and obedience."[22] Sykes asserts that Forsyth "will have no truck with the suggestion that the church is, or should be, a democracy,"[23] and draws attention to Forsyth's position on democracy in so far as "a democracy recognises no authority but what arises from itself, and a Church none but what is imposed on it from without."[24] For Forsyth, therefore, democracy responds to a self-founded authority while the Church draws its foundation in Redemption.[25]

19. Jenkins, *Church Meeting*, 24.

20. Jenkins, *Church Meeting*, 25.

21. Forsyth, "Moral Authority," 73; see also Forsyth, *Church and the Sacraments*, 3–28.

22. Forsyth, "Moral Authority," 73.

23. Sykes, "P. T. Forsyth," 10.

24. Forsyth, *Principle of Authority*, 253. Emphasis removed from original.

25. Forsyth, *Principle of Authority*, 253. An exploration of the concept of democracy in the Congregational tradition can be found in Norwood, "Democracy in Church Government."

It is perhaps not surprising then that the Congregational approach to the Church Meeting distances itself from the norms of participatory equality as illustrated in democratic society. This, of course, is not to give rise to the introduction of differing classes of Church Members, but rather to ground practice in the theology of the Church Meeting.

In considering Church Meetings, the process of voting and decision-making is conceived as significantly different to the approach employed in the British secular establishment. Elaine Kaye concluded her 2008 Congregational Lecture exploring *The Church Meeting in Congregational Tradition and Practice* with the assertion that the "world assumes that decision-making must be achieved either by giving orders or by majority voting."[26] Kaye draws on the discernment of the Holy Spirit, "focusing on what God is doing not what we think God should be doing."[27] In this way, Kaye echoes Routley in noting the similarities with the Society of Friends, in "attentiveness and listening to what others are saying"[28] and then "by gathering up 'the sense of the meeting.'"[29]

Routley stands firm, perhaps more clearly than others have, to the model of a common trajectory of a Meeting or discussion in so far as he asserts "that where opinion was divided the 'cloud remained on the tabernacle and the children of Israel could not go forward.'"[30] This understanding he further explores in terms of the penultimate, or eschatologically orientated, nature of Church order, especially seen in "the attachment of too much importance to single decisions."[31] Dealing with matters in a timely and appropriate manner are, for Routley, important considerations for the Church Meeting. A sense of perspective is sought, he writes, "to leave a free passage for the Holy Spirit's working."[32] The trajectory of a particular decision is not, he asserts, one of earthly measure but is eschatologically directed: "We must not be misled by personal zeal into thinking that the world will come to an end if this special decision does not fall our way."[33]

26. Kaye, "Gospel Obedience," 23.
27. Kaye, "Gospel Obedience," 23.
28. Kaye, "Gospel Obedience," 23.
29. Routley, *Into a Far Country*, 136.
30. Routley, *Into a Far Country*, 136.
31. Routley, *Into a Far Country*, 143.
32. Routley, *Into a Far Country*, 144.
33. Routley, *Into a Far Country*, 144.

The purpose and approach to decision-making is one that has been open to interpretation among scholarship within the URC. Studies have been carried out considering the approach taken in making decisions. These have been concerning moral issues, with marriage, divorce and remarriage in the URC the focus of Richard Goldring's doctoral thesis, while the issue of Human Sexuality is the subject of Nick Brindley's masters thesis, and an important consideration in doctorates by Romiley Micklem and Keith Riglin. By rooting their studies in these moral questions, these authors have considered the URC's approach to decision-making authority and the Church's ability as a conciliar Church to agree and enforce policy.

While Riglin grounds his thesis on the apparent inability to reach resolution on the various case studies he provides, Micklem takes a largely conceptual approach to the question of authority in the denomination, drawing on the URC's Human Sexuality debate in support of the conclusion that there is "not only a crisis of authority but a deeply-rooted crisis of self-understanding which constitutes a failure of the tradition."[34] Meanwhile, for Goldring, the General Assembly's "difficulty of reaching a decision on a controversial area" such as the question of remarriage, and the potential for future "failure to give a specific ruling" concerning "sexual morality" leads him to question whether the URC is anything more than a "federation of independent churches."[35] Brindley considers this in terms of a Church that prefers unity over doctrinal pronouncement and suggests, therefore, that such a view of a federation of Churches has "condemned the URC to a state of confusion and decline."[36] This is, he asserts, a result of the URC's "failure adequately to resolve the different views of Congregationalists and Presbyterians on the nature of authority in the Church."[37] For Brindley, unity is inferior to doctrinal ruling as an aim of the ecclesial community, a view which seems fundamentally counter to the *Basis* and the URC's *raison d'être*.

While both Goldring and Brindley take issue with the nature of the relationship between the Councils, they both assert this nature to be intrinsically flawed and problematic. For Brindley, Goldring, and Micklem, each of whom are addressing specific (and controversial) moral and

---

34. Micklem, "Failure of Moral Discourse," 248.
35. Goldring, "Attitudes to Marriage," 373.
36. Brindley, "URC Sexuality Debates" (1.§5).
37. Brindley, "URC Sexuality Debates" (1.§5).

pastoral issues, where a range of opinion is possible or legitimate, the failure to make definitive policy is seen as a deficiency in the denominational structure. While Brindley, Goldring and Micklem each perceive institutional failure to be the cause of their frustrations, based on the assumption that the Church should have a single view on every subject of controversy, an "epistemological crisis" (to borrow Micklem's phrase) of their own creation may surround such an approach to URC polity. It may be that they expect the URC to be more defined by these types of questions than the *Basis* ever imagined it would be, or that they perceive a definitive stance on ethical questions as the primary focus for the Church's authority.

Routley's assertion of timely and appropriate action, and his negative view of too much importance placed on reaching a single decision on contentious subjects, therefore, provides an antidote to the claims of Brindley, Goldring, Micklem, and Riglin who appear to place overbearing importance on reaching single decisions on matters of policy. Where decisions are unable to be reached, or the outcome is not to our preferred way, the Church has sought the voice of the Spirit and either it has been inconclusive, or our own interpretation of the Spirit's will has not accorded with that of the Church. In either way, Routley posits, the Church has not failed but has sought the mind of God.

Of course, in a modern society where technology and communication speed up many forms of social interaction beyond that which Routley experienced, we may want to hold onto his words as a template rather than a fixed pattern. Sometimes legislation, mission or safety dictate that decisions must be made quickly. Routley appears not to consider such a situation to be plausible and, if he did, how the Church would be best to respond. It is clear, however, that he advocates a model whereby divided opinion among the membership is undesirable and suggests that in such an event no decision may be made. In the contemporary URC, such an approach has been adopted under the title of Consensus decision-making.[38]

The Consensus approach to decision-making has been part of the General Assembly's Standing Orders since 2007. While the Assembly's Standing Orders are not binding on other Councils of the denomination, Local Church Meetings, observing the principles of covenanted fellowship, are prime locations in which to see consensus operating almost

---

38. GA Reports (2014) 61–64.

intuitively. The Local Church is a community of those participating in Christian life and sharing a common focus. Therefore, it seems that this is the location in which consensus will find its strongest expression, in comparison with other Councils where "formal rules of debate make little provision for those whose hesitant, inexperienced voices find it daunting to compete against more eloquent orators."[39] In theory, the participation of the full community in the discussions, debates and decisions ensures that there is opportunity for the Church Meeting to come to one mind, without division. Routley draws on his musical expertise to put this quest quite eloquently: "It is death to the chamber-music of a church meeting if a single member takes offence, refuses to listen, hogs the conversation, tries to play a solo or walks out of his part because it is temporarily uninteresting or inconspicuous."[40] As Jill Tabart wrote in her book *Coming to Consensus*:

> Expecting one point of view on a particular issue will "win" assumes a triumph over those who obviously must "lose". Yet unity and humility are key characteristics of the body of Christ. Our desire to seek God's will as a community will surely be stronger than our personal passion to see a particular position prevail. There can be no winners or losers.[41]

However, the application of the consensus decision-making process to facilitate discernment has not been universally appreciated in the URC. In reflecting on the General Assembly meeting in 2014, the Moderators felt that "clearly it stumbled" and that "people didn't understand" the consensus process while a Synod Moderator felt that the denomination was "still practising consensus." One General Assembly Moderator believed that a lack of openness to hearing the movement of the Spirit by the Council's participants would always impact the consensus decision-making process and affirmed that such an approach was fundamental for consensus to be applied: "Consensus decision-making will always struggle with that [lack of openness]; it's to do with the emotive nature of the system."

The principles of the Local Church Meeting, centred on covenant, with Christ in the midst, apply too across the conciliar structure of the URC. When the Synod, Assembly Executive, General Assembly (or any of

---

39. Tabart, *Coming to Consensus*, 7.
40. Routley, *Into a Far Country*, 138.
41. Tabart, *Coming to Consensus*, 42.

their committees) meet, the central focus remains the Upper Room and the empty tomb rather than the Boardroom and the ballot box. "Unless, therefore, what we say and do in Church Meeting is in harmony with the Spirit of Jesus Christ as the Scriptures declare him we can be quite sure that it's not the Holy Spirit which is leading us."[42] The authority which derives from the URC's structure thus relies upon Christ's presence and the covenanted mutuality between the members of the Councils. With the principles of the Local Church Meeting becoming easier to apply within the wider Councils since the introduction of the consensus decision-making model, the URC has sought to redress the way in which its order reflects the "outward expression of the Christian life of its members."[43]

Connecting Councils

The authority of the URC's conciliar structure is a matter of considerable importance within the life of the denomination. Tensions between Councils on the question of final authority have been an issue since the denomination's inception. As could be seen from the correspondence prior to union, the perceived loss of the autonomy of the Local Church Meeting was seen by Congregationalists to be one of the sticking points in the *Scheme of Union*. This can be understood when, as Alan Sell wrote of traditional Congregationalism, "there can be no such thing as a Congregational churchly body in the sense of a 'third church' subsisting between the local church and the Church catholic."[44] Caryl Micklem wrote in the *New Christian* in May 1967 expressing concern about the nature of oversight that the *Scheme* provided:

> The first thing is to decide who are the shepherds and who are the sheep. Begin at the top, with the General Assembly, and say that they are the shepherds. What, then, is one lot of sheep (the Provincial Synod) doing playing shepherds to another lot (the District Council)? And so on down the line.[45]

In a letter in the URC Archive, Micklem later wrote to Huxtable giving yet further elucidation about his concerns with the proposed structure:

42. Jenkins, *Church Meeting*, 27.
43. Jenkins, *Church Meeting*, 23.
44. Sell, *Saints Visible*, 107.
45. Micklem, "Note," 4.

> While the Basis for Union carefully avoids using the word "Court", I do feel that the constant harping on the word "oversight" gives too much ground to those (and I'm sure they exist) who believe that the Councils of the Church ought to be an *ascending* sequence rather than (as I should prefer to say) a *widening* sequence.

Alongside this, a movement of Congregationalists objected to the *Scheme's* proposals and sought avidly to build up greater support for their position. The Congregational Association was formed during this time to spearhead these objections and while they were unable to prevent union with the Presbyterians, a number of Congregational Churches did not join the URC.[46] A pamphlet and postcard campaign began by way of informing Congregational members and eliciting their support. One such postcard invited people to sign against a statement that declared "I am opposed to any scheme of union which results in moving to Area, Provincial or National Councils, the control which the local Church Meeting now exercise over its own affairs and property."

After comments on the *Scheme* were requested from Churches and Session in 1967, the Joint Committee received a summary report compiled by E. C. D. Stanford. In this report, found as part of the URC Archive, difficulties with the *Basis* included concerns from Congregationalists about the authority of the Church Meeting, "especially in relation to its internal affairs, its membership, its call to a minister, and its right to decide who shall preside at sacraments"; but also about the General Assembly and the way in which it relates to Local Church and "the meaning of the phrase 'final authority', particularly in a 'downward' direction."

Concerns about structure were not, however, limited to Congregationalists. Presbyterians responding to the draft *Scheme* felt that with a District Council and Synod between the General Assembly and the Local Church, the *Scheme* was "too expensive in time and money" and that "operations between local church and General Assembly could be carried out with simpler machinery." There were also responses that queried the authority of the Church Meeting "in relation to that of the Session" (the Presbyterian term used for the Elders' Meeting) and stated that the draft *Scheme's* proposals for Moderators of Synods were considered "unacceptable." Stanford's report comments that Presbyterians believed that the introduction of Synod Moderators would create an office "too similar to that of bishops."

---

46. Argent, *Transformation of Congregationalism*, 511–12.

The introduction of the Moderators to the *Structure* was as a result of the interplay between Congregational and Presbyterian polity.[47] Drawing on the role of Moderator, that had been part of the CUEW's structure since 1919, the *Scheme of Union* brought Moderators into a relationship with a Council so that their office was held in relation to the conciliar structure. Moderators were instituted to "stimulate and encourage the work of the United Reformed Church within the province or nation," "preside over the meetings of the synod and exercise a pastoral office towards the ministers, CRCWs and churches within the province or nation," and "suggest names of ministers to vacant pastorates" by meeting "together at regular intervals for the better discharge of their duties" (§B.2.(4)) As Officers appointed by the General Assembly, the Moderators link the Synod and the denomination. Their monthly meeting is not a conciliar body, and its authority comes through the structural imperative that they should meet to discharge their duties.

The role of the Moderators' meeting in the URC has changed in recent times. While the Moderators' meeting had an important role in providing for the movement of Ministers, changes in 2004 altered the process used by the Moderators to introduce stipendiary ministers to vacant pastorates.[48] Having once had the role of introducing ministers, this altered procedure removed "the need for Moderators to introduce one to the other on their behalf" and withdrew "from Moderators a gate-keeping role which had become suspect when viewed from the perspective of current equal opportunities thinking."[49] This shift meant that for some Moderators they had "to introduce to pastorates ministers where [they had] little or no confidence that they [were] the right person in the right place."[50] Peel argues that such a change, whereby a Synod Moderator's input into the process was ostensibly abandoned, means that "a vital part of the Moderators' *raison d'être* has vanished."[51] While the procedural significance has been removed, the role of the Moderators' meeting to know every pastorate and every Minister across the denomination still allows

---

47. An examination of the place of Moderators is available in Peel, *Story of the Moderators*.

48. Peel, *Story of the Moderators*, 72–74.

49. Peel, *Story of the Moderators*, 73.

50. Peel, *Story of the Moderators*, 74. Peel quotes an unnamed former Synod Moderator.

51. Peel, *Story of the Moderators*, 74. Emphasis original.

for the Moderators' meeting "to approach ministers"[52] and to maintain some of the discernment that a former Moderator felt had become little more than a "clearing house for ministers."[53]

Writing in the Newsletter of the Congregational Order Group in May 1953, John Weller drew on the thoughts of Bernard Lord Manning to comment that the quarrel over bishops was "not with government by bishops, but only with salvation by bishops" adding that the quarrel is "with the claim that episcopacy—and the threefold ministry in its historic form—is of the 'esse' not the 'bene esse', of the Church."[54] Although Weller was considering Archbishop Fisher's call to introduce episcopacy into the Free Churches, his call was to let Moderators become "what they are!—not, of course, prelates in a Roman or Anglican sense, but fully Congregational bishops, having the same function and standing within the province (or county) as the local minister has within the local church."[55] This understanding echoes, in form if not in name, that of the URC's view of the Moderator, acting within the Synod as the pastor to the ministers and Churches.

There is a compelling argument from Congregational sources, such as Weller and Manning, that the Moderator may have a role in "government" but not concerning "salvation." The role of leadership may therefore be fulfilled by the Moderator but that this extends to matters of institution and good order. The URC structure authorises the Moderators' meeting to be, "for the better discharge of their duties," the gatekeepers of the process for ministerial movements and settlements. With a more involved engagement in the provision of ministry as a Moderators' meeting and in Synod discussions concerning deployment, Moderators may have gained a greater role in the functions of ministry within the denomination's life than had been initially envisaged, providing a function that could be perceived further advanced than "government" and potentially as salvific. While the *Structure* falls short of giving them this salvific purpose, an increased role in ministerial movement and discipline relative to what the original Congregational model contained, suggests that URC Moderators, at least when acting as a meeting, have significant authority within the *Structure*.

52. Peel, *Story of the Moderators*, 73 (§8).
53. Quoted in Peel, *Story of the Moderators*, 74.
54. Weller, "Some Notes," 3.
55. Weller, "Some Notes," 3.

However, the Moderator also has a role within the conciliar framework as the president of the Synod. This conciliar framework is described in the *Structure* as consisting of "four parts" with each "possessing such authority, under the Word of God and the promised guidance of the Holy Spirit, as shall enable it to exercise its functions and thereby minister in that sphere of the life of the United Reformed Church with which it is concerned" (§B.1.(3)). The relationships between the Councils, alongside the understanding of a Council's sphere of influence, are therefore significant to understand the structural authority of the URC.

Conciliar Spheres

The "parts" of the URC that are considered by the structure (§B.1.(3)) consist of:

(a) the church meeting and the elders' meeting of each Local Church;

(b) the council of each district to be known as a district council and of each area of ecumenical cooperation to be known as an area meeting;

(c) the synod of province or nation to be known as a provincial or national synod; and

(d) the General Assembly of the United Reformed Church.

Within the *Structure*, each of these Councils is given definition of its "consultative, legislative and executive functions" (§B.1.(3)), and these functions illustrate the sphere of a Council's action. The functions of the Local Church begin with the task "to further the Church's mission in the locality" (§B.2.(1)(i)) and ground the functions of the Local Church within the pursuit of locally focused action and activity such as the calling of a minister (§B.2.(1)(vii)), elect elders and officers (§B.2.(1)(viii)), admit members to the membership roll (§B.2.(1)(ix)) and, with the Elders' Meeting, to have oversight of the finances and property maintenance of the Local Church (§B.2.(1)(xiii)). This contrasts with the functions of the General Assembly whose role it is "to oversee the total work of the church" (§B.2.(6)(A)(i)) and thus to deal itself with the widest sphere of the Church's life.

One notable function possessed by the General Assembly is "to alter, add to, modify or supersede the Basis, Structure and any other form or expression of the polity and doctrinal formulations of the United Reformed Church" (§B.2.(6)(A)(xi)). This function, which allows for constitutional amendment, is supplemented with a further process that defines the actions to be taken in case of such an amendment. The process broadly follows a provision known in the Church of Scotland as "the Barrier Act," whereby the General Assembly is compelled "to consult the wider Church before innovating in the areas of worship, doctrine, discipline or church government."[56] The inclusion of this procedure in the URC's *Structure* came from the PCE provision and ensured that the wider Councils were consulted and that decisions were needed by Synods (or in exceptional cases also Local Churches) to confirm any change.[57] Amendments to this procedure were made in 1984 after it was recognised that the consultation process did not require the Assembly to adhere to the consultation's outcome.[58] The process now stipulates that if more than a third of responses from Synods (or Local Churches) have resolved against the proposed amendment "then the Assembly or the Mission Council, as the case may be, in its concern for the unity of the church shall not proceed to ratify the proposal" (§B.3.(1)(f)).

The facility to consult with other Councils is also a component of the *Structure* of the URC. As with constitutional amendments, consultation should take place "to discover the mind of the other councils or of local churches likely to be affected by the decision" (§B.4). Unlike the "Barrier Act" provision for constitutional amendments, these consultations are not binding on the Council. It is, therefore, for the Council concerned to interpret the consultation's outcome and discern a direction to be taken. Any decisions made on the basis of a consultation, however, should not be to the detriment of the denomination's unity and peace.

Thus the relationship between the Councils and the understanding of their spheres affects the authority that the denomination's structure holds. Alan Sell argues that "[o]nce the theological judgment is made that each council of the Church is competent to seek and discern the mind of Christ under the guidance of the Holy Spirit, there cannot be a hierarchy of 'church courts' . . . [because the Councils'] concerns and interests will quite frequently overlap."[59] This is significant insofar as it

---

56. MacLean, "Presbyterian Governance," 10–11.
57. PCE, *Book of Order*, 78 (§340).
58. GA Reports (1984) 15–17; GA Record (1984) 15–16; GA Record (1984) 28–29.
59. Sell, *One Ministry*, 115.

flattens the structure and gives no greater role in leadership to the members of the Councils, but rather emphasises the interrelation across the structure and establishes both a particularity and a commonality between the work of Local Church Meetings and the General Assembly. Likewise, while Caryl Micklem, quoted earlier, wished the URC's structure to be a "widening sequence" of Councils, absent of hierarchy, Riglin asserts that the URC "is an hierarchical church, but its hierarchy is that of councils not of individuals."[60] The hierarchy of Councils can be demonstrated in the *Structure* where the General Assembly is to "act as the central organ of [the URC's] life and the final authority, under the Word of God and the promised guidance of the Holy Spirit, in all matters of doctrine and order" (§B.2.(1)(xii)). This places the Assembly as the final location of authority within the URC structure and with this, the final point of appeal. "The decision of the General Assembly on any matter which has come before it on reference or appeal shall be final and binding" (§B.5.(2)). This may suggest, as Riglin asserts, the hierarchical nature of the URC, with other Councils being "inferior" to that of the Assembly; this being an echo of the conciliar structure of the PCE.[61]

Such inter-related Councils, familiar internationally in Churches such as the Uniting Church in Australia, is well understood as being "neither top down nor bottom up" and evidences "the body of Christ itself, variously angular, overlapping, tangential and organised by the Head."[62] In such a way, the denomination "lies between the congregation and the universal church" where a diversity can be experienced and brings "the presence of other congregations to bear on the life of the local congregation."[63]

Therefore, it is possible also to regard this function as fulfilling the sphere of the General Assembly namely the oversight of "the total work of the church" (§B.2.(6)(A)(i)). It is only with this widest remit, as opposed to highest, that the denomination's polity may allow for the Assembly to hold the entirety of the URC's doctrine and order. This is done, therefore, within a principle of finality and certainty. When held within the sphere of the URC, all Councils remain within the total work of the denomination and as such are encompassed within the Assembly's authority. It

---

60. Riglin, "Animating Grace," 106.
61. PCE, *Book of Order*, 78 (§339).
62. Thompson, *Disturbing Much*, 260.
63. Ensign-George, *Between Congregation and Church*, 149.

seems only right that the Assembly is, therefore, the body responsible for the consistent and universal oversight of the URC's policies, polity and practice.

Although the Presbyterian strand of the URC's heritage is clearly present in the contemporary polity of the denomination, the fear of the loss of independency, and thus the objection to any form of structural authority have been shown to have been issues at the time of the URC's formation. Congregational objection to Scottish plans to unite the Congregational Union of Scotland and Church of Scotland were, wrote Helen Woods in the Newsletter of the Church Order Group, "almost all based on the dogma that the local church should have complete autonomy."[64] Thus the tension between a structure that provided resource to the local and one that prescribed action to the Local Church is inherent in the URC's *Structure*, and runs through the denomination's core. It is in recognising that the Church is derived from Christ that the Church's conciliarity is given an authority. It is this source that any Council or officer must draw upon in locating the authority of the structure of the Church, and upon this "only in virtue of the authority of Christ."[65]

The significance of the URC being a conciliar Church is something that characterises a "fundamental" principle of the denomination. An Assembly Officer asserted that "giving up the conciliar stuff would be—that's fundamental and the rest of the world's come in our direction" while an Area Minister believed that the loss of conciliarity would significantly alter the denomination's identity: "Once you break the principle you are actually changing the Church in a very fundamental way and I don't think when looking at relatively small practical issues we would appreciate quite what a difference it would make."

Although conciliarity is believed to be fundamental to the URC's life, it was also recognised that this was not always an easy principle to sustain. Unquestioning support of the denomination's Councils is not always forthcoming, with suspicion frequently roused amongst those in Local Church about the operation of the wider Councils and scepticism about the conciliar apparatus. One Local Church minister commented that "[t]hey have, what I call, a healthy cynicism to authority in the URC." The development of an "us and them" mentality between the Local Church and the wider Councils is clearly visible across the denomination, with

---

64. Woods, "What is Amiss in Congregationalism?," 3–4.
65. CUEW, *Christian Oversight*, 4.

scepticism being commended by one Assembly Officer, who indicated that this was grounded in the conciliar life of the denomination: "it has to do with never getting the balance wrong between the authority of the Councils" a reality recognised by a Synod Moderator who admitted that: "I have to say, in my own mind sometimes that, that awareness slips, and I think it probably slips in other people too, so people do see them as a hierarchical structure, as it were."

With such an admission by an experienced Minister, there is little surprise that there is confusion about the ways in which different "spheres of responsibility" are seen to interlink as part of a non-hierarchical polity. This is especially true when considering where authority is located in the structure and the ways it is demonstrated. An understanding of conciliarity, characterised by a covenantal relationship, is required to consider the wider effects of decision-making and actions in the life of the denomination. The suspicion of other Councils can be a stumbling block to the ways in which the conciliar structure can operate.

> And if we could get rid of the "us and them" then the conciliar system would work better with less silly people making points or not being willing to think about others in terms of other churches and people; sometimes [they] can only see their own local church and don't see the effect of what they would like to happen for them on others and it would be good if the attitude was "well, somebody has come in with a wider perspective; let's listen and assume that they're trying to do the best for everybody not assume that we know better because we're local and our church is the most important in the URC," sort of thing.

Conciliarity, therefore, is about mutual recognition of responsibility while also ensuring there is a covenant between bodies to safeguard the best for all. Yet this suggestion is that a mutual recognition is lacking, characterised by the "us and them" mentality that exists between the Councils. A similar view expressed by a Synod Clerk asserted that the Synod was "still needing to break down 'us and them.'" Such comments echo those made in *Reform* in the 1970s where "[t]here is no 'them' only 'us' in a District Council"[66] and evidence that such perceptions of conciliar relationships are long standing. That so many Local Church members are oblivious to the wider conciliar operation until they require it does little to break down the perceived hierarchy that exists. Furthermore, the

---

66. *Reform* (November 1976) 28 (Stephen Orchard).

perception in the Local Church that the wider Councils are "hierarchical" may also suggest that, for Local Church members, these Councils have a greater authority over the local than is in fact the case.

On the one hand, it is apparent that URC members are "not trusting a decision unless we have been involved in it personally," and that Churches contain those who personally dislike having external influence on a Local Church when they hadn't themselves been involved. A comment made at General Assembly in 1974 and published subsequently in *Reform* shows this to be a long standing issue: "I always fear any committee of which I am not a member."[67] However it is also recognised that "[t]here's no way on God's green-earth [Local Church members] could be involved in every decision." This dualism of both requiring participation yet recognising limitations is a significant tension in the discussion of participation in the wider Church.

However, alongside the physical pragmatism of not being able to participate in every decision there exists an apathy towards the wider Councils. One Elder in Local Leadership perceived that the congregation "don't care about what happens at Synod," with focus instead on knowing "who would bury them." The Church Secretary of another Local Church felt that the Synod had "no benefit" to the Church and this resulted in "very few people interested" in the wider Church. Part of this problem has been fuelled by a lack of knowledge about what is being required of the Council. When a complex matter comes to the Synod or Local Church for consultation or discussion, there can be a sense in which this does not come to the Councils in such a way as to make debate or discussion easily achieved. When complex legal or procedural matters (such as those concerning the Ministerial disciplinary process) have come to Synods for consultation, the necessary complexity of the process concerned has caused the Synod members to be confused by what has been asked of them and to lack the requisite knowledge of the implications of the changes. Aware of this difficulty a Synod Moderator posed his opinion on how such matters should be addressed:

> I think we should either say, "if we're going to consult people let's make sure there is a briefing sheet which gives you an idiot's guide, so you actually know what is happening" or say "nobody is going to understand this or read it so let's just do it at General Assembly." I think we mishandle it by doing the formal stuff but actually it's window dressing.

67. *Reform* (June 1974) 7 (Charles Haig).

The idea that in some ways the formal process is "window dressing" may be unfair to the denomination itself, but has the effect of requiring participation even though it is unwarranted or seen to be inappropriate. The same seems to be true when initiatives are proposed from Church House on behalf of Assembly committees. Reflecting on the accusation of "Initiative Overload" an Assembly Officer outlined the position as she had experienced it in connection with the Local Church:

> They don't want to be bothered, they don't want to be consulted, they don't want any more questionnaires, they don't want any more programmes, no more ideas; they want to be left alone which is actually one of the functions of wider church governance is to leave them alone—it's a really important one. So not to lumber them with anything that isn't necessary. So that's the compliance kind of stuff, we just take care of here so that they're not burdened with it; keep the Charity Commission happy on various things.

The balance between full participation and involvement, therefore, becomes one of pragmatism and of ensuring that the Local Church is enabled to participate when it can, but not to overload it unnecessarily.

The loss of District Councils from the structure has been lamented as it felt that they had been "a very, very useful point of contact" and that the loss of this Council had resulted in Local Churches being isolated and the structure of the denomination losing a useful place for consultation. Whether or not District Councils would have resolved these challenges, the issue of the participation of Local Churches in the denominational governance remains unresolved.

The current, pragmatic, view holds the sense of the Local Church as in a one-directional, passive relationship with the wider Councils and where apathy is prevalent. "But they have to care" said an Assembly Officer of improved communication from Church House, "if they don't care, there's nothing can be done to force them." Likewise, when suggesting that Synod or Assembly officers could make themselves better known to Local Church members, a Church Secretary echoed similar apathy towards participation: "But if the Churches are invited to all meet, to meet the person not many will turn up either . . . [and] what I will say to the other people, 'I'm not going'; so I don't know what you can do really."

It seems that this sentiment—that there is nothing that can be done to improve participation—holds the denomination's activities in limbo. On the one hand, "conciliar life requires that active commitment" to the wider denominational life and engagement in its programmes. Yet "there's a huge issue to be got over there—prejudice and projection and so on—of local people to the wider" which appears to fuel a degree of conciliar apathy and prevents Local Churches from benefiting from the denominational structures.

Conciliarity is therefore a significant component of the URC's understanding and manifestation of authority. It is through these meetings and the decisions made by conciliar bodies that Local Church members most often experience the denomination's authority, even where that is not directly but is as a result of the ripples through the *Structure*. In fact, it seems fundamental to the denomination that where a polity of concentric spheres exist and are defined by the denomination's founding documents, the importance of the authority of these Councils will be significant not only in the formalised documentation but relevant in the empirically realised life of the denomination.

Participatory Conciliarity

Conciliarity is perceived to be a significant part of the life of the denomination. It is not only part of the decision-making structure, but it says something that was significant about the URC. As both a valued possession and a crucial aspect of the denomination's identity, conciliarity is overwhelmingly regarded as the way by which the denomination functions and through which authority is exercised. Even when considering whether the URC would remain the same if conciliarity were replaced with a form of Episcopal office, the principle of authority expressed through the Councils of the Church is unanimously endorsed as what constitutes the URC. It is through the expression of coming together as Christ's body to share in the decision-making processes that the URC demonstrates the way in which the Local Church, Synod and Denomination are each meetings of the Church, involving those from all spheres in being the Church in the world.

The involvement of each Council in discerning the will of Christ emphasises the principle of "one body, many members" as an expression of denominational polity. Through the active involvement of Local Church members in the widening Councils of the denomination, the ability of conciliarity to have overlapping responsibilities and functions ensures that authority is spread throughout the denomination rather than held in any single locus. While each conciliar body holds to its specific responsibilities, the interconnectedness of the conciliar structure ensures that authority has a number of locations and differing foci with each keeping the balance while the complete system contains the fullness of the denomination's authority. While conciliarity comprises the formal locus of authority in the URC, empirical study has demonstrated its importance as a key part of the URC's identity and being for those involved in the Church.

However, while it is expected that conciliarity would have a key place in the minds of those involved in the denomination, what may not have been expected is the extent to which the idealised conciliarity stated at the time of the URC's formation, and amended occasionally since then (including the significant changes of *Catch the Vision*), would be seen to be deeply problematic for many Local Church members. The perceived distance between the Local and Synod—let alone between the Local and the Denominational—in the mind of those involved in Local Churches has led some to question the relevance of the structure and of conciliarity itself. With such claims as "Who are this General Assembly to tell us what to do?", it is clear that there is a significant ecclesiological question about the work of the denomination as a conciliar body.

Such queries come from a variety of positions and apply to all such questions of conciliar authority. First, there is the questioning of the Assembly's right to make a decision on a matter. This addresses the sphere in which the Council is operating and the extent of its authority on a given topic. The effect of such a question is to ponder the legitimacy of a Council's action. The question of legitimacy is wrapped up with the question of whether the Council holds the authority to make a decision and, therefore, whether the sphere of the Council's responsibility matches that which the Council is seeking to exercise.

Although Councils operate in their own sphere, there is an extent, discussed previously, in which the functions of bodies are distributed with dovetailed responsibilities. Given this interconnectedness, there is the possibility that such decisions are seen to sit in more than one location. When considering the Roll of Members in a Local Church, there is an overlapping remit of the Elders' Meeting and Church Meeting. The Elders' Meeting are, "in consultation with the Church Meeting . . . to advise" (§B.2.(2)(vi)) while it is for the Church Meeting to act "always on advice from the elders' meeting" (§B.2.(1)(xi)). While these functions in the *Structure* ensure that there remains a dialogue between the bodies in the Local Church, these dovetailed functions may be understood to possess differing emphases. The extent to which one body may advise and another act on advice may lead to questions of whether one or other body is extending its own authority.

Within the *Structure*, the functions given to each Council are defined. This ensures that Councils are given legitimate contexts in which they are permitted to hold authority. However, due in part to the flexibility of overlapping functions and to the ability of different spheres (Local or Synod) to establish structures and procedures that are most appropriate to their context, there are a number of opportunities for claims of illegitimacy in the Council's sphere of decision-making.

Such questions may be particularly pertinent in contexts where authority is delegated to committees rather than to the Council itself. One such example would be the relationship of Assembly Executive to the General Assembly. Where it could be recognised by some that Assembly Executive "can act on behalf of Assembly but is cautious in doing so" it is similarly recognised that Assembly Executive carries the authority of the General Assembly. As such, this dualism of a committee acting with delegated authority of the Council establishes a complex network of legitimacy. If Assembly Executive makes a decision on one matter which is deemed to hold the authority of the General Assembly, why might it be cautious about making other decisions? The logical progression is that Assembly Executive has the authority of Assembly, delegated to it in the *Structure* as "power to act in its name," and therefore it has the legitimate authority to act as the denomination's "final authority" (§B.2.(6)).

The non-prescriptive practice in acting cautiously, however, does not negate the delegated authority held by Assembly Executive. Other bodies exist elsewhere in the denominational structure whereby committees (or sub-committees) possess delegated authority to act on behalf of the Council. The questions raised by such delegation, therefore, pose whether there is in fact a legitimate use of authority which can be recognised for a given matter and where, or how, might such a decision or action be appealed or justified.

While such claims may be made, questions of polity are raised. The understanding of the URC's ecclesiology which focuses on a "one body, many members" approach suggests that the understanding of Councils (or committees) acting on behalf of the URC is right insofar as each body has its sphere clearly delineated. In such a context, the coming together of a group of people to meet and decide in Christ's name is an act of the Church universal for the sphere in which the decision has been made.

However, it is the scope for disagreement and human fallibility, as well as the blurred lines between conciliar responsibilities and functions, which lead to difficulties with recognising this approach as entirely legitimate. Where authority is thus delegated, and not subjected to the scrutiny of the full Council, it is necessary to recognise that there is a greater risk (but not necessarily a greater propensity) of bias to lead decisions in a particular direction. Whereas a "full" Council may discern a different approach, the delegated body will, by definition, consist of only a subsection of the Council's members (or even a different membership). Therefore, any body acting with "delegated authority" reaches its own decisions based on its reduced membership yet with the authority of the delegating Council. While officially such decisions affect the wider sphere, they are made on its behalf by a sub-section. Such delegation, therefore, removes from the full Council the ability to make decisions on particular matters. However, it must be questioned whether it is logically possible for such delegation to reflect legitimate authority of the Council when the Council is not involved in its own decisions and the sub-section are not a group in their own right. A Synod is not a sub-section of the General Assembly, but is its own entity and makes decisions as such, even if these are functions given to it in the *Basis* by the authority of the General Assembly.

The second area raised by the question of "Who are this General Assembly to tell us what to do?" is that of the authority of the Assembly to instruct other parts of the denomination. This concerns the influence of one Council on the other. This was, most certainly, the implication of the question raised at General Assembly. In a denomination in which Councils are regarded as disparate and separated, and where the Local Church focuses its energy on the local mission and activity of the Church, programmes supplied by Church House and the wider denominational structure itself are regarded as largely irrelevant, whereby "most members at a Church couldn't care less about the denomination." A sense of disempowerment with the denomination and the lack of denominational focus was attributed to two factors: the elimination of District Councils and the move to biennial General Assemblies. Both of these changes, introduced as a result of the *Catch the Vision* process, although now partly reversed, reduced the opportunities for networking beyond the Local Church and have therefore affected the extent to which Local Church members may encounter the breadth of the denomination's conciliarity. Such networking has the potential to bridge the divide between Local Church members and other Local Churches and Councils, recognising that where such networking occurs, barriers to the wider bodies—such as unfamiliarity—cease to be issues.

These divisions between the Councils exist because of the damaged relationship between the Local and the wider Councils, but such divisions question the ability of one Council to influence another. A sense of apathy towards the wider Councils exists, which proliferates the opinion that the work of Assembly has no bearing on the life of the Local Church. Local Church members find the discussions taking place at denominational level to be "irrelevant" to the questions that they are seeking to address and are therefore reticent to be involved in the debates. This may further become accentuated as a result of the Covid-19 pandemic and the needs and concerns of Local Churches. The relationship with the wider Councils appear to be characterised largely by discussions which are deemed to be irrelevant—either on certain topics or in geographical particularly—or on decisions made by wider Councils that affect the way in which the Local Church operates.

Although the topic falls largely into the discussion of legitimacy, the relevance of the decisions taken deserves a brief mention. As part of the conciliar life of the URC, the concentric spheres of influence of the denomination's Councils extend from those that affect only the local mission of the URC through the regional Synod to the denominational policy of the Church. The task of the wider Councils is to "provide a forum for concerns brought forward by local churches" (§B.2.(4)(v)) and "to consider and decide upon issues and representations duly transmitted by other councils." (§B.2.(6)(xx)). The transmission of these concerns and issues can therefore be sent through from a Local Church where the issue is affecting their life. In such cases, while a debate at General Assembly may not have a bearing upon the life of one particular Local Church, the need for the Assembly "to consider and decide" on the matter has been taken through the progression of matters through the Councils. This is the method agreed by the denomination for such issues and asserts that the Council has the authority to remit or decide on a particular matter.

However, although such a process is in place, the questions about it highlight the lack of knowledge of the URC's conciliar structure. A Church Secretary who believes that authority is located "where your heart and your Sundays are spent" is also one who states that "Synod wise, I think they're pretty powerful . . . They probably pack a punch." This understanding of conciliarity is both illustrative of many encountered in Local Churches and yet lacking understanding of the conciliar structure and its actions. Where matters have been transmitted to the wider Councils for discussion or decision, the conciliar structure is fulfilling its function of consultation and involving the widest possible number in the decision. For the same reasons that delegated authority was considered not to be the optimal approach to achieving the full authority of the Council, the transmission of matters to a wider Council and their sending out through the Barrier Act provision for consultation or decision ensures that when a decision is reached it secures the full authority of the denomination. It is therefore right that in the case of matters that have a wider remit than the Local Church, even if that need was recognised in the Local Church, the Council with the widest responsibility for that aspect of the URC's life is responsible for the decision and involves members accordingly.

In some ways, however, it will always be considered that the actions of the General Assembly are occasionally dealing with matters that are perceived to be of little relevance to the Local Church. This is akin to how the concerns of one Local Church may seem irrelevant to the concerns of another. As the Assembly has a wider sphere of influence and its own set of functions, it has its own agenda that it has to enact on behalf of the denomination. This occasionally leads to discussions around subscription to legal measures or to funding for programmes provided by the denomination. While such topics are deemed to be irrelevant to many in the Local Church, their importance as part of the work or legal status of the denomination requires that they be carried out, and this is done for the benefit of the denomination as a whole.

Just as the claim of conciliar irrelevance can be attributed partly to a lack of understanding of the URC's structure, so too can a lack of understanding describe a view of intrusion into the life of the Local Church. The concern of an Elders' Meeting about whether their Synod would take away a bequest they have received is indicative of such concerns. However, such a view is not without its grounding in reality and Local Churches have felt themselves disadvantaged by the actions of the wider Councils. Although Local Churches are regarded each as part of the URC, it's clear that, nearly fifty years on, it's possible to have a sense of the antecedent tradition from which the Local Church has come. While each Local Church is therefore treated equally, whether from Congregational, Presbyterian or Churches of Christ tradition, the experience of the members in Local

Churches previously affiliated with one of these traditions has instilled in some the particular expression of churchmanship associated with that antecedent tradition. Therefore, while the "one body, many members" paradigm may suggest that Councils are formed of members of the URC, and that a reciprocity occurs between the conciliar bodies, experience of a Presbyterian or Congregational background may influence an understanding of the URC's polity and how it works in practice.

Therefore, it is possible that where claims of intrusion into the life of the Local Church are found, an understanding of Local Church autonomy exists which is neither realised in the URC's *Structure* nor strictly speaking from either the antecedent Congregational or Presbyterian denominations. Although the decision-making responsibilities of the local Church Meeting were never removed, staunch independency had been reduced in the Congregational tradition by the formation of the Congregational Union and then latterly in the Congregational Church. In both cases, the presence of Congregational Associations in the regions in addition to the presence of Moderators from 1919 sped to completion a widespread loss of what was perceived as local independency within Congregational polity. While the wider bodies of the CUEW and CCEW facilitated regional and denominational activity, the Local Churches were responsible for their lives in the locality.

In reading the *Structure* such an understanding is still true in the URC. However, within the life of Local Churches the perception arises that wider conciliar activity is encroaching upon the Local Church. In some cases this is arguably true and for good reason. Amongst other things, the need to establish Safeguarding principles and the request to provide financially to the denomination feature as important ways in which the wider Councils facilitate the work of the Local Church. However, such provision is not always seen as beneficial to the life of the Local Church. When seen in this way—either through a claim of irrelevance or without knowledge of the conciliar structure—the authority of a wider Council to have an effect on another is doubted.

The third way in which the claim of "Who are this General Assembly to tell us what to do?" is evidenced is in the understanding of the polity which is persistent through a lack of participation in the conciliar structure. Although there are limitations set by the General Assembly on its own membership, there is also a distinct apathy towards being involved in the life of the Church. With awareness that Local Church members "don't want to be bothered," Assembly Officers are aware that in Local

Churches there is a desire not to be distracted from the Local Church's needs and actions. Energy needs to be where the Church is focused.

The lack of engagement echoes the difficulty highlighted with the lack of relationship between the Councils of the Church. It is difficult to ascertain whether the lack of involvement has led to apathy or vice versa. The move towards reducing down the involvement asked of Local Churches is both a reflection of the move to reduce the burden on those in Local Churches and a reflection of the changing form of wider Church governance. Through the removal of District Councils by *Catch the Vision*, those involved locally were released from the burdens of further meetings and responsibilities. However, these reduced the opportunities for people to be involved in the conciliar structure of the denomination and to become educated in the ways in which the conciliar bodies link with one another. By attending District Councils, Elders from a Local Church could see that there was a connection between the Local and a wider Council and be educated in the wider implications of Local Church decisions.

The loss of District Councils has removed such opportunities to interact and to have a continual awareness of the conciliar relationship in which Local Churches are involved. Without a regular wider conciliar engagement, Local Churches have lost this emphasis on corporate conciliarity and have become increasingly insular in their outlook. The Church Secretary who emphasised the Sunday focus of the Church as grounded in the locality is not overstating the perspective of many, and the Assembly Officer's view that Local Churches did not want to be "bothered" by denominational initiatives emphasises the isolation wanted by Local Churches.

Participation in the wider Councils now means involvement at Synod and General Assembly. With Assembly reduced to biennial meetings for the period of a decade, although now back to annual meetings, the number of Synod representatives able to attend has been through a period of reduction. Where Synods have sought some continuity, this has further reduced the number of possible attendees. In 2014, out of a total of twenty-two representatives, seven General Assembly representatives (four ordained, three lay) from one Synod had attended the previous General Assembly in 2012 as representatives from the Synod. Where such a pattern is replicated, of the eleven lay representatives, only eight might be new to Assembly, while some of those may well have attended in previous years or places. Averaging only four potential new involvements from a Synod each year, such a role does not involve large numbers of Local Church members.

However, Synod attendance is similarly difficult with one representative from each Local Church attending, often for a number of years. Like Assembly participation, this limits to a small number those in the Local Church those who know about the Synod's role and activities directly. Likewise, with meetings occurring twice per year and in Local Churches big enough to host larger gatherings, the awareness of the conciliar role of the Synod is less diminished than that of District Councils who met with greater frequency and were able to meet in a larger number of smaller gatherings. Although continuity is a valuable commodity in improving memory and identity, the low involvement of wider Church Members does create a limitation.

The assertion of "Who are this General Assembly to tell us what to do?" does suggest also that while participation is constrained by numerical attendance and frequency, involvement in the Council by the person meant that they were not "them" but "us." The participation in a Council makes an individual part of that Council and involved in that sphere of the Church's life. The participant cannot distance themselves from the Council's actions for they have been part of it and must speak not of "them" but of "us." The authority of the wider Council is based on the membership of those involved and is not held by a body separate from those meeting. When the Assembly meets, with its many members, it is the General Assembly and holds that authority. Although participation may be restricted, involvement as a constituent part of the Council's authority and decision-making is not to be ignored.

The authority of a conciliar denomination, therefore, is characterised by the relationships between the Councils, the understanding of their functions and the reliability and participation experienced within the wider Church. Where there has been a combination of polities, it could be argued that such conciliarity may be less clearly understood. However, while the United nature of the URC highlights these misunderstandings and knowledge deficiencies, it also highlights a number of aspects of conciliar polity that may resonate within purebred Reformed ecclesiologies. The apparent distance between Local Church members and the wider denominational decision-making requires knowledge or process to circumvent any experiences of disempowerment. Whether this is addressed by more frequent meetings of relevant Councils, or a better communication process, there remains the need to keep Local

Church members not only appraised but connected with the conciliar structure and to the relevance of the denominational architecture.

Yet, the recognition that it is in the Local Church where relationships are formed, where mission takes place, and where the ministry of Christ is most tangibly realised, focuses the minds of Local Church members into the important role of looking after the Local Church. Very few Church Meetings will ever consider the financial arrangements of a Synod or Assembly, expressing concerns for cashflow or for recruitment or staffing plans, yet many will consider in depth their own finances, their viability, and the numbers of members and attendees to sustain the Local Church. It is within the local context that members focus their attention, and the wider Council, Conference, Classis, and Assembly needs and concerns remain an often theoretical benefit or an unwanted imposition.

6

Personal Authority in a Conciliar Polity

REFORMED IDENTITY IS CHARACTERISED by the presence of conciliar bodies to underpin ecclesial structure and form the basis of Reformed ecclesiology. Such conciliar bodies act in authoritative functions to ensure the necessary oversight of the work of the denomination. Within these Councils rests the authority of the Church, and from which decisions can be made, appeals can be heard, and theology and ecclesiology can be agreed and enacted.

Although Episcopacy is found in Churches which are both United and Reformed, such as the Church of South India, conciliarity rather than episcopacy is a prevalent polity in Reformed Churches. By definition, such conciliar ecclesiologies place an emphasis on the role of Councils to provide *episcope* rather than place this upon individuals. The Reformed principles of conciliarity, therefore, place a heavy dependence upon the role of the Councils to act as executive and judge. This is a collective act, and uses discernment within the gathered community to decide the route to take. There is a view within such conciliarity that suggests that the episcope of the Church rests within the Councils and not, as in other traditions, in individuals called, ordained or consecrated for that role.

However, United and Reformed Churches call individuals into roles that mean that they take responsibility for certain conciliar roles or functions, and become involved in local, regional or denominational roles where they have a remit for activity. In even the most cooperative and egalitarian of traditions, where individual leadership is frowned upon, individuals still find themselves in some role which distinguishes them from the members. Prior to union with the URC, the Churches of Christ had a form of peripatetic lay ministry, while the Quakers have Meeting Clerks. Even if there is little distinction sought between individuals, there remains these distinctions of role.

In order to consider authority in a United and Reformed context, a view of corporate committees and Councils is not enough. It is also necessary to consider the ways in which individuals play their part in the life of ecclesial communities. The breadth of involvement includes ordained and lay office holders, paid staff, and a large number of laity in Local Churches. All of these individuals play their part in Church life. However, some influence the life of a Church in different ways. Naturally, this aspect highlights the different forms of being "in authority" and being "an authority." It is the effect of the individual on authority that we explore in this chapter.

Ministry of God's People

The URC confirms that "[t]he Lord Jesus Christ continues his ministry in and through the Church, the whole people of God called and committed to his service and equipped by him for it" (§A.19). This ministry, located in the body of the Church, is provided through the body of the membership of the Church. In this way the "priesthood of all believers" relates to the understanding that it is through the whole Church, as Christ's body, that the priestly actions of Christ are performed. Daniel Jenkins asserts "unambiguously that the primary human reality in the Church is not the ministry but the congregation. Or since the term 'congregation' has also become excessively rigid and stereotyped, perhaps it should be said that the primary reality is the common life of the people of God."[1] Thus through the centrality of the "people of God" as the primary reality of the Church, the "priesthood of all believers" becomes a logical progression by which Christ's ministry is exercised through the body of the Church. Particular ministries may have a place in the Church, but they are part of the whole ministry of Christ through the Church.

This is especially pertinent when beginning to explore the place and role of particular ministries. The *Basis* recognises that to equip "his people for this total ministry the Lord Jesus Christ gives particular gifts for particular ministries and calls some of his servants to exercise them in offices duly recognised within his Church" (§A.20). Some people,

---

1. Jenkins, *Protestant Ministry*, 34.

therefore, will be called to serve in the recognised formal ministries of the URC: Minister of Word and Sacrament, Church Related Community Worker (CRCW), and Eldership. Although there are different callings, there are not, Daniel Jenkins asserts, different orders: "All believers belong to the *laos*, the community of the people of God, and all have gifts appropriate to their calling."[2] While recognised ministries may set some apart to fulfil their calling, this does not create a "hierarchical order": "The minister does not stand with the Word and Sacraments over against the Church but with the Church under the Word and Sacraments."[3] This is echoed in the *Basis*, where it states that "Christ gives himself to his Church through Word and Sacrament and through the total caring oversight by which his people grow in faith and love" (§A.20). Ministry of Word and Sacraments, therefore, is a gift given to the Church to administer and not a separate "reality apart from the Church."[4]

Ministry, therefore, is a continuation of the authority of Christ in the Church. It is through the "priesthood of all believers" that the authority of Christ is expressed in the Church and by which the particular ministries of the Church are called and authorised. The Church, therefore:

> having solemnly acknowledged their vocation and accepted their commitment shall appoint them to their particular ministry and give them authority to exercise it within the church, setting them apart with prayer that they shall be given all needful gifts and graces for its fulfilment, which solemn setting apart shall in the case of ministers and elders be termed ordination and in the case of church related community workers be termed commissioning. (§A.20)

This setting apart into ministry gives authority which is exercised in the context of the Councils of the Church, and therefore with Christ, to carry out the particular ministry to which they have been called. Elders are set apart after the discernment of Church Meeting and their election to the Elders' Meeting (§B.2.(2)). CRCWs, like Ministers of Word and Sacraments, are set apart (commissioned) after a process conducted by the wider Church. This discernment seeks to establish whether a candidate is called to community work as a ministry of the Church. Unlike Ministers of Word and Sacrament, CRCWs are not commissioned "to

---

2. Jenkins, *Protestant Ministry*, 35.
3. Jenkins, *Protestant Ministry*, 36.
4. Jenkins, *Protestant Ministry*, 37.

conduct public worship, to preach the Word and to administer the Sacraments" (§A.21) but are commissioned to foster links between the Church and community as an authorised ministry of the URC. CRCW ministry is restricted to two posts per Synod (totalling twenty-six posts across the denomination) and as a result has a much lower profile than Ministry of Word and Sacraments. Therefore, because of its prevalence, unless mentioned otherwise, focus in what follows will be directed towards the Ministry of Word and Sacraments.

The process of acknowledging vocation is itself a process of authority in the life of the Church. The testing of call, considered through the various committees and Councils of the URC, forms what Keith Forecast describes as "an intricate process of discernment and by a period of training."[5] Aubrey R. Vine comments that "no one can be final judge in his own case, even in a matter of this kind"[6] and that a minister must be "willing to prove his call to those competent to judge."[7]

Therefore, the discernment process includes the participation of the various Councils of the Church, including the Local Church, Synod and General Assembly. In each sphere, the Council (delegating the task to a committee or separate group) judges whether the candidate is to be considered for ministry and transmits their approval to the next Council for further consideration. The General Assembly's Assessment Conference, made up of those from a denominational panel along with specialists representing the Education and Learning Committee and Ministries Committee, meets with candidates and discerns whether there is a call to ministry and ascertains any training or study requirements. The final stage of the discernment process takes place towards the end of the training whereby a candidate seeks a pastorate in which to minister. With the concurrence of the Synod, the discernment of the pastorate in offering a call to a Minister concludes the "intricate" process of discerning vocation.

The authority of an ordained minister, therefore, comes with that of the entire denomination. Ministers are ordained to serve within the URC, and through the assessment, a candidate gains the authorisation of each of the Councils of the Church. At ordination, suggests Tony Tucker, "[t]he intention of the act is to ordain to the ministry of the whole

---

5. Forecast, *Getting the Name Right*, 34.
6. Vine, "Congregational Ministry," 7.
7. Vine, "Congregational Ministry," 8.

Church."[8] However, he subsequently argues that this intention is yet to be realised: "In reality the authority conferred by [the URC's] ordinations was proportionate to [the liturgy's] acceptance within the wider Church" and this lacks full recognition among ecumenical partners.[9] Thus, the ordination of URC Ministers, conducted with the authority of the denomination, occurs within the "priesthood of all believers" held within the ecclesial body of the denomination. It is this priesthood, held corporately as a denomination, which is maintained and not that of the Church Catholic.

Therefore, the authorisation of ministry recognised by the URC, in Ministers of Word and Sacrament and CRCWs, confers the authority of the denomination to be set apart "to do what laymen may indeed do if need be; but [the minister] is set apart to give his full time and energy to the work of God, having received God's own call to do so, and in the confident hope that his ministration will be the more effective because of his calling, his gifts and his training."[10]

Ministry of Word and Sacraments is not, therefore, an essential characteristic of the Church, but is a significant feature in the good order of the denomination.

However, the challenges of numerical decline of members and Ministers within the URC has led to the need to consider further the question of Lay Presidency at the Sacraments and the role of local leadership. Such a policy on lay presidency has always been part of the denomination's *Basis* as a continuation of widespread practice among Congregational Churches prior to Union in 1972. The URC's policy in the *Basis* allows "for the recognition of certain members of the United Reformed Church . . . to preside at baptismal and communion services where pastoral necessity so requires" (§A.25). Such recognition is carried out by occasional authorisation by the Synod (previously the District Council) in consultation with Local Churches.

In describing the practice of the Churches of Christ, William Robinson asserts, "there would be nothing invalid in a layman celebrating the Eucharist if the Church appointed him to do so, as the sacrifice of praise and thanksgiving is performed by the whole Church as the priestly

---

8. Tucker, *Reformed Ministry*, 138.
9. Tucker, *Reformed Ministry*, 139.
10. Vine, "Congregational Ministry," 10.

body."[11] Such an understanding returns to the concept of the "priesthood of all believers" and an understanding of the role of the Church in embodying the act of the sacraments. Therefore, while a Minister of Word and Sacraments may, in the words of Vine, be considered "more effective" in their administration of the sacraments, the appropriate authorisation of Lay Preachers to preside at the Sacraments is itself a reflection of the priestly act of Christ's body, the Church.

The role of the Minister in the URC can be summarised, as Daniel Jenkins wrote of the Protestant ministry, as "the person in the midst of the particular church who is the representative of the Great Church, bringing to bear upon the affairs of the particular church the insight of one whose duty it is to see it in the setting of the whole."[12] In reflecting the authorisation of the wider Church to the particular, and in presiding at the Sacraments, the Minister brings to the Local Church a representative of the Great Church through Word and Sacrament. Such authority, derived from Christ, reflects the "priesthood of all believers" and places in the Local Church a duly authorised individual whose call has been discerned and whose qualification assured on behalf of the whole Church.

Individuals with Authority

As explored previously, authority can be seen to reside also with individuals, with some being "in authority" while others are "an authority." Although the conciliar structure of the URC was where authority was grounded, discussion of authority in the denomination incorporates the role of individuals, with this being encapsulated in the URC as "personal leadership within conciliar government." An Assembly Officer remarks:

> But in the main I think people in our Local Churches, if you use the word authority might think in two directions: one is the Church Meeting; the other is, I think some Churches would want to give some authority and leadership credence to the Minister.

Being an Office Holder in the denomination, however, does not give the individual authority to act beyond constrained limits: "we don't have

11. Robinson, "Church Order," 5. Robinson is talking about the approach of the Churches of Christ to Lay Presidency, but in highlighting the whole Church as priestly he emphasises the role of the ecclesial body.

12. Jenkins, *Protestant Ministry*, 44.

the authority here to speak on behalf of the United Reformed Church in terms of controversial things where the Church has lots of opinions. There's a line in there somewhere" stated an Assembly Officer whose role it was to give leadership to the denomination. At a local level, a Church Secretary echoes that the conciliar strength came by nature of a "decision everyone has made, not just one person."

The role of a Minister in the life of the Local Church is seen as continuity. In a context in which no Minister is in post, it can be felt by members that "the continuity is missing" in the life of the Church. Members can be focused on the Minister, finding the lack of one disorientating, but then have little acknowledgement of the role of the Elders in the leadership of the Local Church and in their continuity of service. However, in other contexts, members look to the Elders rather than the Minister at the point of difficult decisions and recognise that it is "inevitable" that decisions will be made by individuals, even ones outside the Local Church. A level of pragmatism is also present: "There are certainly people who have got a greater persuasive authority and who are perceived as being folk with authority; and of course if you perceive somebody as having authority then you give them authority."

Thus whereas those in authority may perceive themselves to be devoid of such standing, this view insists that by nature of being perceived as such, these individuals hold authority. The downside is that outside formal office, this authority cannot be universally acknowledged, but it does not negate the authority that some individuals hold, whether by nature of an office or not.

Therefore, the distinction between those who are "in" authority and "an" authority, as explored earlier, becomes noticeable in practice. For those who are perceived as holding authority but are not formally recognised as such, it is an expression of "an" authority which leads them to secure obedience through their "greater persuasive authority."

However, the place of ministers in the conciliar life of the denomination, "represented in those places where decisions are made," ensures that those accountable to and responsible for the life of the Church are involved in the discussions that affect them. However, it is also the case that certain Ministers, including those who are Church House staff, lose their right to participate in the conciliar functions. However, whether such a role disenfranchises the Minister from the decision-making processes seems uncertain: "Well, structurally, it would appear so; but by the nature of authority it hasn't. It has actually made me more influential and therefore the challenge for me is to be aware of that and to not misuse that."

This raises a warning about the influence that such a role offers: "The tendency as an individual, the tendency to sin would be that I then misuse the position that I'm in to suit my agenda and that's something we carry within the Local Church or wherever."

While the role of some individuals has an emphasis on strong leadership and an authoritative role, some of those believed to be roles of authority recognise that this is not always easy. At a senior level "[t]hose of us who clearly have authority are very good at ducking it in the URC and denying that probably hasn't helped" while a Synod Moderator laments that "those who you think ought to have the authority to hold the organisation actually don't seem to be doing so." In contrast, a Minister acting in a regional role within a Synod notes that "[s]ometimes it feels like I've got a lot of responsibility and not a huge amount of authority."

While such rationale is never made explicit in his doctoral thesis, Keith Riglin's analysis leans heavily upon an understanding of URC practice though an Episcopalian lens. This he does largely by drawing on the question of personal episcope as understood during the English Reformation seeking to place contemporary discussions in the context of that period. Riglin draws on the process of discussion arising from the *Covenant for Unity* proposals in the late 1970s and early 1980s which sought to bring together a number of denominations in England. When exploring the *Covenant for Unity*, Riglin draws attention to the URC's insistence that episcopacy was encapsulated within the denomination's Councils and in the role of the Synod Moderator, contrary to the clear guidance laid down by the body overseeing the covenanting process. He asserts that the URC "continued to regard its own practice of ordination to the ministry of Word and sacrament as already fulfilling 'the episcopal role . . . in a conciliar manner'"[13] while clarification had been made "that 'episcopal' did indeed mean a ministry 'distinguishable from the presbyteral ministry and from corporate and conciliar forms of oversight' and thus, however else moderators of the synods of the United Reformed Church could be affirmed, they could not be affirmed as bishops."[14] Yet, as highlighted by his example of seeking authority of a Synod Moderator over the decision of the Local Church, Riglin confuses the issue by evaluating

13. Riglin, "Animating Grace," 95.
14. Riglin, "Animating Grace," 99–100.

the solution in terms of the personal episcopacy of the Moderator rather than through addressing the topic in terms of the URC's understanding of conciliarity. In considering the URC's authority in light of an historical Protestant understanding of personal episcopacy, Riglin overemphasises the role of Episcopalian understandings of authority in his exploration of authority in the URC, and fails to regard his understanding within the lens of the *Basis*.

Yet the wider episcope remit can be seen in the role of the Synod Moderator. For a Church Related Community Worker (CRCW) acting as an Interim Moderator of a Local Church in ministerial vacancy Synod Moderators are the "URC's version of a Bishop." Such similarities can also be seen by Synod Moderators who feel that, in terms of their relationship with the Synod, they have a role that has a number of parallels within a Church of England Diocese but this is not a straightforward parallel to a Diocesan Bishop. For a Synod Moderator this can lead to a situation where the multifaceted nature of the role does not find a straightforward comparison: "I often think that, as a Synod Moderator, occasionally I am a Diocesan, often I'm a Suffragan, as often as not I'm an Archdeacon and occasionally I'm a DDO (you know, a Director of Ordinands)." This wide remit, encompassing a variety of activities emphasises this breadth of responsibility. It is such broad responsibilities that show that, perhaps in support of Riglin, "Moderators, and others, do have some scope to offer personal leadership."

Individual Influence

In many Local Churches, there is an emphasis placed on the presence of a Minister of Word and Sacraments. The narrative of a lack of Ministers and the implication that this is a problem in the life of the Church becomes a frequent concern among Church Members, with such situation seemingly problematic. One Church Meeting has been observed to raise concerns for another Local Church which was without a Minister, offering pastoral prayers to "hope they have a Minister soon."

A similar sentiment, although not the same tone, is frequently voiced around Lay Leadership in Local Churches. In a Church led by an Elder in Local Leadership, many such Elders in Local Churches without a Minister are authorised to preside at the Sacraments (Baptism and Holy Communion). Although the Local Church is receiving ministry through the Lay Leader, who is able to fulfil the functional roles of a Minister such as presidency at the Sacraments and Chair Elders' and Church Meetings, this does not always satisfy the Local Church. In such circumstances where a Minister is not in post, it is not unusual to observe a frequent and fervent lamentation about the lack of Ministers in the denomination. While such a view is directed outward towards a lack of Ministers, the emphasis in the Local Church is focused strongly on having someone that the members can call their own Minister. Although grateful for receiving ministry from their Elder in Local Leadership, the evidence would suggest that the Elders—or the members—often do not equate this role with that of ordained ministry. Such a ministry is becoming increasingly prevalent in the denomination, reinventing the Congregational ministry of Deacons, yet is now regarded as a second-rate or substandard ministry, where it seems in many ways to be a good and favourable option.

However, the effect of a Minister within a Church is significant. Ministers take a lead in guiding the Elders' and the Church Meetings through a number of items on vision and strategy. In many cases, Ministers are the impetus behind introducing many new ideas and themes to Elders' Meetings. These ideas are tested on the Eldership who then, often without exception, consent to the plans being put to Church Meeting or for further work to be done by the Minister. This seems to be the case even when Elders have little idea of what is taking place. In one instance, a Church Meeting was presented with a plan for mission and is informed by the Minister that this had come from the Elders, yet it becomes apparent in a subsequent Elders' Meeting that not all of the Elders have understood the basis of the plan. The centrality of the Minister, therefore, is as a leader in the Local Church, providing themes and ideas and mobilising support from across the Church community. The Minister has a significant influence on the life of the Church.

Beyond a Local Church, the Synod is home to the ministry of a Synod Moderator. The Moderator, therefore, has a wider sphere of influence than that of a Local Church Minister. In this role, the Moderator is involved in discussions between the Synod and the Local Churches concerning provision for ministry. The Moderator, therefore, meets with the Local Churches to discuss the options available and to discuss any possible changes that may need to be considered, or to act as broker between parties when there is a breakdown of relationship between a Church and a Minister. Immersed in the pastoral life of the Synod, it is not entirely unsurprising that the Moderator may take a lead when it comes to discussing the pastoral life of the Synod. Even when not in the chair of a committee meeting, this important and significant experience ensures that wise guidance can be offered and in some cases leading the meeting even when others might have the formal role.

Other office holders, in Local Churches, Synod and Denomination, also hold influence. The place and role of Synod Clerks has been described as "part of the glue that keeps the denomination together." When the denomination was seeking to ascertain a standardised job role for Synod Clerks, there was some rejection of the imposition of ideas about the job role from the wider Councils. Such a role has been recognised by Synod Clerks as oversight although there is a recognition that the Synod Moderator and Synod Clerk should ideally have complementary skill sets.

The staff of the Denomination and Synod (and where appropriate, also of the Local Church) have an influential position in the life of the Church. Each Assembly Committee relates to a department at the denomination's Church House in London. From here employed staff manage the programmes of the committees and carry out the day-to-day work of those committees on behalf of the denomination. As these staff oversee the programme implementation and the department's practice, Church House staff hold the potential to exercise considerable influence in the URC and further afield. At Synod level, the administrative and programme staff meet together as Synod staff to discuss strategic direction and practicalities. They may deal with strategic planning, the planning of the Synod meeting, or the practical questions surrounding appointment processes for new office staff.

In all cases, the influence of individuals can be significant. It is possible that staff members take decisions without consulting other officers or the relevant committees which lead to practices that are not in line with where the relevant committees or bodies understand them to be. Other officers, such as those working under remits of training, mission or evangelism are similarly open to influencing policy and practice. The inclusion of Area Ministers in some Synods has added a level of seniority and influence among Ministers in pastoral charge. Other officers also have influence and can be found to use groupings of these ministers or other officers to develop strategy outside the conciliar process through the influence and contribution of such Ministers. Although there is nothing to prevent such interaction, and to garner such wisdom, when these office holders are then creating and validating a wider strategy or policy direction, the conciliar bodies have ceased to be involved.

Yet, not all influential individuals are in positions of office. The role of the Church Meeting is to allow members the opportunity to share in discerning the will of God in their locality. Sometimes these Meetings can be influenced by the contribution of one or more individuals. In one example, a Church Member read a statement prepared ahead of the meeting, using especially emotive language in such a way as to shift the entire mood of the Meeting. It disrupts the Meeting and leaves those leading the Meeting unable to detract from the emotive direction taken. While not all such involvement has a detrimental effect, the influence of such participation can be seen to affect the Meeting.

However, there are moments too when individuals are shown not to have influence. The Nominations process has been shown to lack knowledge of individuals being suggested for committee appointments. This highlights the knowledge base of those charged with Nominations. However, a lack of knowledge about candidates suggests too that these individuals are not necessarily influential or from cliques or non-conciliar networks, known widely among those tasked with seeking nominations. Although this lack of knowledge about candidates is a challenge to the task of the nominations process, it does suggest that personal influence or status may not always be a factor in the appointment of nominations.

So far, influence has been considered in terms of the office held by the individual. However, the role or office held by an individual does not necessarily correspond with the personal influence an individual may possess. In some situations, individuals participate with one office or role but also simultaneously fill another influential role. In the period 2013–2016, one Moderator of the General Assembly also filled the role of denominational Treasurer. At one point during the 2014 General Assembly, the Moderator was involved in chairing a discussion that included a large financial component. The same Moderator was also in the chair for a debate at Mission Council about the work of the Joint Property Strategy Group. In both cases, although chairing the sessions in the role of Moderator, the effect of this person being the denomination's Treasurer potentially influenced how the discussion progressed. In the discussion at Mission Council, the Moderator provided input gained as Treasurer in addition to his role as chair. In this case, the Moderator's position as chair of the session ceased to hold its independent nature when input from the other role began to influence the discussion of the matter before Mission Council.

However, the URC has struggled recently with the question of personal influence. In discussing the place of the influence given to "expert voices" in Mission Council, there has been an understanding that specialist knowledge needs to be weighted in debates and discussions. Assembly committees had indicated to the Nominations committee that the expertise of new members was to add balance and continuity to the committee, while elsewhere Committee Convenors were keen to "respect and value longer serving committee members." Therefore, maintaining the place of expert and experienced voices in the work of the denomination is important and deserves appropriate weighting. What remains unclear is who defines "expert" and who mediates when "experts" offer apparently contradictory advice.

The Legal Adviser is one such expert available to the denomination. However, criticism has occasionally been voiced that the Legal Adviser may act beyond their remit in offering opinion to the Church. For some, this role has always been seen as one of legal advice or opinion, not as a Council member with personal opinions. A question therefore arose from the distinction that the Church could be informed by legal opinion and not influenced by personal opinion wrapped up in apparent legal advice. The challenge of such expert opinion was compounded at the General Assembly when three experts, the Legal Adviser, the Clerk to the Assembly, and the Clerk-elect were offering contradictory advice to the Assembly around the approach to be taken concerning constitutional arrangements for Same Sex Marriage. In this case, the expert voices were not of one mind about the course of action that would be constitutionally required if the denomination were to consent to enacting the Same Sex Marriage legislation. The Assembly was not given opportunity at that stage to make up its own mind on which advice to take as definitive, and individual expert opinion was clearly divided. Such division may not have been seen to rest exclusively on legal grounds, but also on ecclesiological—and therefore, theological—grounds.

The influence of individuals is a significant factor in the way in which the denomination acts authoritatively. The operation of the Church is dependent upon the influence of Office holders and non-office holders alike, and the evidence suggests that this influence comes from all manner of people, not just those in high profile roles. Such influence, therefore, plays a significant role in the way in which the Councils and committees function and the way that URC programmes are run and disseminated throughout the denomination. It is essential, therefore, to bear this in mind when exploring the role of authority in the denominational structure, and for such considerations to be recognised despite a tradition which is not grounded in, or receptive to, individual authority.

7

Deciding with Authority

AUTHORITY IS NOT ONLY demonstrated in the structure of an organisation, but through the ways that decisions are made. This can encapsulate not only thinking about the ways in which decisions are achieved, but also thinking about the principles that are important in decision-making. Such principles can be shaped by common ecclesial understandings of good order or by understandings about what it means to be open to the Word of God.

Both a United and a Reformed aspect bring principles for inclusion. Within a Reformation heritage, the idea of being a dissenting voice, held with conviction, while open to differing or diverse voices is an important principle. Yet this is also complemented with the desire to collaboratively seek a common voice as a group. These two seemingly contradictory principles highlight some of the reasons why Reformed Churches have a propensity to divide. However, in living out a unity in the gospel, it's clear that United Churches are drawn to the idea of finding commonality and consensus. Conscience in what is being discerned, together with the need to be clear together in what is being agreed, naturally places a tension in the life of the Church. However, this also establishes a framework with which decisions can be reached and recognises key understandings of ecclesial discernment and authority. A decision of a body which is authentic to its membership and satisfies a common mind is an authoritative decision. Informed, as Church decisions are, by the need to further the mission of Christ's kingdom, such principles encapsulate the ultimate goal of ecclesiology—regardless of polity.

However, what is being decided can often be impacted by how this takes place, the process used in seeking a mind and the ways in which such decisions can be trustworthy and accountable. Some of this is influenced by structural factors, not only linked to the ways ecclesial communities are woven together but also the relationships of decision-making bodies and individual authority. In many ways, the ways that decisions are reached, and how they are understood and regarded by the Church are a culmination of the ecclesial history, tradition, and polity which forms the denomination. It is only through the structure that the decisions can have any authority, yet only through these decisions that the Church can chose to act. Without making decisions or acting, ecclesiology itself is little but a shell awaiting its moment to act, or a palace awaiting the pronouncement of the monarch.

Whereas some matters of ecclesial authority are dependent upon questions of doctrine or ecclesial structure, this type of authority is one of process and procedure. It is, in many ways, the minutiae of debates and discussions, and the practices which inform and shape the organisations decision-making. It is a type of authority which can be seen as procedural and, at times, obstructive, referring to the process as the way to complete or decide a piece of business in good order.

However, it is this authority that is so routinely present in the contemporary Church, and is open to so many varied applications. It is useful, therefore, to have some of these applications considered and to see how practical outworking of United and Reformed ecclesiology affects the practice of authority in the Church.

Being Conscious Together

To consider what authority decisions have in the life of the Church, it is necessary firstly to address principles important to decision-making. Within the context of a United and Reformed Church, it is important to keep the idea of seeking a common position—or voice—which is one of Christ in the gathered community. In nonconformist thought, a key principle is that of conscience.

Within contemporary culture, conscience has an individualistic focus, concerned with the self and the personal relationship with the world around. This understanding has become part of the "changing intellectual and social realities" of the contemporary world.[1] However, for Nonconformists, the matter of conscience runs deep within the veins of a tradition that rejected state interference in matters of faith in 1662. What today we recognise as conviction and integrity was for Nonconformist forebears a matter of firm and justifiable conscience against a curtailment of religious liberty. The Nonconformist witness in Britain grew out of acts of conscientious objection. As inheritors of this tradition, the importance of conscience runs deep within the URC's self-understanding as well as its polity.

Understanding the role of conscience for those dissenters of the seventeenth century requires recognition of the way in which conscience relates to society. Both Hobbes and Locke draw out the social nature of conscience. For Hobbes, "conscience is a social, communal phenomenon" and the significance of conscience lies in "liberty of action and confession."[2] It is not enough to hold something personally, but rather to act and confess accordingly. While conscience is, according to Hobbes, "an innate human faculty for distinguishing between good and evil"[3]—an Augustinian approach adopted previously by Calvin and later by Oman—there exists the tension between personal, human conscience and the interaction in social and communal encounter. Tralau notes that "Hobbes emphasises that conscience can err, and that following one's individual conscience would mean that few people would obey the law."[4] Whereas laws are established for the benefit of all, based on communal conscience, Hobbes therefore suggests that individually consciences are not always in line with that of the legislative frameworks. Participation in a community is therefore the method by which an individual's conscience may be kept in check. The only conscience that supersedes the individual member of society is, for Hobbes, that of the sovereign, being "the will that becomes law."[5]

Yet however commendable the personal conviction of good and evil may be, the true sense of the conscience in Hobbes is when something is known by at least two people. In such a case "they are said to be

---

1. Bradbury, "Non-Conformist Conscience?," 47.
2. Tralau, "Hobbes Contra Liberty," 61.
3. Tralau, "Hobbes Contra Liberty," 70.
4. Tralau, "Hobbes Contra Liberty," 70.
5. Tralau, "Hobbes Contra Liberty," 70.

CONCIOUS [sic] of it one to another."⁶ This relocates the personalised nature of conscience as being something that affects more than one person. Thus, in terms of Hobbesian philosophy, while conscience originates in the individual, its manifestation is only possible through the social.

The nineteenth century was a period of active social conscience within Nonconformity. During this period, Nonconformists made claims for justice and equality within society. This age of the Nonconformist Conscience, examined comprehensively by David Bebbington, provided an impetus to social improvement and gave voice to the marginalised.[7] However, by the 1930s, an article in the *British Weekly* was claiming that the Nonconformist conscience had lost its impact in society. In an 1938 article entitled *Where is the Nonconformist conscience?*, J. D. Jones comments that "Nonconformity is no longer united politically. We are deeply divided."[8] Such comments suggest that by this time, the socio-political unity on which nineteenth-century Nonconformity had centred had now disappeared. Jones concludes that "[i]t may be that it has in a measure ceased to be the Nonconformist conscience, because it has become the national conscience."[9]

The effect of the Nonconformist social conscience, grounded in an imperative to seek justice even if this meant dissenting from the predominant socio-political norms and expectations, cannot be ignored. Much of the work of the Dissenting Deputies grew from this conviction, and, if Jones's suggestion is true, found its way into the national conscience. Such suggestions, however, may not be justified.

The Nonconformist Conscience, therefore, played a role in the nineteenth century engagement with the state. In the twenty-first century a different approach is taken. A Joint Public Issues Team (JPIT)—an ecumenical collaboration between the URC, Methodist Church, Baptist Union, and (since March 2015) the Church of Scotland—addresses issues relating to Church and Society and provides a public voice to those speaking as a body of non-Anglicans. If J. D. Jones was correct, it could be argued that there would be no need for JPIT. Therefore, the role of the Christian conscience, with a strong influence by Nonconformists, remains strong.

---

6. Hobbes, *Leviathan*, 43 (VII.§4).
7. Bebbington, *Nonconformist Conscience*.
8. Jones, "Nonconformist Conscience," 423.
9. Jones, "Nonconformist Conscience," 423.

While the Calvinistic conscience sought to convict the believer of their dependence upon God in redemption, the personal nature of conscience as it developed in the seventeenth century became "a principle of both ecclesial and political polity."[10] The political dimension became apparent through the so-called "Nonconformist conscience," where social action was located, while the moral aspect of the conscience, illustrated through individual conviction, led itself towards the ecclesial polity adopted by Independents and subsequently Congregationalists. In his examination of baptismal practice, Bradbury notes that "[t]he Congregationalist movement manages in many places to hold together individuals within one local congregation who held two differing perspectives."[11] In the modern period, the role of conscience became "the full and all-embracing liberty of the children of God,"[12] opening up "the right of different religious groups to co-exist within society, and for individuals to have the freedom of association to join whichever they find best fits their individual conscience (or none)."[13] The role of personal conviction as an expression of the individual conscience, therefore, highlights the ecclesial significance of the conscience.

The freedom afforded to the individual in their conscience and convictions ensures, therefore, that such co-existence is possible in the Church. As Forsyth noted, conscience "does not give laws either for action or belief, it receives them" and as such "conscience is not a legislator, it is a judge."[14] The receiving, rather than the legislating, aspect of conscience gives the individual the freedom to discern God's Spirit, even if this creates differing perspectives within the Church.

In exploring the place of conscience in the URC, Bradbury notes that the denomination has recently used the term *integrity* rather than the previous terms of *conscience* or *conviction*.[15] In the 2007 *Commitment on Human Sexuality*, the URC General Assembly acknowledged differing views on the topic of same-sex relationships and accepted that these views are held "with integrity." It went on to state that Christ calls people

---

10. Bradbury, "Non-Conformist Conscience?," 38.
11. Bradbury, "Non-Conformist Conscience?," 38.
12. Oman, *Natural and Supernatural*, 326.
13. Bradbury, "Non-Conformist Conscience?," 51.
14. Forsyth, *Principle of Authority*, 240.
15. Bradbury, "Non-Conformist Conscience?," 50.

into unity and to assert that further exploration, under the guidance of the Holy Spirit, is needed.

The *Commitment* "leaves the URC without a stated policy, and living with the recognition that individuals, and congregations, will respond differently to one another regarding this issue."[16] The intent of the *Commitment* is to hold differing views on this issue while remaining united as one denomination. Just as the URC holds to the belief of both infant and believer's baptism, this allows the denomination to recognise and hold "a wider range of understandings . . . than some individuals in their personal conscience can."[17] Conscience thus has an ecclesial impact. Acknowledging its importance has led the URC to develop a polity which provides for a wide range of perspectives and belief.

Bradbury concludes his examination of conscience in the URC by raising a concern about the effect of this shift towards personalised conscience on ecclesial authority.[18] Where the Church has historically held "The Conscience" as a corporate conviction, the space that is opening up provides a new challenge to the Church. No longer does a Nonconformist conscience define the polity of the Church, the Church embraces the gamut of convictions held with integrity. The URC, therefore, ceases to hold a single policy on particular issues, but by maintaining a degree of personal freedom is effectively without a policy.

The question this lack of policy raises is a significant one for authority: how can it be decided whether there has been a breach of orthodoxy and therefore whether disciplinary action is required? The URC's understanding of personal conviction within the *Basis* offers some initial thoughts. The existence of a *Conscience Clause* within the *Basis* allayed concerns of Congregationalists who feared "that they might be found wanting in terms of their orthodoxy"[19] while giving freedom to regard personal convictions "as ultimately subordinate to the church."[20] The *Basis* reads:

> The United Reformed Church, believing that it is through the freedom of the Spirit that Jesus Christ holds his people in the fellowship of the one Body, shall uphold the rights of personal

---

16. Bradbury, "Non-Conformist Conscience?," 50.
17. Bradbury, "Non-Conformist Conscience?," 49.
18. Bradbury, "Non-Conformist Conscience?," 51–52.
19. Bradbury, "Non-Conformist Conscience?," 48.
20. Bradbury, "Non-Conformist Conscience?," 47.

conviction. It shall be for the church, in safeguarding the substance of the faith and maintaining the unity of the fellowship, to determine when these rights are asserted to the injury of its unity and peace. (§A.10)

The role of the Church to "check" this has already been explored in connection with the discernment of the Spirit. The role of the Church to discern when personal conscience is out of line with the beliefs of the denomination is significant. The presence of this clause in the *Basis* has a number of results. One such result is the provision of the "right to record in the minutes dissent from any decision of the Assembly."[21] This allows, if the Moderator permits, for members of Assembly to have their names recorded if this is within the *Basis*'s assertion of unity and peace. In a later paragraph concerning baptism, the *Basis* "spells out that the two historic positions on the administration of baptism can both be held within the one church and that no individual will be forced to act against their personal conviction."[22] In this way, the *Basis* states the validity of the two positions and requires local Churches to provide for both, but declares that "it shall not be such to which conscientious objection is taken either by the person administering baptism, or by the person seeking it, or by the parent(s) requesting it for an infant" (§A.14). Thus, in addition to its stance on dissent from the Assembly's decisions, the denomination has given clear direction on the approach to baptism and the URC's policy on its administration concerning personal conscience.

This presents issues for the authority of the Church. However, as the *Commitment* has shown, a new approach has increased the permutations available for personal conviction within the denomination. Forsyth claimed that "Authority and Freedom, however antipathetic for abstract reason, are conjoint and inseparable"[23] and thus while the liberty of conscience frees the believer to "freedom in Christ for Christ and the kingdom,"[24] he asserts that "[t]he last authority is not demonstrable, it is only realisable, as *the* religious experience of the conscience."[25] This leads to a tension between personal conscience and the "last authority" which, for Forsyth, is sourced and experienced in Christ. He further argues that

21. GA Reports (2014) 68 (§9c).
22. Bradbury, "Non-Conformist Conscience?," 49.
23. Forsyth, *Principle of Authority*, 328.
24. Cornick, "P. T. Forsyth," 165.
25. Forsyth, *Principle of Authority*, 365.

what is understood as "external authority . . . is not external enough" and preferred that "a Calvinistic God should rule men than they should be their own authority."[26] The tension between holding a personal conviction and claiming it to be an authority for conduct and faith is therefore the challenge to the Church.

Within an ecclesial polity in which the integrity of differing perspectives is affirmed, the ability for "the church . . . to determine when these rights are asserted to the injury of its unity and peace" are restricted. With a perspective that allows for multiple positions, no one position can be maintained as a position of the Church. Perhaps Bradbury's observation that "matters that the Church has determined are (for the time being at least) indifferent" (i.e., not essential to faith) gives a framework in which ecclesial authority may be assured.[27] When the Church has regarded a matter as indifferent, freedom is given to the individual for personal conviction to be released from its subordinate position under the authority of the Church. The rise of the individual conscience is thus to the detriment of ecclesial authority, which now finds itself subject to the authority of personal conscience. The shift towards individualism is noted also by Bradbury who comments that:

> We cannot extricate ourselves from the culture in which we exist, and the notion of conscience is now largely an individualistic one, whereby the inner thought or feeling of an individual human is that which determines their "conscience". Any conception that "conscience" in some way has a direct relational nature with God has by and large gone.[28]

Although writing in a different age, Forsyth was also concerned about the erosion of the Christian faith by the rise of the individual:

> Protestant theology is founded upon authority as much as Catholic. It starts from something given. It is not the discovery of new truth so much as the unfolding of old grace. Christian truth is as unchangeable in its being as it is flexible in its action. Surely this is so. Surely Christian truth *is* something fixed. It is not just what every many troweth. Individualism there is mental anarchy. There must be authority. And by authority is meant

---

26. Forsyth, *Principle of Authority*, 322.
27. Bradbury, "Non-Conformist Conscience?," 52.
28. Bradbury, "Non-Conformist Conscience?," 47.

something outside our personal opinion, will, vision, inclination, or taste.[29]

When the *Commitment* is considered in light of Forsyth's concerns, the Church's determination of "matters indifferent" is a crucial factor in asserting the location of an authority in line with Christian truth. It is in the "unfolding of old grace," the connection with the authority of Christian truth, expressed through the freedoms of personal conscience that the truth of the Gospel may become manifest. Oman considered that "the true quality of the conscience is not alone to be an ever enlarging sense of the inadequacy of the attainment of what we see, but also a hungering and thirsting after a fuller discernment."[30] The quest of the conscience in the Church, therefore, is to seek after the truth and moral authority "for, while it does not claim that its verdicts are infallible, it insists on their right to be regarded as sacred . . . [and] we can escape only by finding a higher truth to which to transfer it."[31]

Within this framework the Church has created an open policy on Human Sexuality, for example, by categorising the matter effectively as indifferent to the substance of the Church's faith, and in asserting that personal conviction on the topic—of whatever perspective—is of no challenge to its unity and peace.[32]

The existence of the *Commitment* as a policy of the URC both asserts the place of personal conscience and establishes a future pattern for the resolution of contentious topics. However, it has been demonstrated that this pattern is not without implications for the Church's authority. The inbuilt provisionality that "what is sacred to-day be secular to-morrow"[33] gives to the Church both a freedom and a challenge; space to discern the call of Christ.

Seeking Consensus

Within the context of a United and Reformed denomination, the principles of consensus are ones that resonate with what it means to be people gathered to discern and serve the Word of God. In focusing on a model

29. Forsyth, *Principle of Authority*, 395.
30. Oman, *Natural and Supernatural*, 314.
31. Oman, *Natural and Supernatural*, 317.
32. GA Reports (2007), Document 2, 7–9.
33. Oman, *Natural and Supernatural*, 326.

of decision-making built upon consensus, the URC places this approach at the centre of what it means to make decisions. When used to its fullest, it provides an opportunity for a breadth of experience and perspectives to be shared, and to provide an opportunity for the Holy Spirit's guidance to be discerned. One comment made at General Assembly, asserting the conciliarity of the Church, called upon the Church to "hear voices that are least heard." In the Local Church, this includes hearing from those who disagree or have strong opinions against the prevailing mood of the Church. The Elders of one Local Church were struggling with how to ensure an open discussion about the Church's mission and were asking "how do we deal with people's ideas?", while also recognising among themselves that they, as an Eldership, had not fully explored the possible direction.

A leading reason behind the use of consensus points towards the unity of the Church. In order to secure the Church's peace and unity, a diverse set of opinions are held together in one decision. However, a Moderator of General Assembly posed the question of unity, "if we want consensus, what kind of consensus do we want?" When consensus is used as a sign of unity, its limitations are most prominent when it fails to produce any form of decision by consensus. This is where the Church's disunity becomes visible.

Yet while a body may agree a matter through consensus, this decision will encapsulate a vast number of individuals with varied commitments to the decision. Consensus seeks approval but recognises that this approval is diverse rather than monolithic, with some being fully committed to the proposal while others have stood aside from their objections to allow consensus to be reached. It is recognised by Quakers that "[t]oo often, it is said, such differences may not be sufficiently heard, so that a true unity may feel out of reach."[34] The decision by consensus recognises that there are not winners or losers but that a way forward together has been reached and a proposal has been agreed by all.

The principles of consensus decision-making were adopted by the URC's General Assembly, and commended to the other Councils of the Church in 2007. However, this move has led to a difficult transition period within the denomination, with perceived complexities of the consensus processes leading to a lack of awareness of its operation. Consequentially, some questions have been raised about its effectiveness.

---

34. Mace, *God and Decision-Making*, 66.

This was highlighted particularly after the General Assembly in 2014. During the final morning of the Assembly, the consensus process descended into confusion as attempts were made to complete the business under tight time restrictions. In doing so, the membership of the Assembly became confused about which stage of the three-tiered consensus approach (Information, Discussion, Decision) the debate had reached. Members of the Assembly expressed concerns about the validity of the process both on the floor and, subsequently, in *Reform*. Retired Synod Moderator Peter Brain went as far as to suggest that "The [consensus] system was probably worth trying and has been found wanting."[35]

At other points during the Assembly, ignorance or a lack of understanding of the consensus method within the membership of the Assembly led to a confusion as to how to address the matters being considered. One decision was avoided through the action of a single member of Assembly preventing agreement from being reached. The following day, the Moderator admitted that there was a misunderstanding of where the consensus process had found itself during that debate and the decision session was "re-run," this time resulting in a resolution that recognised the member's dissent but did not prevent the reaching of agreement.

The displeasure at the managing of the consensus process within the General Assembly came only a few months after a discussion at Mission Council noting the end of the role of the denomination's Consensus Adviser. This role had a dual purpose: to offer advice to the Moderator on the consensus process during debates at Mission Council and General Assembly, and to ensure the written process was kept adequately up-to-date based on experience of using consensus in the Church. During its discussion, members of Mission Council expressed concern that the Adviser role had ended when the Church still had so much to learn about the consensus approach. The Moderator asserted that the Officers of Assembly were capable of holding the advisory role to oversee the conduct of consensus at meetings and that a separate adviser would not be necessary. In addressing the concerns about the lack of strategic development, any development of the consensus process within the denomination would be led by a small ad hoc group set up to look at the process and who could offer any proposed amendments to Mission Council for their consideration. Such a process was used after the 2014

---

35. *Reform* (September 2014) 10.

General Assembly and amendments proposed by the Clerk were brought to Mission Council in November 2014.

A lack of knowledge of the consensus process in a number of observed meetings led to considerable discussion. After questions had been raised at General Assembly about how to abstain from a decision made by the Assembly, Mission Council discussed the process for consensus. The decision of Mission Council was to rename part of the decision-making process with the hope that this would improve understanding of the process. This "passed, recognising disagreement" tagline replaced the earlier text that read "resolved by agreement."

In light of the aim of consensus to move away from the idea of "winners" or "losers" it may be argued that this practice of the consensus decision-making process has significantly altered the theoretical underpinning of the consensus approach. The use of the language of "passed" and "failed" has, therefore, moved the process away from mutual resolution and towards one of win or lose. The lack of knowledge about the consensus process and its underlying theory, which would have been subject to the advice of the Consensus Adviser, appears to have significantly altered the basis under which consensus seeks to operate.

On the one hand, the rationale for the use of consensus decision-making is very strong. It highlights the method by which the Spirit may be discerned and thus it may be possible to seek a deep and profound understanding of the direction God is willing the Church to take. Consensus sits well with the desire to remain together in unity and peace and is an approach that can bring about outcomes that are positive for all people involved.

However, the reverse is also true and its propensity for matters to be held back by a minority can lead to difficulties. The change to the Assembly Standing Orders to allow for "passed, recognising disagreement" is, in some ways, a pragmatic approach to resolving this problem. However, approaching the perceived problem of the consensus decision-making through an amendment to the process, rather than to better education regarding the decision-making method, is perhaps indicative of concerns about consensus as a methodology rather than exclusively about the need to improve the process.

The consensus methodology relies, predominantly, on an openness to the views and opinions of others and to discerning how best to proceed. This matches the need to be open to discerning the Spirit in the gathered community to listen to the ways in which Christ is leading the

Church, recognising that there may be a difference of opinion but that through discussions the outcome can become clear.

In addressing the difficulties with the consensus method, the URC has taken steps to ease the process but in doing so has begun to disassemble the basic premise that underpins the process. By allowing the consensus method to have a "disagreement" aspect, the URC has stepped away from consensus as a concept and has developed its own understanding which allows for division. A simple majority vote may, unless unanimous, be considered as "passed, recognising disagreement" and therefore the use of consensus to resolve a matter has now lost its fundamental benefit.

Reaching Decisions

In seeking to ensure that decisions within an organisation are authoritative, the challenge to its officers is to ensure that the decision-making process is legitimate. Such processes may take a number of forms. But unlike the structural authority of the Church, the aspect of authority present in the decision-making process is dependent upon procedural authority and the approach taken within the life of the Church to making decisions.

The observation of the decision-making process, therefore, is a significant insight into the way in which the URC reflects its own practices and its own understanding of the principles of decision-making in its life. Unlike the process in a secular organisation, the act of decision-making in the life of the Church is considered an act of discernment of the movement of the Holy Spirit. This relies upon approaching the meeting with the openness to listen for God's Spirit and to the possibility of being led wherever the Spirit leads.

In July 2014, the URC's General Secretary took the opportunity to remind the General Assembly that "The Spirit moves when a Council of the Church gathers." This echoed a comment made by another representative to the Assembly who asserted the conviction that the "Holy Spirit speaks through all people." Discerning the Spirit's call upon the life of the Church is achievable through meeting in Christ's name to discuss and decide. The adoption of residential weekend Synods remains popular because they "integrate decision-making and inspiration," a combination that allows for the Spirit's inspiration to flow creatively into the life of the decision-making body.

The making of decisions within a desirable timeframe, however, is reliant upon a number of considerations. In some contexts, observation indicates that Councils or committees have been asked to consider making decisions on matters on which they are not ready to decide. In the case of Local Church Elders and Members, there was some desire not to tackle the questions asked of Local Churches in the Assembly instigated consultation on Same-Sex Marriage. One Local Church Elders' Meeting believed that this consultation was occurring while they had "too much on [their] plate" and that it was a topic which they wished to "take seriously; but not for now." Another Eldership was informed by the Chairperson that they "*had* to discuss" the topic, although it was abundantly clear that the Elders were far from believing this discussion to be coming to them at an appropriate time.

Another aspect of the timely nature of decision-making concerns the processes employed in order to conduct the business and to ensure that it is not rushed or discussion prematurely curtailed. In some cases, a meeting chair may apply some pressure upon the group by suggesting that, being conscious of the time, "we don't *need* to have a coffee break." Although such rulings from the chair might limit the unnecessary interruptions of the business that sometimes occur, this can apply a level of pressure to come to a decision, using the participant's comfort as an incentive. When such restrictions are employed it is clear that a degree of coerciveness is being applied to the participants, not to make a particular decision but to deal with the business swiftly.

Yet what is "timely" is also connected with what is "ordered." One way in which the two are interrelated is in the handling of business by the correct body. The Mission Council Advisory Group (which was disbanded when Mission Council changed to Assembly Executive) was a group of Mission Council members appointed to consider items of business and make decisions about how best to proceed with the items in the larger body of Mission Council. Their task was not to take a view on the matter of concern, but to ensure that its consideration was timely and in the best order possible. This can be the case for any such Business committees, deciding agendas for other bodies. A discussion about the work taking place to forge closer links between the five northerly Synods of the URC in May 2014 concluded with recognition that it was for Mission Council to make a decision on any proposals from the Synods, and not to be made ahead of time. Similarly, Assembly Executive acts to shape resolutions to General Assembly when it seems appropriate for the Assembly to make the decision rather than to decide on the Assembly's behalf.

Likewise, within a Synod and a Local Church, there are occasions when bodies have recognised that decision-making responsibility lay elsewhere. A Synod Pastoral Committee needed to remind itself to direct a decision to a Local Church Meeting and not to make that decision on its behalf while in a Local Church, an Elders' Meeting insisted that it should direct a number of decisions on items to the Church Meeting to gain the approval of the Church membership. Such action recognises the decision-making limitations of the body within the context of the conciliar structure.

However, while ensuring that business is not rushed or prematurely curtailed, it may be possible for business to be perpetually referred elsewhere for consideration or for a body to claim that a further period of consideration is required. On some matters a legitimate case might be made for further consultation or discussion. However, one Elders' Meeting, wishing to delay further its decision on a matter, was reminded by the Minister that some elimination of options to facilitate discussion by the Church members was needed. The Elders were asked whether they needed to carry out a "full assessment or grab the nettle" while being posed the question "where is the process of elimination going to go?" The solution mentioned in the meeting was the suggestion of seeking assistance from an outside facilitator; such a facilitator never appeared.

One aspect of the ordered nature of decision-making in the Church can be observed in the formality or informality afforded to the business of the meetings. In some meetings, Standing Orders defining the rules for debate and decision are laid down and are applied rigorously. General Assembly's Standing Orders apply equally to Assembly Executive and are offered for adoption by all Councils of the URC. Sometimes, not all participants in these Councils have been fully aware of the rules around debate, and the decision-making processes, and it's not usual for bodies to remind their participants frequently of the Standing Orders so that they may make the most of their membership. Despite being guided to become familiar with these approaches to debate, by their very nature, however, these Standing Orders are "not the lightest of reads." As a result, it's been recognised that members might not enthusiastically take up such invitation.

However, alongside the formally ordered approach to business, a number of informal approaches can be observed. On occasion this has shown itself as disordered mayhem, whereby the participants have disregarded the chairperson and split themselves into a number of disparate and uncoordinated group discussions occurring simultaneously. In one particular example, after such a period of disordered discussion around the room, the chairperson brought the meeting to order and insisted on discussion being "through the Chair."

However, other approaches cause questions to be raised about the validity and legitimacy of the Church's decision-making. A number of decisions in committee and in the Local Church Councils are made with silent, tacit consent. Most notably, but not exclusively, this occurs when bodies are concurring to the minutes of the previous meeting. However, it's not unusual for even this process to be circumvented. In one case, it was noted by the chairperson that the minutes had been signed prior to the meeting even though they were only then coming for approval. In one Church, while the Elders' Meeting minutes came on paper to the Elders, minutes of the previous Church Meeting were read aloud to a Church Meeting where they were then tacitly approved. While such an approach is not unique, it does place members in a position where they are unable to consider in advance the record of the previous meeting.

In some cases, Councils are required to approve formally the work carried out for them by other bodies. A number of Church Meeting items seek approval of recommendations from the Elders, ranging from buildings and finance through to questions about worship. The way in which these items of business use the time resources of the Councils has led to the Assembly introducing in 2014 a category of *En Bloc* business. This enables the clustering of a number of resolutions which are then approved collectively with a simple majority vote. The *En Bloc* process allows for the Moderators to decide whether to place business into *En Bloc*, although there is provision for a matter to be withdrawn from *En Bloc* if a number of Council members request opportunity to discuss the matter. This approach increases time efficiency yet can also lead to the bypassing of debate especially where this may reduce the likelihood of an uneasy and time-consuming debate.

Where Church Meetings had business referred to them from other bodies, the Church Meeting was usually invited to approve the items as transmitted from other places. When these were offered to Church Meeting, the recommendations from the Elders were often sufficient with little or no ensuing discussion. In one Church Meeting, a presentation by an Officer was concluded with "The Elders have approved this . . . so hopefully none of you have a problem."

Other considerations of the legitimacy of decisions being made can be seen where the time or information available have not been sufficient to make a timely and orderly response. In a Synod Trust Executive meeting, a discussion about a new categorisation for a Fund became increasingly difficult as the Directors were not in possession of the complete information relating to the proposal. Other committees, particularly those considering Nominations, similarly lacked information, both about the roles they were seeking to fill and the potential candidates.

The lack of gender diversity within the spheres of the URC's life also provides an interesting comparison. From experience of observing Assembly and Synod based committees and Elders' Meetings in Local Churches, the gender diversity of those present at the meetings in the different spheres illustrates inconsistency in the gender diversity in the Church. In the committees of the General Assembly and a Synod, observations suggest that of the participants 67 percent were male while 33 percent were female. However, in the Local Church, this was reversed with 67 percent female and 33 percent male participants. This disproportional diversity was especially pronounced where, in three Assembly committees, female attendance was observed to be less than 25 percent of the committee attendance, while in one meeting, there was one woman present out of eight attendees (12.5 percent).

While the data alone gives an indication of a problem with gender inclusivity, it hides the complexity of the gender diversity and the diversity of participation in meetings. Further research would be required to provide quantifiable data in this area. However, it does go some way to show how the structures of the Church do not reflect the local expression of the URC in terms of gender diversity. The inconsistency of the ratio of women/men across the spheres of the denomination suggest that, at the very least, participation is skewed away from some and in favour of others.

The different involvement of gender and personality types can lead meetings to have a different qualitative feel and tone. Some discussions, for example, can lead into a more emotive discussion and this can make any decisions more difficult to achieve. At one Church Meeting, after a male Church member presented an impassioned—arguably aggressive—pre-prepared statement that invoked strong and emotional language, the tone of the meeting shifted considerably. In chairing the meeting the Minister remarked "this was an excellent meeting . . . and we've veered off and got emotional."

When time is short or information not fully available, a variety of responses can emerge in the various Councils. Some have opted to facilitate small-group discussions in order to allow clarity of consultation, allowing these to feed into the wider debate. However, in using small-group discussions in Mission Council, concerns were been voiced about the legitimacy of the groups' output. In a comment made at Mission Council, a Synod Moderator expressed concern that "feedback from the groups is being taken as the prospective view of Mission Council" and asserted that this approach should not be seen as a decision forum but rather as making use of Mission Council in its conciliarity. It has been highlighted within the URC that a clearer delineation should be present marking the distinction between the "discerning" (or decision-making) and the "discussing" (or debating) modes that small group discussions are prone to move between.

Occasionally, however, business is remitted elsewhere for further discussion or decision. Having been unable to develop further their resolution on funding ministerial formation, the Education and Learning Committee withdrew their resolution at General Assembly in 2014 and took it back to the committee for further work, while additional business, including a resolution examining the age limitations on acceptance of candidates for Non-Stipendiary Ministry, was remitted to Mission Council for further discussion. At Mission Council, this same item was then forwarded as an inter-committee task requiring additional work and examination and for this to return for debate and decision at a later stage.

One area, which was growing but slowly, was to explore the possibilities of finding a new pattern of working that could make for easier decisions with less dependency upon meeting in person. When researching the doctorate on which this book is based, much was made of online platforms such as Skype to be methods by which meetings could happen without needing to be in the same room. The market has grown considerably in recent years, with an increased selection of providers including Zoom and Microsoft Teams. The increased use and availability of technology far exceeds that of previous generations and that brings new challenges for Church life.

Councils and committees often need to conduct their business between meetings. In these cases, modern technology has allowed for the successful process of decision-making to take place using email. This was seen in connection with the role of a Synod Pastoral Committee to concur with the process of calling of a minister to a pastorate which was conducted by email communication. In other contexts, however, communication by email has not been as successfully utilised. In one Committee, members found that it was an impersonal and insensitive method by which to carry out their business, mentioning confidentiality and the ability to discuss openly without committing such musings to writing. The value of this method, therefore, relies upon the nature of the business being transacted by the body concerned. It is also, one may argue, difficult to understand such approach within the principles of collective discernment in the way in which the Church has hitherto understood it, and in line with the principles of discerning a consensus.

The argument for the increased use of technology is strong. It allows for meetings to take place easily, without the need to travel to a particular location, and without the associated expense of time and money. The impact of the Covid-19 pandemic has certainly been to invite Churches, and other institutions, to experience and evaluate the possibilities of remote meetings. In the case of one writing group creating material for the URC's *Stepwise* programme, the restrictions in early 2020 resulted in meetings taking place entirely online. Through a period of just over four months, it was possible to convene for intensive working in excess of twenty-five times, mixing between small group conversations and whole team meetings. Instead of participants travelling for a meeting, the increased technology allows participants to remain in their homes (or offices) and save time and energy, especially among an older demographic who may find lengthy or frequent travelling unsustainable. The cost saving on the committee budgets, too, would benefit the denomination. Practical realities make the pursuit of such technology worthy of consideration.

However, significantly, the arguments against such an approach are grounded in the traditional understanding of what it means to discern the will of God in the gathered community. To what extent, it could be asked, does a meeting across the miles constitute meeting? This echoes John Huxtable's response to criticism around absentee voting at the time of the URC's formation. There has been increased discussion about whether a "virtual" meeting constitutes a meeting of people who can gather in Christ's name, seeking the mind of Christ. It is essential, in all modes, that the fundamental purpose of meeting is to discern how the Spirit is leading the meeting and what is the direction to be taken. Whether this can be carried out over a virtual or technological means is perhaps subject to further study.

A number of practical matters also bear consideration. First, there had been a decision by some committees not to use email as a medium for making decisions between the meetings because the physical meeting was less likely to lead to misinterpretation and did not place into writing thoughts that would otherwise be mentioned in passing. Secondly, there was a feeling that to do it this way was not to allow gathered discernment to take place as everyone was considering response in their own time and away from a designated space allocated for discernment. Thirdly, although technology is increasingly and affordably available not everyone involved in the life of the Church has either the access or the inclination to utilise such technology. Whereas meeting together is expense neutral to the participants through the paying of travel expenses, the provision of appropriate technology could not always be freely available to committee members.

Although there appears currently to be a discrepancy between the practical desire to conduct business through the use of technology and the practical application and theological underpinning of discernment, neither of these need be a permanent bar to the use of technology. Although the technological solution used for electronic voting at the General Assembly in 2014 was not fit for purpose, other solutions are available that can cope with such demands. As experience has shown through the pandemic, a huge influx of users to online platforms for meeting—socially as much as for business—has made the idea of an "online meeting" much less alien to the wider population. It will be important that an understanding of the *Meeting* aspect, notably discernment, is firmly held and a judgment made into the key principles that may apply to the use of technology.

The decision-making process, therefore, demonstrates the many ways in which the Church seeks to discern the will of God and to base its policies and practices on legitimate process. Where there have been attempts to improve the discernment process, such as through the adoption of consensus decision-making, these have not always been seen to be practically easy to operate. The constitution of committee meetings, which may have vast gender imbalances, and the lack of input from a variety of voices can lead to a discrepancy between the view of a Council and the work carried out on its behalf. Although the URC seeks to draw on legitimate process, the practical application of this does not always achieve the desired outcome.

Trusting Process

An ecclesial structure dependent upon the participation of a number of people in conciliar government requires an extensive and deep rooted need to place trust in others. However, conciliar government relies upon a communal nature and the accountability of one member to another. Therefore, the question of trust brings with it the question of accountability. It is the conciliar structure, therefore, that invites participants to be open and responsive to one another (in response to the Holy Spirit) and to be mutually accountable to one another within a Council and across the various Councils.

The delegation of conciliar responsibilities to committees raises a question about the ways in which Councils are accountable for the decisions they make, and as a result, reflect some questions of trust. Both those involved in the acceptance of Candidates for ministry, and those involved in the Ministerial Disciplinary Process are aware of their roles acting on behalf of the General Assembly. The Assessment Board, which assesses the suitability of candidates, makes decisions for the training of ordinands and does so by maintaining a link with Assembly policy through the Church House Secretary for Ministries. A participant in the disciplinary process noted that a disciplinary panel were independent of any process before and after the panel, leaving pastoral considerations to others in the process. In doing so, the participant noted, the Local Churches on the receiving end of a disciplinary decision were not involved in the process, and were left with the decision made by the Assembly's panel. This delegated nature of these functions, although subject to appeal, are carried out on the authority of the General Assembly. A recent increase in the number of appeals to the assessment process has the effect of challenging the authority of General Assembly through the Assessment Board's decisions. Such appeals may, however, be indicative of a need for the decisions of the Board to be more widely accountable.

Similarly, a regional leader offers an observation on the way that the concurrence to a call of a Minister has altered since *Catch the Vision*:

> It used to be the case that, when there were District Councils, the District Council would concur with the call of a minister.

Now, that role has been given to the Synod but a key difference is that it is now done by the Pastoral Committee of the Synod, not the Synod in full Council, whereas actually, at District level, it was done by the District in full Council—wasn't always done brilliantly, they often needed more information than they got, but it was done by a Council.

The actions of a Synod Pastoral Committee "do get reported to Synod and Synod does have the opportunity to raise questions, but effectively it's a delegated authority to the Pastoral committee." Compared with that of the full Council, this process lacks the full transparency of conciliar operation.

However, the need to fulfil the increased functions within the Synod and Assembly timetables requires the use of delegated bodies to carry out the work of the Council. Assembly Executive fulfils this role on behalf of the General Assembly and, alongside the Assembly, commissions work to be carried out by committees and task groups. It was felt by a denominational leader that task groups have received a greater trust in recent years:

> I think latterly we've [the URC] done better about receiving what the taskgroups say and engaging with it instead of saying "Who are you? Who appointed you? And, What's this paper? We don't want this paper". I've experienced a lot of that but I don't think it happens quite so much anymore.

An increased trust in these groups and individuals illustrates how trust is important in the internal relationships of the URC, demonstrating how such characteristics are important in maintaining the cohesion of the denomination's conciliar framework. "If we can't trust the people who we're asking to act on the authority of the Church Meeting, or whatever Council it is, then I think it does make people feel uneasy." While this trust is necessary, one Church leader is certain that such trust could not be left untested: "There's a healthy amount of scepticism that makes for good accountability and you don't get away with anything; that's fine."

Yet across all spheres of the URC's life, there is talk of the need to increase trust in others within the structure. At the General Assembly, the Moderator invited the Assembly to "trust others to deal with detail" when considering referring a matter to a consensus facilitation group. Likewise, a member of a Synod executive body suggested that the committees acting on behalf of the Synod should be trusted, and that members of the Synod should "accept the care and good intentions of fellow members." Meanwhile, some members at a Synod meeting were keen to ensure that, affirming the *Basis of Union*, the Synod should be "trusting the Local Church to make the decision." Within a Local Church, a Church Meeting was asked to agree to whether they were "willing to trust the discussion of the Elders."

Where trust exists characteristics of authority—such as cooperation, coercion, acquiescence—are magnified in their ability to affect the relationships that affect decision-making. Decisions of leaders and Councils are more likely to be respected and followed if there is trust in the relationship. Trust in representatives in government, company boards or church Councils, as well as trust in the collective parliament, board or Council will add value to the authority of that body and facilitate the propagation of its decisions and policies. The absence of trust will not lead to the absence of the structural authority these organisations employ, but diminished trust will affect those matters which are open to debate or require an element of goodwill.[36]

In many ways, the process of "dissent" in the decision of a United Reformed Church Council is not only a sign of disagreement with the outcome, but is a sign of doubt in the motivation or competence of the body on the matter concerned; it expresses distrust in the Council's mind at this time. Dissent to an individual decision is likely, therefore, to be related to the motivation rather than the competence of the body, while a fundamental distrust of a body's competence (as well as its motivations) will lead to a wider ranging dissent.

Therefore, trust is invoked as a means of remitting decision-making or further work to non-conciliar groups in the Church. Trust is continually regarded as a value to be afforded to other bodies and individuals. However, this often comes without explicitly reflecting on their body's own trustworthiness or the impact of trust in their relationships.

Yet, the actions of a body do enable its trustworthiness to be assessed. Three prominent areas of action feed into this assessment. The first of these relates to the approach taken by the Councils and committees; the second considers the membership of the Councils and committees; and the third relates to restrictive actions taken by the Councils and committees.

When considering the approach taken by a series of Councils or committees a number of competing factors are present. The role of the

36. Bos et al., "Procedural Fairness," 1450; See also De Cremer and Tyler, "Trust in Authority."

Council or committee is a primary driver for the approach it may take: Is it for decision-making? Is it for agenda planning? Is it a consultative or strategic thinking body? Each of these roles suggests a different approach to the agenda item, and the Council or committee may move between roles for different items of its business.

One challenge comes when consultative activity is understood—rightly or wrongly—to provide definitive solutions. Assembly Executive (and Mission Council before it) acting as the General Assembly, fulfils a number of functions on behalf of the denomination as defined in the *Structure* (§B.2.(6)(A)). One way it fulfils these functions, given its smaller size, is to facilitate conversations and consultation. However, a number of concerns about the use of these consultations to inform committee work have been raised. A Moderator of General Assembly, concerned about the way in which these consultations are used, commented that "we don't trust that this information has been weighted appropriately." Elsewhere, recognition has been made that the feedback from such groups can often be from the "loudest and the person with the pen." Such concerns highlight the need to take such feedback as informing discussions but not defining a position. While such consultation produces valuable input, it is still necessary to test the mind of the Council if the body is to reach a "considered consensus view" on a matter.

The membership of the bodies working on behalf of the Church is the second factor relating to trustworthiness. The gender balance has already been discussed in connection with the legitimacy of decisions and their effectiveness. The various processes by which members are brought into membership of committees are managed, in most cases, by Synod or Assembly Nominations committees. These committees, acting on behalf of the Councils, address a number of issues and seek to create a balanced committee structure that complements the wider conciliar structure. Members of the Nominations committees include representatives from geographic or Synod areas. In an ecclesial context in which the perception is that "people are getting too old for roles," these nominations processes face increasing pressure and difficulty in filling spaces on committees.

The practical realities of these procedures, however, illustrate some weaknesses in the processes. The first of these is demonstrated by an overwhelming lack of knowledge about the constituencies from which representatives are drawn. In the case of seeking individuals who are ministers, there is frequently a good—although not detailed—knowledge of many possible candidates to fill places. However, when seeking names of non-ministerial individuals who may be able to fulfil specific roles, there is a diminished awareness of possible candidates, with those already known through Local Church offices (such as Church Secretaries and Treasurers) being those who might be capable of filling the vacancies.

This difficulty adds further to the challenge to meet the URC's diversity policies to ensure a balance of male/female, lay/ordained, and the inclusion of representatives of different ethnic groups. This is further accentuated when names are suggested, and consideration is focused on a process of "best match," even if this does not fulfil the URC's own policies on the gender balance and lay/ordained/ethnic makeup of committees. Even when the Nominations Committee had been directed to address the low female ratio in the URC Trust, appointing only women until the balance was equal, when names came from Synods for approval by General Assembly in July 2014, this was not achieved.

This feeds onto the third aspect which considers the trust afforded to other Councils or committees. This is illustrated in how a Council or committee prevents another competent Council or committee from discussing or decision-making. This is most notable in the way in which some Councils or committees seek to limit the scope or facility for discussion of the other Council or committee. This is a risk for Business committees whose task it is to ensure the efficient use of time. The inclusion of challenging business *En bloc* is one way in which difficult—or contentious—business can be managed. However, it is also possible to question the "timely" nature of a piece of business, and therefore close down discussion. During a consultation period on the best approach for the denomination around Same-Sex Marriage, a resolution being brought to Mission Council concerning Same-Sex Marriage in Scotland needed to be considered by Mission Council Advisory Group. Conversations attempted to edit the substance of the resolution in order not to preempt the consultation taking place across the denomination. Despite a desire to remove any resolution from the Mission Council papers, an amended form of the paper and resolution came before Mission Council in November 2014.

Therefore, an understanding of "trustworthiness" may be informed by the ways in which committees and Councils can be seen to act in these three areas. However, trust is informed not just by the way in which the bodies are seen to act, but in the ways in which they hold themselves accountable to the wider conciliar structure. This additional consideration makes it possible to recognise the extra-conciliar bodies as separate from the decision-making Councils while also seeking to ensure the role of the Council as overseer of the body's work.

One innovation begun at the 2014 General Assembly meeting included the use of parallel sessions. In these sessions, which broke the Assembly into meeting in several parts simultaneously, Assembly Committees could present their work carried out to date and be available to engage in conversation with members of Assembly. The Assembly Arrangements Committee was clear in its thinking that these were full sessions of the Assembly, not fringe meetings, and were part of holding Assembly committees accountable for the work in which they were engaged. It allowed "members of Assembly to engage directly" on items not subject to resolution of the Assembly.

One way in which the extra-conciliar bodies lack accountability is the way in which business is kept separate from the Councils. Lengthy discussions at Elders' Meetings about policies and practices do not always get relayed to the Church Meeting. One Elders' Meeting conducted a lengthy discussion about the membership roll and, by resolution of the Elders' Meeting, agreed to remove three names. There was no suggestion that this would be sent as a recommendation to be adopted by the Church Meeting.

In commenting about the *En bloc* approach taken to resolutions, the Moderator of General Assembly remarked that of the resolutions brought to be decided by the Assembly "some are more worthy of Assembly time than others." In a Synod executive meeting, a Synod Moderator similarly observed that the Synod meeting often left "more important items sidelined by more urgent." Both of these statements assert the practical reality of conciliar life whereby limited time must be used most effectively. However, the implications are that somehow these items are either being considered without being duly accountable or are being neglected as other, more pressing, business is transacted. The *En bloc* approval of the Education and Learning proposal at the November 2014 Mission Council, having been subject to lengthy debate without reaching a resolution at the 2014 Assembly, is particularly good example. Despite new proposals being developed by the department, Mission Council consented to the proposals *En bloc* without raising debate or question of the altered proposals. Such situations suggest that the accountability of these proposals and the decisions of Councils and committees are affected as much by external factors as by the best efforts of the Councils.

However, while accountability is lacking in some areas, the desire for accountability in other parts of the Church's life can lead to extensive and prolonged discussions. These occur where business is brought from Elders to Church Meeting to ensure the conciliar bodies are fully appraised of the work being carried out in the Church's name. When the Elders "bring to you to ratify or otherwise" as was remarked at one Church Meeting, the conciliar bodies are given their opportunity to hold the committees to account.

Trust and accountability, therefore, remain two sides of the same coin. The way that the Councils and their extra-conciliar bodies and committees develop trustworthy relationships and accountable operations demonstrate the extent to which they may be seen as authoritative in the Church. Where trust and accountability are lacking, regardless of the strength of the doctrine, identity or polity, so too is a body's authority.

Thus, together with other decision-making considerations, it is clear that principles of consensus, trust, and procedure play an important role in ecclesial authority. The discernment of God's Spirit in the Church is most effectively led by appropriate process and procedure. Yet, this is reliant upon individuals being convicted of the competence and motivation of others—in turn informing trustworthiness—whilst seeking the peace and unity that comes with consensus. Authority is not only reliant upon the ecclesiological architecture that holds the Church but is impacted by the quality of the decision-making such architecture accommodates. While Councils may err in their discernment of God's Word, the authority of their decisions are dependent not on their decisions themselves but on the process, trustworthiness and unity that their decisions encompass. If they can be empirically observed to be authentic and true, they ensure they are authoritative.

Conclusion

The Contemporary Quest for Authority

THE THIRD DECADE OF the twenty-first century brings with it a number of challenges for authority. The Covid-19 pandemic which impacted worldwide during 2020 highlighted a number of social, economic, and political questions affecting global communities. The imposition of lockdowns and "social distancing" in multiple settings around the world forced the need to rethink interactions and communal activities putting distance between individuals and groups. Technology has stepped up to fill the gap that such distancing has created, with online meetings and video calls becoming ubiquitous and providing a viable alternative to "in person" interaction.

Additionally, questions of authority have been raised through the actions of politicians and governments. In Britain, the referendum on membership of the European Union which took place in June 2016 overshadowed two General Elections and the service of three Prime Ministers before "Brexit" took place. Meanwhile, in the United States of America, Donald Trump's election as President resulted in a radically different form of politics.

In Britain, the Parliamentary expenses scandal of 2009 undermined the position of authority in institutions. Subsequently, the Leveson Inquiry looked into the "culture, practices and ethics of the press" while the investigations into the Jimmy Savile sexual abuse scandal raised questions about actions of individuals at the BBC. Frank Furedi remarks that the increase in the calls for inquiries in recent years has been to "legitimise opposition criticism of government" while "governments use inquiries to show that they, too, are interest in the truth, and thereby legitimise their standing."[1] Challenging though such scandals become, through laying bare the failings of the institution by the process of an inquiry, the institution can itself regain (or seek to regain) legitimisation. Furedi recognises Weber's argument of such a quest for legitimisation as the "main political challenge facing modern society."[2]

Shifts in the early part of the twenty-first century, therefore, bring into question the social, economic and political challenges which face communities worldwide. This is no less true for the Church and examples from within a United and Reformed context can help illustrate how these are becoming manifest in communities and institutions. While history has been a major element in where authority has been found and how it has been expected to be seen and experienced, the rapidly changing social, economic and political contexts in which the Church finds itself will require a further story to be written of ecclesial authority in the coming years. In this concluding chapter, these three aspects will be considered using examples from recent experience, with a consideration of where this quest for authority might lead in the coming years.

Social Meeting in Virtual Ways

In terms of social challenges, the move to ensure that there has been social distance observed through the Covid-19 pandemic has been an interesting challenge for Churches. The URC has not been immune to such needs, however it has found itself challenged by the practicalities of such operation.

The interconnectedness of the conciliar bodies in Reformed Churches is grounded in the relationships which exist between the members of a fellowship. Prior to the pandemic, concerns had been raised by URC members who, recognising the importance of meeting together, had questions about the way in which technology and budgetary constraints were affecting the future pattern of meetings and leading to reduced opportunities to meet together. One Church House staff secretary suggested that "actually we do tend to meet together as a Church less often, and that, I think, disadvantages our conciliar structure in terms of building the relationships that allow us to operate that system with, with trust." A Minister in a regional role similarly drew out the issues of the

---

1. Furedi, *Moral Crusades*, 89.
2. Furedi, *Moral Crusades*, 89.

technological advances and their effect on the discernment process so important to the conciliar approach to the URC's polity:

> That is going to become more of an issue in general because of Skype and things, and as a denomination we are going to have to start making decisions about when it is appropriate and when it is not appropriate to have Skype contact as part of discerning the mind of Christ.

This Minister went on to assert that "[i]t's all about being together discerning the mind of Christ and I think that is going to become more and more of an issue." The relational effects of meeting together to discern Christ's mind, which are so key to conciliar principles, are therefore considered to be of central significance to the life of the Church. Such experience reflects the comment from John Huxtable, mentioned previously, whereby both "Church" and "Meeting" are key to the theological understanding of what it means to meet and discern. For a Synod Moderator, the role of the discernment process reflects much more than a simple majority decision and led to a focus on seeking the mind of Christ when approaching their decision-making. He claimed that in this process, the gathered Council were doing this "because they're grounded in worship and the authority of Christ and they're trying to live their community life consistent with Christ's authority." The importance of conciliarity becomes apparent, therefore, in this collective discernment where the Council becomes "a discerning body; yeah, discerning where we are as a group of people."

This view was, until early 2020, a credible position. Church Meetings were only to be considered if the Meeting took place in person, with the idea of proxy or remote votes considered an anathema to the conciliar operation of the quest for discernment in the gathered community. This position was reiterated in November 2015 by a paper taken to the URC's Mission Council and agreed under *En bloc* business that

> Mission Council affirms the long standing practice of the United Reformed Church and its predecessor denominations, that postal and/or proxy votes are not permitted in the councils of the church on business which is subject to discussion. . . . The views of absent members may be made known to those present before any decision is made, but only those present should make a decision.[3]

3. MC, Minutes (November 2015) 8.

The resolution affirmed the position that "[t]his is because we believe such meetings are to seek the will of God, and everyone present is open to the possibility of changing their mind in openness to the Holy Spirit until a decision is made." However, the need for such a resolution and paper was recognised as coming from a challenge of the contemporary age:

> [T]he world around us has changed, and the climate in which we now find ourselves is one in which the prevailing mood is directly opposed to this thinking. There are a great many organisations, from political parties and trades unions to special interest groups (such as the National Trust and the WI [Women's Institute]) which encourage their thousands of members to participate in mass votes by postal or proxy voting. It is also the case that a greater proportion of our members than ever before come from backgrounds outside our tradition, and that we live in an age increasingly assertive of democracy and rights, and an increasingly litigious culture.[4]

The supporting paper argued that the need for the resolution was because previously the need to formally record such a position had not been necessary, but that "[i]t is no longer so self-evident as to not need saying."[5] It also recognised that this position was necessary where there were discussions to take place around a resolution, rather than in the case where there was to be a straightforward vote on a proposal, noting that provision exists within the General Assembly Standing Orders for a postal vote to elect Moderators in need of an unexpected election and that Local Churches make allowances for the election of Elders by postal votes. This, the paper argues, makes sense in such circumstances for "[w]hen matters are not subject to discussion, it easier to see how postal/proxy votes are reasonable."[6]

This reinforcement of the voting position considering in-person attendance and participation was further supplemented by a paper which was due to be discussed at Mission Council in March 2020. In this paper, the authors outlined a case where a vote had taken place in a Local Church where a member was participating through a virtual medium where only the Chair could interact with the member while others present in person could not. Question had arisen as to whether such votes could be counted.

---

4. MC, Paper M4 (November 2015) 123.
5. MC, Paper M4 (November 2015) 124.
6. MC, Paper M4 (November 2015) 124.

CONCLUSION 191

Building on the resolution of November 2015, this paper proposed that there be a reiterated position made by the URC to clarify that votes could only be valid when in person, although it requested that more be done to explore the virtual context for participation.

The meeting of Mission Council in March 2020 was, ironically, cancelled because members were unable to meet in person due to the Covid-19 pandemic. As a result, this paper was not presented nor the resolution put to the vote. However, as the Covid-19 pandemic became more protracted and in person activities were subject to cancellation, the General Assembly meeting for July 2020 was transferred to a virtual meeting. Mission Council met prior to the General Assembly to transact the denominational business, while General Assembly convened to receive the Roll of Assembly and to induct new Moderators and a General Secretary in worship. At the start of the meeting of Mission Council, the Clerk of the General Assembly proposed a set of "Standing Orders for Virtual Meetings" which were adopted by the online meeting to sit alongside the "Standing Orders for Physical Meetings." These rules for use in virtual meetings became available for the Church to use, and subsequent meetings of Synods and Mission Council have taken place with these Standing Orders as a basis.

The contemporary challenge of virtual meetings, however, isn't solely about the question of practicalities. There is the question of discernment through the medium of virtual gathering. The experience of virtual meetings, whereby a group of people gather online through an appropriate platform, obviously has a different feel to that which can be experienced in person. The atmosphere produced through an online call cannot (currently) replicate that which would be experienced in person, with tools used for transactional business insufficient for some of the more nuanced interactions required in Church meetings. Practicalities play into such engagement, with sound and vision problems (both too little or too much) becoming stumbling blocks for good interaction. However useful the technology can be for enabling meeting, the quality of the interaction itself lacks the subtlety of in person meeting.

One important consideration for challenges of virtual meetings comes down to the immediacy of online and virtual media and the accentuated discomfort with silence in digital format. Any period of silence may be explained by technical difficulties—such as poor network connectivity or a muted microphone—rather than as a space provided for reflection or discernment. One Synod Moderator observed that meeting in this context has a tendency towards functionality over discernment and makes it difficult to provide a valuable silence: "God can work in busyness and quiet, but we must do our bit to let God speak." The need to ensure that there is a suitable environment being framed by the meeting, with the opportunity for silence as well as spoken word, is an important consideration. Despite marked improvements in virtual connectivity and appropriate technology in recent years, providing a meaningful context for discernment remains problematic within a virtual meeting environment.

Although some Christian traditions struggled with the closure of their Church buildings for corporate worship, many nonconformist Churches found themselves making arrangements to "meet" virtually for regular worship. Like a radio broadcast, many congregations were able to comfortably participate in worship wherever people were based, or at whatever time people accessed the worship materials. This raised some ecumenical discussion about provision of "virtual" Holy Communion, with a variety of practice growing from ecclesiology. The Methodist Conference in the UK confirmed the position agreed in 2018 "that presbyters and other persons authorised to preside at the sacrament of the Lord's Supper are not permitted to use electronic means of communication, such as the internet or video-conferencing, in order to invite those not physically present with the presiding minister to receive the elements."[7]

The URC, however, recognised a diverse practice among its Churches and the lack of restriction preventing a virtual Communion service. A paper, authored by the Revd. Dr. John Bradbury in a personal capacity prior to his induction as General Secretary, outlined a theology of Holy Communion for the URC. In this paper, Bradbury outlines fifteen theses which centre on a United and Reformed perspective of Holy Communion and provides a summary of the Reformed tenets that underlie discussions about a virtual act of Communion.[8] Bradbury is clear to state that "what we determine to do in abnormal times and as an exception to normal practice, must not define what we do in normal times." Yet the paper gives rationality to practice, arguing that "God uses that which is less than perfect as instruments of grace through the work of the Holy Spirit in any celebration of Holy Communion." He recognises that

---

7. Methodist Conference, "Faith and Order," Resolution 31/2.
8. Bradbury, "Covid-19."

the "tendency to prioritise inclusion in the sacramental life over strict adherence to Church order" gives opportunity to share in a virtual act of Holy Communion, echoing the Reformed basis that "Holy Communion is always the act of the gathered people of God . . . not normally understood to be a vicarious act." Thus, in arguing for the need to be careful about setting precedent, Bradbury is clear that United and Reformed authority is not contradicted by the practice of virtual communion during a period of global upheaval and specific need for the community of the Church to gather around Word and Sacraments.

The pertinent challenge that comes as a "new normal" is established after the period of pandemic restrictions is about whether the methods used in the extreme circumstances of pandemic have sufficient standing to be of value in the future of the Church. Transactional decisions can be made, whereby a simple majority decision needs to be taken. But to what extent can a virtual meeting truly discern the will of Christ in a gathered community that gathers not in person but through virtual means? To what extent is the meeting that everyone has logged into the same meeting if it does not take place physically together? If it is possible to consider virtual worship as part of one gathered community, can this same principle apply to discernment of the will of Christ in the same gathered community?

Economic and Legal Implications for the Church

In any formalised discussion of authority in the Church, finance is given little if no coverage. It is rarely, if ever, mentioned in constitutional documents, and is given little place in theological and ecclesiological discussions. However, through ethnographic study it is clear that issues around finance are omnipresent yet with minimal, if any, acknowledgement.

Earlier, authority was defined as having the effect of securing voluntary obedience. This means that through its use, some form of action could be secured. The role of money in such an exploration, therefore, cannot be ignored. As such, financial implications have led to outcomes being altered or an alternative achieved. In all spheres of the Church's life, matters of finance, resources and legalities inform and direct discussions about the future of the Church, its ministry, mission and day-to-day operation.

The changing demographic of the URC in recent years has led to the subject of finance and resources becoming prevalent in conversations about the Church's life. The contributions made by Local Churches into the denomination's Ministry and Mission (M&M) Fund provide for the "financial resources needed to train, equip and remunerate ministry, to support centralised services, and the world-wide work of the Church."[9] In a context in which finances are stretched in all spheres of the denomination's life, income to the M&M Fund provides the denomination with its centralised finance to support the denominational work of the Church. However, while the M&M Fund provides the denomination with its income, the Local Church supplies finance to the fund, where, "[e]ach Synod has the responsibility for agreeing with its local congregations the share which each will take in meeting the budget commitment."[10] It is, therefore, within the Synod and the Local Church where the commitment to contributions to the M&M fund resides.

The M&M financial commitments on the Local Church have been largely equated to a share in ministry, with an expectation of return in terms of the ministry offered to a Local Church. The M&M contributions, however, are not conditional on ministry offered or provided and there is a recognition that the share of M&M and of ministry are not always linked. This results in Local Churches claiming that when they are without a Minister, or when one is off work on long-term sickness, they are being disadvantaged financially. Local Churches are certain in their commitment and assert that "we have to pay Synod" while also questioning the amount that is to be paid. Meanwhile, in other contexts, a lack of Ministers "to go around" has been attributed to lack of money within the denomination. Whether or not this is factually accurate, there is awareness within Synods that finance does have an impact on deployment and that money sets an emphasis for scoping. Thus, while M&M is not linked to the expectation of ministry, it is becoming important in the provision of ministry that a Local Church is being offered.

Although income is used by Local Churches to scale the provision of ministry, the lack of funds available for pieces of the Church's work similarly act to restrict the decisions available. The location of funds in Synod Trusts rather than in the conciliar structure means that the Synod or General Assembly have very little funds of their own. This places

---

9. URC, "Ministry and Mission Fund," 1.
10. URC, "Ministry and Mission Fund," 1.

reliance upon the various Trust bodies to approve the spending of funds by the conciliar bodies and removes the Councils from making some decisions without Trust approval. An agreement by a Trust, however, can result in funds being made available to projects that were otherwise unlikely to be funded.

As well as financial considerations, the use of other resources, such as buildings, has an impact in the life of the denomination. The URC Trust has considered the use of Church House (the denomination's central office in London) to ensure that it is used appropriately for the Church's needs. This mirrors conversations in Local Churches who are dependent upon rental income or are relying upon a share of proceeds from a property sale to provide finance for other work.

The significance of finance and resources can be seen in the way in which they are dealt with in the life of the Church and their effect on the governance of the Church. In some cases a Local Church may assert that finance is the "most important" item at their Annual General Meeting while elsewhere there is a feeling that the future plans are too finance driven.

However, the impact of finance also impinges directly upon the conciliar governance of the denomination. The costs involved in the conciliar governance leads some in leadership to ask "How much does this Church want to spend on governance?" while those charged to provide the conciliar governance for the Assembly are similarly aware of the contradictory demands for the General Assembly when cost are placed beside benefit. At the Synod level, the use of residential Synod Meetings which seek to increase conciliar involvement are considered expensive, while the suggestion has been made that the finances could be more appropriately used for missional activity.

In terms of legal requirements, the denomination has a number of factors affecting its life. The impact of charitable legislation on the denomination serves as an illustration of the various considerations that are now part of the URC's decision-making. Such considerations are apparent in, but not restricted to, the legal bodies that form part of the denomination's life. In both Synod and URC Trusts, the legal requirements of charity legislation (most notably the Charities Act 2011) form an important consideration. Within their concerns, the significance of Elders as Trustees and the responsibilities of Trusteeship features in attempting to understand the impact of the charity legislation in the life of the denomination, notably its governance. Unlike the conciliar bodies, the Synod and denominational Trusts are not linked to one another, are "not hierarchical" and, therefore, the URC Trust is not where the decisions of Synod Trusts can be appealed.

One noted tension in the existence of the legal framework affecting the Church is that it impacts on the perceptions within the URC of independency, both from the state and of Local Churches from the wider denomination. This can be seen in discussions within Synods that recognise that with the complexities of denominational polity and legal statute there is uncertainty regarding where authority lay between the Synod, the Local Church and the Trusts. While those involved are committed to ensure that the correct decision-making processes are followed, each situation requires a reconsideration of what process should be followed or adopted to maintain practices that are within the URC's polity and the law.

Other legal matters that are observed in the life of the denomination include those of Health & Safety and Fire safety, Data Protection, the charitable registration of Local Churches, volunteer and safeguarding policies, employment legislation, and financial commitments to pension provision. Each of these areas have differing impact on the life of the local, synodical and denominational URC, with some affecting every Local Church while others are the concern of denominational Officers.

Throughout the Covid-19 pandemic, the UK Government (either centrally or through the devolved nations) continued to impose regulations which impacted the life of Churches. The closure of Churches has been addressed previously. However, the regulations affecting places of worship stipulated behaviours and actions needed for the benefit of Public Health, and provided a number of matters for Churches to consider. Restrictions on the numbers of attendees at weddings and funerals, the need for social distancing, and the avoidance of congregational singing, imposed further legislative considerations on Churches. Synod Moderators, however, provided regular updates to Local Churches to add support to Churches seeking guidance in their particular context.

Likewise, Churches, together with other businesses and organisations, were given opportunity to be placed on a Job Retention Scheme and furlough staff members. In these cases, the UK Government provided financial support to pay the employees while work was unable to be carried out. Some faith groups took up this opportunity, with some Higher Education Chaplains being put on the Job Retention Scheme, and some employees of the URC across the organisation (although not

Ministers) were placed on this scheme. The financial support from the UK Government was much needed in the moment of the pandemic, although there was some feeling in the URC that there was potential to use the scheme more widely, including with Ministers, some of whom found their role diminish with the lockdowns and restrictions imposed through 2020. Whether mission or finance were at the centre, it seems that finance was certainly a consideration in questions of the provision of ministry.

Financial and legal matters, therefore, appear not to feature in the formalised ecclesiological considerations, yet have a practical bearing on the life of the Church. This may not be unexpected. However, it would be short-sighted to consider this only as a sub-category of discernment; being part of the knowledge gathering that leads to the discerning of God's direction for the meeting. Economic and legal matters have a deeper significance than being part only of the data gathering ahead of a decision. In some cases, financial and legal constraints directly affect decisions whereas in other cases they are part of a range of possible considerations.

The practical rather than ideological nature of finance is probably the reason for its absence as a conceptual source of authority in the URC. Because it is associated with enabling action, money does not feature as an ideological principle for the denomination. Unlike secular organisations, the Church's assets are not counted in monetary form but in terms of members, and its success is not indicated by shareholder dividends. However, the Church's status as a charitable organisation, evidenced by the significant roles held by the URC Trust and Synod Trusts, has led to the increased need to consider the denomination as operating both for the purposes of God and to satisfy charity law. This may well point to the increased authority of finance in the denomination's work.

However, a further suggestion for the increased role of finance as a source of authority may be put down to concerns for the future of the Church. Such concerns may align themselves quite closely with the concept of unity insofar as the growth, rather than the death or separation of the Church, is to be understood as an authoritative influence on the URC. As the decline of Churches may be perceived as failure to live up to the call to unity and to bring all into one fellowship, sustaining the fellowships in their financially troubled states may be the solution to ensure compliance with the authority of unity. The presence of finance as an authoritative influence, therefore, shows how such practical difficulties are being addressed in the pragmatism of Church life.

The inclusion of finance as an authority could pose the question of other such factors—context, demographics, membership numbers. Yet, while the impact of these are felt in all Councils, finance remains a consistent factor impacting upon the Councils and committees of all spheres of the denomination; the same could not be said of other such factors. That money has such an impact in the life of the Church is lamentable. Where money—or more often than not, a lack of money—has an impact on the decisions and discernment of the Church, it has been allowed to secure obedience to a given direction. Where funds become yet further stretched with challenges of Pension costs and diminished congregational giving, decisions will be made that will not only be influenced by finance, but by the spectre of an ecclesial financial crisis.

Participation in Conciliar Government

Although the Church may not need to address the type of political challenges facing governments, a number of factors from the political sphere do play into the life of Church governance. In a participatory, conciliar Church, there is a definite need for there to be a relationship between the membership and the governance structures. This requires active engagement in the structures, together with a level of understanding about how these structures operate. This gives members opportunity not only to participate fully, but to appreciate the ways and means the Church uses to make decisions.

This understanding of the URC's authority is informed deeply by the antecedent tradition from which the Local Church has come. It's been said that "if you look at an individual Church you can generally tell whether it was Presbyterian or Congregational." This affects the relationship between the Church Meeting and the Elders: "Part of the variation is to do with the history, so whether it was a Presbyterian Church or not. So Presbyterian Churches have got a greater tendency for the Church Meeting just to rubber-stamp what the Elders say."

Within a Local Church context, the antecedent traditions become apparent with the differing historical polities—Congregational or Presbyterian—becoming more noticeable. However, the relationship between Elders and Church Meeting is understood to be of complementary functions rather than being defined by historical definitions. Instead, it is understood that these two bodies dovetail together to form an effective leadership of the Local Church. This is demonstrated in "an Eldership which takes a lot of responsibility and leadership, and a Church Meeting which makes the ultimate decisions." This is substantiated by recognition around the Church that authority within the URC resides in the Local Church. One Church Secretary remarks that "[t]ruthfully, it's where your heart and your Sundays are spent." Therefore, it is in the local expression of the URC, in the Local Church with its Church Meeting and Elders' Meeting, where people meet Sunday by Sunday, that a strong locus is found for authority in the URC.

However, this is not always the case and some believe the authority resides with the Synod. An Assembly Officer notes that "[a]nytime [a Local Church] want to move, the Synod is there saying yes or no" while a Church Secretary, uncertain about the particularities of the Synod's functions, perceives that "Synod wise, I think they're pretty powerful . . . They probably pack a punch." This is echoed by a Local Church Minister who felt that the Synod is where many would locate the function of oversight.

Those who have experience of the wider Church structure have perspectives informed by their experiences. Examples exist where Local Churches had not always felt that the Synod had been especially helpful in its dealings with the Local Church. For one Church Secretary, the focus needs to be on ensuring that the Local Church operates to the best of its ability, while the Synod's support feels less secure: "And think probably Churches in similar situations to us may well feel like that—feel a bit let down—therefore think, provided we're getting on, we're, you know, coping then that's what counts."

A similar sentiment can also be heard elsewhere: "I don't think we get enough guidance or help from Synod . . . from our Moderator." Such Church members also remark that they are not aware of news in the Synod, saying "I don't feel that as a member of the congregation we hear an awful lot about what is happening." There is often a consensus among members that not much is known about the wider Councils, especially the General Assembly. However, such members do ponder whether that is the fault of the Assembly or their own fault for not asking more questions.

The role of General Assembly and Assembly Executive (previously Mission Council), however, seems to be less contentious. There is recognition around the denomination that the final authority of the URC resides with the General Assembly and, in the words of a Church House Secretary: "The ultimate authority in any decision that needs to go that far is General Assembly. Whether that is General Assembly or whether it's [Assembly Executive] acting as General Assembly doesn't make any difference, ... it's General Assembly decision."

Yet, despite this final authority, the perspective of the General Assembly's role is consistently seen to be one of steady direction and not to "interfere" in business in which it does not have direct responsibility. In the majority of issues affecting Local Churches, namely "buildings or deployment policies, it is for the Synods to do." In other matters, focus is on keeping to Synod and Local decisions, and on consulting where necessary. In drawing on the requirement to consult as found in the *Basis*, a Synod Moderator comments that a signal is sent that "we're all in this together and it's not one Council acting in a hierarchical way, it's saying 'This is our sphere of influence; this is what we presume; but we want to check with you.'" Some senior Church leaders are challenged by the situation the Church's Councils find themselves in. One such leader described the consultation entered into in response to the debate on Same-Sex Marriage as evidence that the General Assembly is not "competent to make a policy decision regarding Same-Sex Marriage on its own," echoing the earlier views of Micklem, Riglin, and Brindley. However, the use of a consultation ensured that the Assembly was not acting "high handed" by seeking the opinions of the wider Councils of the denomination. Yet criticisms exist and some believe that "sometimes authority is actually about making the tough decisions" and that in this example such authority was lacking. Yet such a consultation process would be expected of a Local Church if its decision affected the wider Church: "We can uphold the right of Church Meeting to make decisions about things but if the things that it does impacts on the wider Church then the wider Church needs to be able to say so. So, ultimately that takes us to General Assembly."

The role of an Assembly Executive in the polity of the denomination has been open to more discussion. Pragmatism recognises that, in the CTV period when Mission Council met multiple times between General Assembly meetings, "[i]t is necessary, I think, because we can't wait, for two years, and to be honest Assembly is, to a certain extent, unwieldy and there is only so much Assembly can do." The distinction between in the two bodies was categorised: "General Assembly is about strategic direction and matters of principle and high level policy, and Mission Council is about implementation. It can act on behalf of Assembly but is cautious in doing so. Then when something's really important says 'Sorry, we're going to wait; I know it's two years, but we're going to wait."

Since the change to annual General Assembly, a reduced membership, and once annual Assembly Executive meeting, such observations are less pertinent. However, it's clear that the structure of the biennial Assembly and Mission Council structure created an issue that was unexpected when it was adopted, and yet highlights a reason for the return to an annual Assembly.

In considering how Mission Council, and now Assembly Executive, can function, one Assembly Officer notes that this body can do more to facilitate the work of the Assembly: "I don't share people's disquiet about Mission Council; I think Mission Council should do more to set Assembly free to discuss the big things." This sentiment is echoed by others involved in the Committee structure of the denomination who consider the Assembly Executive as the location where committee work can be placed in the "big picture" of the denomination's work and look to Assembly Executive "to broaden the debate" on the committee's work.

However, the use of an Executive for General Assembly does not always achieve what had been desired through the use of a smaller, more agile membership. Instead of Mission Council setting strategic direction and mission, this had not been well achieved. One long term participant in Mission Council reflected on its role:

> I think (I've had a number of conversations with people) and I don't think we've really felt that it's lived up to its potential, Mission Council, because the idea is that, you know, it should provide some sort of strategic leadership in Mission. I mean, it does it from time to time certainly. But consistently? No.

However, while an Executive may not historically have fulfilled the desires of senior Church figures, either to free the Assembly or offer strategic leadership, its size in comparison with the wider life of the URC offers alternative perspectives that might not be heard from a smaller group. With a transition to Assembly Executive from Mission Council, some such ideas visions may yet be realised. However, the size and dynamism of an Executive creates challenges too: "If it gets much smaller you start leaving people out. But it is too big to do its work very easily, gets bogged down, and lots of people don't speak."

For some, an Assembly Executive can be seen as too small "if it's making decision for the whole denomination" while for others it can be shaped into "a more streamlined body which in a sense wouldn't be a very representative Council of the Church, but then it's not supposed to be a representative Council of the Church; that's General Assembly." That Mission Council has been adapted to become Assembly Executive, such a function is needed in the contemporary structure of the URC, whereby it can ensure that the agenda of the General Assembly through its programmes, activities and policies are overseen between the meetings of the Assembly.

Yet while such concerns of the central bodies affect those who participate in them, there is a sense in which such views are not shared in many Local Churches. An observer at Mission Council, a Church House staff secretary employed by the General Assembly in a role that sees him working closely with those across the denomination notes that "the reality, I think, my experience has been that most people in the Local Church are not concerned about Mission Council at all, in fact, they're probably not really concerned about General Assembly too often either." In the Local Church, the wider Councils mean "Damn all!" to some members, while for others who are part of the Synod and Assembly spheres, there is a deep respect and love for the way the denomination's conciliarity considers the Church's business.

The place of the General Assembly, its constraints and limits, and its ability to carry out detailed work is largely understood by those who have experience of the wider Councils. Those involved only at Local Church contexts are much less likely to have any perspective on the role or actions of the General Assembly. In these situations, it's clear that the Assembly is, largely, perceived to be irrelevant to the life of the Local Church. As one Church Secretary notes: "So if you're a Church whereby you're getting everything you want, or say you need, so you've got a vicar [sic], you've got, you know, good flock, you've got youth, you've got this, that and that, and everything's going well for you, sure whatever [General Assembly] said, I'm aiming for it."

These observations from within the Church's life, reflect the challenges of wider engagement in the life of the denomination, and highlight the apathy and ambiguity about the conciliarity of the Church. These are not necessarily a result of the antecedent traditions of individual congregations, although this undoubtedly plays its part. In terms of the URC's practice, there is a distinct ambivalence within the Local Church to the wider functioning of the denomination. Part of this is a result of the perceived distance from the central organisation of the denomination and the uncertainty among those within the Local Church about the URC's operation and nature.

The URC's conciliar structure connects a number of spheres with the participatory nature of the denomination's structure linking each of the bodies. Local Church members are those who sit on committees of Synods and the General Assembly, and it is members from the Local Church who are present at General Assembly, as at the Local Church meeting, to make decisions affecting the life of the denomination. This relatedness ensures that the conciliar bodies of the denomination are not separate from the life of the Local Church, but are intrinsically connected to it. However, the reality of much of the Church's life does not demonstrate any recognition of this relational nature of the conciliar structure.

A prevailing view is not of the General Assembly or Synod as part of the life of the Local Church, but rather as an external body acting independently of the needs and actions of the local. Such a view is similarly seen at Synod in reference to the General Assembly. One comment raised at Mission Council in March 2014 expressed concern that the denomination was making policies centrally and then passing on the cost and resourcing implications to the Synod. Concerns echoed elsewhere talk of the "us" and "them" mentality between the Local Church and the wider conciliar bodies.

The General Assembly, as the body with the widest sphere in the life of the URC, has the widest ranging set of functions and the broadest selection of participants. The Assembly and its actions embody the denomination as a whole and it is seen to act for the denomination. With a number of people committed and participating in the conciliar and committee life of the Assembly, it might be expected that its life is recognised as part of the wider functions of the denomination.

However, the General Assembly, and by extension also the denominational Church House in London, is considered to be distant from the Local Church. Geography is one obvious factor. Church House is located in London, with Synods having offices in regions, and Local Churches in the locality, which means that for many members the location of "Headquarters" in London is physically distant from their experience, a situation exacerbated by little direct contact with Church House. This aspect was subject to work within the URC Trust, with the aim of examining the place and role of a central London office. Such examination, which focused on the function of the building and its reuse in a more sustainable manner, has drawn in the questions of being London-centric.

Such matters have caused much reflection, including a Moderator of General Assembly posing a question about the cost—and by inference, value—of a conciliar structure that is focused on London.

While the perceived cost and geography is one common complaint, the General Assembly's programmes and materials have also been seen to be largely irrelevant to Local Churches. Synod Officers recognise that "most members at a Church couldn't care less about the denomination." For others, the question is more pointed, with a local perspective at General Assembly being asked in terms of the question "Who are this General Assembly who tell us what to do?" Such remarks highlight the way in which an understanding of wider conciliarity is lacking within the life of the Local Church and demonstrate the gaps in the conciliar structure. In a discussion at Mission Council considering the proposal to return to annual General Assembly, comments made emphasised a "strong disempowerment" of URC members under those conciliar arrangements. Discussions around the denomination have also suggested that the URC cannot carry on with its structures as before but must instead explore new ways of doing the work of the denomination.

The local view of the Synod, too, reflects that of the General Assembly. With its role as the intermediate Council in the URC's structure between the Local Church and the General Assembly, the Synod has a duty both directly towards the General Assembly, but also towards resourcing the Local Church. With the Synod fulfilling a regional (or national) role, linked directly to the work of Local Churches, there is an increased likelihood of knowledge or even experience of the Synod as a Council or of its officers within the Local Church.

However, with the removal of District Councils from the *Structure* in 2006, the distance between Local Church and Synod has not been easy to reduce. A number of comments about the need for the Synod to increase its networking function and to act further to involve a larger constituency have been made. About a third of the Synods have run some of their Synod Meetings residentially with the aim of creating a time for carrying out business while also ensuring opportunities for networking. This residential approach has been commended by these Synods as by reducing the impact of travel it gives opportunity to "engage with people" and allows for the meeting of the Synod to take place in alternative formats such as "Cafe-style."

Although the Synods have sought to adapt themselves to make stronger connections with Local Churches, the lack of interaction between Local Church members and the Synod continues to create distance between the two Councils. The introduction of Area Ministers with a geographical role has sought to fill the gap in some Synods, making Synod more visible in the life of the Local Church. In Local Churches, the Area Minister can be noted and regarded as the embodiment of the Synod, offering the possibility of advice on Mission, and can be involved in preparing Churches for the Local Mission and Ministry Review (LMMR) process overseen by the Synod.

However, the Local Church relationship with the Synod is not regarded as universally positive. Many of these challenges are fuelled by perceptions or experiences from history. When a Local Church's contacts within a Synod change at similar times (due to Committee Convernorships ending, the retirement of Staff, or the moving of a Moderator), it can feel like Synods are volatile locations. For some this can be expressed as concern that there is a "large turnover" in Synod Officers and that this gives the impression of the "Synod falling apart." Where such changeovers affect discussions of Ministry and Finance, the perception in the Local Church can be that there has been a large turnover and this makes the Synod seem unstable.

Therefore, the Synod is viewed both positively and negatively by the Local Church. In some Local Churches, the Synod is recognised as having "no authority over the Elders" while concerns are raised in other Local Churches about whether the Synod would take money received in a bequest. This perspective is heightened when the Synod's responsibilities include how best to develop a regional strategy while still allowing Local Churches the independence to operate within their own context. This is particularly true in terms of the provision of ordained ministry (understood in terms of ministerial scoping and deployment) available to Local Churches, which has gained a greater profile in recent years due to high levels of ministerial retirements, and declining membership numbers. Synods are only too aware of this tension when Synod Pastoral Committees meet to consider these questions. Even where the Synod Pastoral Committee can see possibilities for ministerial deployment, where the Local Church concerned objects to the strategy, it leaves the Synod in need of reconsidering its proposals. Likewise, groups of Local Churches often need to work together in new ways and find it difficult to negotiate well for the common benefit. In such cases, while any future proposals may be "better" for the Church in question, it undoubtedly will have an impact on other Local Churches, drawing Synod resources (committee time, money, or deployment) away from other projects and mission foci.

Synods are only too aware of the decision-making authority of the Local Church and this causes a tension. Synods recognise that to "allow Churches to close or 'force' them to close [is] not a benefit" yet assert that there is a need to "allow a Church to make its own decision about call of ministry." A Synod facilitated consultation process with Churches, therefore, gives the Local Church the opportunity to explore their own future, especially recognising that Local Churches often do not want to be told what to do by external denominational bodies.

The conciliar relationship of the General Assembly and the Synod is defined within the *Structure*. However, within all spheres of the life of the denomination, additional bodies exist that receive delegated authority from the relevant Council to maintain its life. In the case of the General Assembly, this consists of Assembly Executive and a number of Assembly Committees. Within the Synod, this includes a number of committees. In both Assembly and Synod spheres, these committees are further supplemented with the Charitable Trusts which maintain the legal standing of the conciliar bodies. This includes the URC Trust and the relevant Synod Trusts. The impact these Trusts have on the conciliar life of the denomination are not insignificant.

The relationship between the Trusts and the conciliar bodies is complex and has become, in recent times, a topic exercising a number of the legal and ecclesiological minds of the denomination. The Law and Polity Advisory Group (LPAG) has sought advice on the legal status of the URC Acts with regard to the Trusteeship of the properties held in trust within the denomination. The discussion places the relationship of the Church to the State (and vice versa), notably the effect of statutory provision on the Church's activities, as an important matter in the denomination's life.

For many, however, the complexities affecting the relationship between the Trust, the Council and Local Churches is not well understood. Local Church buildings are, in most cases, held in Trust by the Synod Trust and, therefore, any changes of use (by hire or sale) are dependent upon their consent. However, the Synod's conciliar bodies are also involved and this creates a three-way relationship between Local Church, Synod Trust, and the Synod (through its Council or delegated committees) who each have distinct roles in relation to such authorisation. In some contexts, the challenges between Charity Law, the URC Acts, and historic trusteeship create a number of tensions in the Church's life.

Such issues are never simple to address, drawing in multiple aspects and heightening tensions—often unnecessarily—between the Local and the Synod.

As the Synod Trust is the legal Charitable Body, it is for the Synod Trust to approve the Synod's budget each year, while the URC Trust approve the denominational budget. As a result, the appropriate Synod or Assembly finance committees have to satisfy the relevant Trust of the value of the work being carried out. It is for the Charitable Directors to be satisfied of the budget, and at times questions may be raised about the spending priorities, about budgeting and about use of resource. The mention of such a veto of the Synod's work by the Directors illustrates the complex relationship of the Trust to the conciliar bodies.

It was asserted in a meeting of the URC Trust that where a Trust Company forms part of the three-way relationship between the Local Church and the Synod, the role of the Trust is to act as mediator of the charitable aims and objectives of the Church. In the sphere of the General Assembly it's also the case that the URC Trust does not operate within a vacuum, entirely separate from the conciliar structure. However, the URC Trust is aware of its actions and "would need strong concerns about General Assembly policy to intervene."

This complex inter-relationship of Synod and Trust body can be a challenge to understand. The Chair of the URC Trust remarked that Synod Trust acts as Trustee for the Church, not as agents for the Synod. As such, they are required to remain both independent from the Synod bodies yet linked closely enough to be part of the denominational framework. In some contexts, the Synod Trust Executive and the Synod Finance committee meet consecutively with a significant overlap in membership. Given the need for these bodies to work closely with one another, advantages are apparent. However, if the Synod Trust is to remain a mediator between the needs and wants of the Synod and of the Local Church, while maintaining its charitable independence, there is the possibility that the near overlapping membership might not provide the level of independent scrutiny and decision-making that might be expected from the three-way distinct structure.

While there is clearly a distance between the Local Church, the Synod and the General Assembly, there exists little enthusiasm to consider any structural changes. Former General Secretary Revd. Roberta Rominger, in her presentation to Mission Council on the work of the denomination's Medium Term Strategy Group (MTSG), commented that natural evolution was necessary in terms of structural changes. Discussing the possibility of a reduction in the number of Synods, there was, she went on to assert, "no appetite for the URC to change the number of Synods." Concerns with making unnecessary changes were echoed by the Synod Clerks who questioned "if it's not necessary, why do it?"

Yet, as previously mentioned, a sense of disempowerment in the work of the Assembly suggest that a reconsideration of the structures of the denomination would be timely. However, such criticisms of the effectiveness of centralised denominational resources and the links with the Local Churches meet difficulties when groups review the existing framework. Nevertheless the reticence for change, as the MTSG has found, suggests that any significant structural changes are unlikely.

Local Churches have also shown a lack of enthusiasm for change. In a Local Church which recently combined into one Church where it had previously been three, concerns have been expressed within the Elders' Meeting that "people want to revert back to safety and security" rather than forging onwards with necessary structural and practical adaptation.

The reticence for change provides a worrying prospect for the denomination in terms of its future vulnerabilities. The practical concerns expressed are legitimate. In the Local Church, Elders are feeling "worn down" and feel that they are unable to go against the tide of the membership who are content with maintaining the status quo. In some contexts, Elders appear adamant that if the membership want something different to the path the Elders have discerned best to pursue then maybe the Elders should relent with the course they are taking and accede to the Members' protestations. This situation affects not only Elders, but Ministers and Moderators too, and this resulting tone of ambivalence and malaise remain a present reality of the challenges that lay before the Church.

One further consideration rests with the concept of memory within the life of the Councils and committees. In more than one place, reference has been made to the changes in memberships of bodies. During Moderatorial tenures, a number of key committees have significant turnover such that only a Moderator and PA may retain unbroken membership of the committee. Meanwhile concerning denominational activity, such as the work of the Methodist/URC liaison group, the ongoing effectiveness of the consultation has been considered to have suffered because of a "loss of memory" over the years. This too is echoed around the denominational structure when it's noted that "things get lost from memory very quickly."

This loss of memory, within the committees and Councils of the wider Church, plays its part in perpetuating the loss of knowledge and awareness that comes with experience of the wider conciliar structure. The reduced frequency of and attendance at General Assembly, and the loss of a sphere of conciliar governance could indicate when such a memory loss became more pronounced, although it seems likely not to be a new phenomenon but one that may have gained a higher profile in recent years.

The challenges of participation in a United and Reformed Church, therefore, have a significant impact from the nature of a conciliar ecclesiology which draws in the membership to engage in the collaborative experience of the Church. The impact of conciliarity, which requires participation, is much diminished by the lack of knowledge of the structure. However, being a United Church, there is much to suggest the lack of purebred polity results in added complications, with little understanding of what is—or should be—in place.

However, the apathy towards a wider structure highlights the passion of members to locate locally rather than be concerned with a wider conciliar community. This may be impacted yet further by the development of online worship and community as a result of the pandemic, and the counter-desire to increase and strengthen relationships that are proximate and tangible. The reduction in movement towards the denominational core may also be practically explained by an increasingly elderly demographic unable to participate more widely, paired with younger participation which links to individuals in the global arena and not with the bodies that provide community. In an environment in which community is at the micro or the macro rather than in the space between, it's hard to see how conciliarity—which is so much more counter-cultural—can spark the imagination of many but the most committed.

Conclusion

While these challenges have been illustrated through the example of the URC, they are not unique to this, or other, United and Reformed ecclesiologies. There are many challenges facing the contemporary Church. They grow out of the history and the identity of a Church, and are helped or hindered by it, but are not exclusively questions of history or identity. In many cases, they are questions of authority.

The Scott Rennie case in the Church of Scotland brought together questions of history, identity, theology and—most importantly—authority. The debates around human sexuality, women in ministry, lay leadership and presidency at the sacraments are all questions of authority. Even in traditions which are less explicit about answering and responding to the Spirit, it is the place of the contemporary Church to be always alive to the Spirit of God. These are questions which are about freedom of expression, power to worship, living in the Spirit of God's creation, and the ministry of the people of God. These are questions of authority.

In many Churches the question of human sexuality continues to be an issue: the ministry of openly gay and lesbian ministers, the marriage of same-sex couples, the ordained or lay ministry of those married in such relationships, the baptism of children of same-sex couples. Many different Churches and traditions continue to have ambiguity or even policy which forbids one or more of those areas. I have seen as Anglican friends have been required to have their civil partnerships "blessed" rather than marry in Church as they would have wished. I read of Anglican Clergy who have entered into same-sex marriages and are now refused a Bishops Licence and therefore struggle to serve within the Church they have called home. I know of friends and colleagues in a number of denominations where same-sex marriages are not yet permissible and where they are unable to preside or celebrate at the marriage of their members, but do all they can to have a Church "wedding" in all but legal standing after a civil act performed by the local registrar.

Anyone who thinks such issues are of history, identity or theology do so by avoiding that the underlying basis of all of these rests in an understanding of authority. A Church's history tells the story of authority and its significance. A Church's identity radiates what authority looks like in a denomination. A Church's theology reflects the authority the denomination wishes to live by. Authority is a matter for denominational bodies, Church leaders, conciliar structures and commissions, but it is also a matter for Local Church leaders, Elders, Deacons, Consistory, Church Councils, Church Meetings, Ministers, Priests and Vicars. History, identity and theology are lived out through the mighty and the mundane acts of all of these bodies and individuals. Yet in a contemporary Church, it is necessary to think of the many members of the whole Church, in their multiplicity, each playing a part in the story of authority.

Authority lies at the centre of what it means to be called together into an ecclesial community. It is, rightly, rooted in the Word of God. Yet other sources of permanence and reliability begin to show. History does not get to be the forever solution and identity doesn't get to be the final answer. Churches which have learnt this, have renewed their identity and started to reframe their history have grappled with what it means to be under authority and to face the contemporary challenges of the world. They have not allowed themselves to be held captive by an authority—an individual, dynasty or heritage—which has turned history into future. Instead, they have allowed themselves to be shaped by the history and identity that has come from past and present and to allow authority to tell a different story. They have been called together in community, in an ecclesiological form, as many generations have before, and have decided what identity, theology and history means as part of a new normal.

Authority is far from lost in our Churches and our society. Authority is in every sinew of our ecclesial communities, telling the story of our past, our present, and defining the direction the Church will take. Rather than be frightened by its apparent lack or its authoritarian impact, our quest for authority requires us to look to what is central in answering the call to follow in the life and ministry of Jesus. We must recognise that we each have a part to play in discerning future direction and making our voices heard, adding our voice, our history, our identity, and our authority to that from years past and together with those who join us around the table. If we regard authority as the freedom to respond, to act and to change direction, our quest for authority need look no further than ourselves.

Bibliography

Airaksinen, Timo. "Coercion, Deterrence, and Authority." *Theory and Decision* 17 (1984) 105–17.
Anonymous. *Heads of Agreement Assented to by the United Ministers in and about London: Formerly called Presbyterian and Congregational.* London: R. R. for Thomas Cockerill and John Dunton, 1691.
Arendt, Hannah. "What is Authority?" In *Between Past and Future*, 91–141. New York: Penguin, 2006.
———. "What was Authority?" In *Authority*, edited by Carl J. Friedrich, 81–112. Cambridge: Harvard University Press, 1958.
Argent, Alan. *The Transformation of Congregationalism 1900-2000.* Nottingham: Congregational Federation, 2013.
Arthur, Gordon. *Law, Liberty and Church.* Aldershot: Ashgate, 2006.
Austin, Victor Lee. *Up with Authority: Why We Need Authority to Flourish as Human Beings.* London: T&T Clark, 2010.
Avis, Paul. *In Search of Authority: Anglican Theological Method from the Reformation to the Enlightenment.* London: Bloomsbury T&T Clark, 2014.
Bachmann, Reinhard. "At the Crossroads: Future Directions in Trust Research." *Journal of Trust Research* 1 (2011) 203–13.
Barth, Karl. *Church Dogmatics. 1/1: The Doctrine of the Word of God.* Translated by G. T. Thompson and Harold Knight. Peabody: Hendrickson, 2010.
Bebbington, David. *The Nonconformist Conscience: Chapel and Politics, 1870-1914.* London: Allen & Unwin, 1982.
Bevans, Stephen. *John Oman and His Doctrine of God.* Cambridge: Cambridge University Press, 1992.
———. "Seeing with a Prophet's Eye: John Oman's Experiential Method." In *John Oman: New Perspectives*, edited by Adam Hood, 117–39. Milton Keynes: Paternoster, 2012.
Bocking, Ron. "The United Reformed Church: Background, Formation, and After." *Journal of the United Reformed Church History Society* 5 (1997) 7–17.
Bos, Kees van den, et al. "When Do We Need Procedural Fairness? The Role of Trust in Authority." *Journal of Personality and Social Psychology* 75 (1998) 1449–58.
Bradbury, John P. "Covid-19, the Church and Holy Communion; 15 Theses: United and Reformed." https://urc.org.uk/images/15-theses-united-and-reformed-john-bradbury.pdf.
———. "Non-Conformist Conscience? Individual Conscience and the Authority of the Church from John Calvin to the Present." *Ecclesiology* 10 (2014) 32–52.

———. *Perpetually Reforming: A Theology of Church Reform and Renewal.* London: T&T Clark, 2012.
Brindley, Nick. "URC Sexuality Debates: An Ecclesiological Reflection." MTh diss., University of Edinburgh, 2012.
Cadoux, C. J. Review of *History and the Gospel*, by C. H. Dodd. *Mansfield College Magazine* 14 (1939) 588–92.
Campbell, John M. *Being Biblical.* London: URC, 2003.
Camroux, Martin. "Ecumenical Church Renewal: The Example of the United Reformed Church." PhD diss., Anglia Ruskin University, 2014.
———. "Why Did the United Reformed Church Fail? I: The Origins of the United Reformed Church." *Journal of the United Reformed Church History Society* 8 (2008) 30–45.
———. "Why Did the United Reformed Church Fail? IV: Where Do We Go from Here?" *Journal of the United Reformed Church History Society* 8 (2009) 210–25.
CCEW. *Declaration of Faith.* Hull: Independent, 1967.
Christianson, Paul. "Reformers and the Church of England Under Elizabeth I and the Early Stuarts." *Journal of Ecclesiastical History* 31 (1980) 463–82.
Church of Scotland. *Acts of the General Assembly of the Church of Scotland 1638–1842.* Edinburgh: Edinburgh Printing and Publishing, 1843.
———. *Compendium of the Laws of the Church of Scotland.* Edinburgh: Edinburgh Printing and Publishing, 1837.
Coates, Tony. "Slack, Kenneth." In *Who They Were: In the Reformed Churches of England and Wales, 1901–2000*, edited by Clyde Binfield and John H. Taylor, 206–7. Donington: Tyas, 2007.
Cocks, H. F. Lovell. "The Foundation in Christ." In *Proceedings of the Seventh International Congregational Council*, edited by R. F. G. Calder, 45–57. London: Independent, 1953.
Cook, Karen S., et al. *Cooperation without Trust?* New York: Russell Sage Foundation, 2009.
Copleston, Frederick C. *A History of Philosophy Vol. 5, Hobbes to Hume.* London: Search, 1959.
Cornick, David. "P. T. Forsyth's Doctrine of the Church." In *P. T. Forsyth: Theologian for a New Millennium*, edited by Alan P. F. Sell, 153–70. London: URC, 2000.
———. *Under God's Good Hand.* London: URC, 1998.
Cremer, David De, and Tom R. Tyler. "The Effects of Trust in Authority and Procedural Fairness on Cooperation." *Journal of Applied Psychology* 92 (2007) 639–49.
Cressey, Martin. "On Being a Conciliar Church." *The Ecumenical Review* 51 (1999) 355–63.
CUEW. *Christian Oversight: Local Church and National Union (Commission 1).* London: CUEW, 1960.
———. *Oversight and Covenant: Interim Report of Commission 1: Some Questions and Answers.* London: CUEW, 1961.
Cunliffe-Jones, H. Review of *Reformation Old and New. (A Tribute to Karl Barth)*, by F. W. Camfield. *The Presbyter* 5 (1947) 24–27.
Dale, R. W. *A Manual of Congregational Principles.* Edited by Digby L. James. Weston Rhyn: Quinta, 1996.
Davis, Thomas Webster. *Committees for Repeal of the Test and Corporation Acts Minutes 1786–90 and 1827–8.* London: London Record Society, 1978.

Dekker, P. "Political Trust: What Do We Measure? Should Politicians and the Public Trust Us?" Paper for the 6th European Consortium for Political Research General Conference, 2011.

Dietz, Graham. "Going Back to the Source: Why Do People Trust Each Other?" *Journal of Trust Research* 1 (2011) 215–22.

Drysdale, A. H. *History of the Presbyterians in England: Their Rise, Decline and Revival*. London: PCE, 1889.

Ensign-George, Barry A. *Between Congregation and Church*. London: Bloomsbury T&T Clark, 2018.

Forecast, Keith. *Getting the Name Right: Exploring the Identity and Role of The United Reformed Church 1972–2012*. London: URC, 2014.

Forster, Greg. *John Locke's Politics of Moral Consensus*. Cambridge: Cambridge University Press, 2005.

Forsyth, P. T. *The Church and the Sacraments*. London: Independent, 1964.

———. "The Grace of the Gospel as the Moral Authority in the Church." In *The Church, the Gospel and Society*, 71–127. London: Independent, 1962.

———. *The Principle of Authority*. London: Independent, 1952.

Friedman, R. B. "On the Concept of Authority in Political Philosophy." In *Authority*, edited by Joseph Raz, 56–91. New York: New York University Press, 1990.

Furedi, Frank. *Culture of Fear*. London: Continuum, 2002.

———. *Moral Crusades in an Age of Mistrust: the Jimmy Savile Scandal*. New York: Palgrave Macmillan, 2013.

Gardiner, Samuel Rawson, ed. *The Constitutional Documents of the Puritan Revolution 1625–1660*. Oxford: Clarendon, 1906.

Gerrish, Brian A. "Introduction: Doing Theology in the Reformed Tradition." In *Reformed Theology for the Third Christian Millennium*, edited by B. A. Gerrish, 1–11. Louisville: Westminster John Knox, 2003.

Goldring, Richard. "Attitudes to Marriage, Divorce and the Remarriage of Divorced Persons in the United Reformed Church and Its Predecessors 1830–1992." PhD diss., University of Birmingham, 1992.

Grdzelidze, Tamara. "Editor's Introduction." In *Sources of Authority: Contemporary Churches*, edited by Tamara Grdzelidze, xi–xviii. Geneva: World Council of Churches, 2014.

Gunton, Colin E. *The Promise of Trinitarian Theology*. Edinburgh: T&T Clark, 1997.

Haight, Roger. *Christian Community in History: Comparative Ecclesiology*. London: Bloomsbury T&T Clark, 2014.

Hall, Basil. "The Presbyterian Church and Its Future." *The Presbyter* 5 (1947) 25–33.

Hill, Craig C. *In God's Time: The Bible and the Future*. Grand Rapids: Eerdmans, 2002.

Hobbes, Thomas. *Leviathan*. Oxford: Oxford University Press, 1996.

Höpfl, H. M. "Power, Authority and Legitimacy." *Human Resource Development International* 2 (1999) 217–34.

Huxtable, John. *As It Seemed to Me*. London: URC, 1990.

———. *The Bible Says*. London: SCM, 1962.

———. *Christian Unity: Some of the Issues*. London: Independent, 1966.

———. "Sermon Preached by the Rev. John Huxtable in Westminster Abbey on the Occasion of the Inauguration of the United Reformed Church on Thursday, 5th October, 1972." London: URC, 1972.

International Congregational Council. "A Message to the Churches from the Seventh Council Meeting at St. Andrews, Scotland June 1953." In *Proceedings of the Seventh International Congregational Council*, edited by R. F. G. Calder, 158–62. London: Independent, 1953.
Jenkins, Daniel T. *Church Meeting and Democracy*. London: Independent, 1944.
———. *The Protestant Ministry*. London: Faber and Faber, 1958.
Jones, J. D. "Where Is the Nonconformist Conscience?" *British Weekly* (24 February 1938) 423.
Jones, R. Tudur. *Congregationalism in England, 1662–1962*. London: Independent, 1962.
Kaye, Elaine. *A Way of Gospel Obedience: The Church Meeting in Congregational Tradition and Practice (The Congregational Lecture)*. London: Congregational Memorial Hall Trust, 2008.
Kennett, Peter Trevellyn. "Autonomy: Cuckoo in the Congregationalists' Nest?" *International Congregational Journal* 4 (2004) 85–102.
Kenyon, J. P., ed. *The Stuart Constitution 1603–1688: Documents and Commentary*. Cambridge: Cambridge University Press, 1986.
Locke, John. "The Second Treatise: An Essay Concerning the True Original, Extent, and End of Civil Government." In *Two Treatises of Government and A Letter Concerning Toleration*, edited by Ian Shapiro, 100–209. London: Yale University Press, 2003.
Luther, Martin. "On Secular Authority." In *Luther and Calvin on Secular Authority*, edited by Harro Höpfl, 3–43. Cambridge: Cambridge University Press, 1991.
Macarthur, Arthur. "The Background to the Formation of the United Reformed Church (Presbyterian and Congregational) in England and Wales in 1972." *Journal of the United Reformed Church History Society* 4 (1987) 3–22.
———. *Setting Up Signs*. London: URC, 1997.
Mace, Jane. *God and Decision-Making: A Quaker Approach*. London: Quaker, 2012.
MacLean, Marjory A. "Presbyterian Governance." In *Legal Systems of Scottish Churches*, edited by Marjory A. MacLean, 1–12. Dundee: Dundee University Press, 2009.
Macphail, W. M. *The Presbyterian Church: A Brief Account of Its Doctrine, Worship, and Polity*. London: Hodder and Stoughton, 1908.
Manning, Bernard Lord. *The Protestant Dissenting Deputies*. Edited by Ormerod Greenwood. Cambridge: Cambridge University Press, 1952.
Marty, Martin E. *Building Cultures of Trust*. Grand Rapids: Eerdmans, 2010.
McIntosh, Peter, and Graham Robson. *Refreshing the Elders Meeting*. London: URC, 1999.
Methodist Conference. "Faith and Order Committee Report (2018)." https://www.methodist.org.uk/downloads/conf-2018-31-Faith-and-Order-Committee.pdf.
Micklem, Romilly. "The Failure of Moral Discourse: The Epistemological Crisis in the United Reformed Church." PhD diss., Heythrop College (University of London), 2010.
———. "Note." *New Christian* (4 May 1967) 4.
Morgan, D. Densil. *Barth Reception in Britain*. London: T&T Clark, 2010.
Nichols, Vincent Cardinal, et al. "Faith Communities letter to the Prime Minister." https://www.churchofengland.org/sites/default/files/2020-11/Faith%20communities%20letter%20to%20Prime%20MInister%20%28ii%29.pdf.
Norwood, Donald W. "The Case for Democracy in Church Government: A Study in the Reformed Tradition with Special Reference to the Congregationalism of Robert

William Dale, Peter Taylor Forsyth, Albert Peel and Nathaniel Micklem." PhD diss., Kings College London, 1983.

Nuttall, Geoffrey F. "Congregationalists and Creeds." In *Studies in English Dissent*, 111–24. Weston Rhyn: Quinta, 2002.

———. *Visible Saints: The Congregational Way, 1640–1660*. Oxford: Blackwood, 1957.

Nuttall, Geoffrey F., and Owen Chadwick, eds. *From Uniformity to Unity 1662–1962*. London: SPCK, 1962.

Oman, John. *Concerning the Ministry*. London: SCM, 1963.

———. *Honest Religion*. Edited by Herbert H. Farmer. Cambridge: Cambridge University Press, 1941.

———. *The Natural and the Supernatural*. Cambridge: Cambridge University Press, 1931.

———. *Vision and Authority*. London: Hodder and Stoughton, 1928.

O'Neill, Onora. *A Question of Trust*. Cambridge: Cambridge University Press, 2002.

Owen, John. *The True Nature of a Gospel Church and Its Government*. Edited by John Huxtable. London: Clarke, 1947.

Paddison, Angus. *Scripture: A Very Theological Proposal*. London: T&T Clark, 2009.

Paton, Lady. "Opinion: The Free Church of Scotland v. The General Assembly of the Free Church of Scotland [2005]." CSOH 46. https://www.scotcourts.gov.uk/search-judgments/judgment?id=3e6186a6-8980-69d2-b500-ff0000d74aa7.

Parry, Geraint. "Trust, Distrust and Consensus." *British Journal of Political Science* 6 (1976) 129–42.

PCE. *The Book of Order*. London: PCE, 1964.

Peel, David. *Reforming Theology*. London: URC, 2002.

———. *Sola Scriptura: The Achilles Heel of the Reformed Tradition?* Cheam: Free to Believe, 2012.

———. *The Story of the Moderators*. London: URC, 2012.

Percy, Martyn. "Authority in Contemporary Ecclesiology." In *One, Holy, Catholic and Apostolic: Ecumenical reflections on the Church (Faith and Order Paper 197)*, edited by Tamara Grdzelidze, 141–47. Geneva: WCC, 2005.

Pooler, Norman. *Introductory Notes on The Proposed Legal Arrangements*. London: printed for the Joint Committee, 1968.

Pope, Robert. "New Genevans." In *T&T Clark Companion to Nonconformity*, edited by Robert Pope, 640–41 London: Bloomsbury T&T Clark, 2013.

———. "Nonconformists and the Holy Spirit." In *T&T Clark Companion to Nonconformity*, edited by Robert Pope, 213–34. London: Bloomsbury T&T Clark, 2013.

Pope, Robert, ed. *T&T Clark Companion to Nonconformity*. London: Bloomsbury T&T Clark, 2013.

Proctor, James. "Religion as Trust in Authority: Theocracy and Ecology in the United States." *Annals of the Association of American Geographers* 96 (2006) 188–96.

Rawlinson, A. E. J., and Nathaniel Micklem. *Church Relations in England: Being the Report of Conversations between Representatives of the Archbishop of Canterbury and Representatives of the Evangelical Free Churches in England, Together with the Sermon Preached by the Archbishop of Canterbury on November 3rd, 1946 Entitled A Step Forward in Church Relations*. London: SPCK, 1950.

Reed, Michael I. "Organization, Trust and Control: A Realist Analysis." *Organization Studies* 22 (2001) 201–28.

Riglin, Keith Graham. "Animating Grace: The Practice of Authority and Order in a Reformed Church." ThD diss., University of Birmingham, 2008.

Ripstein, Arthur. "Authority and Coercion." *Philosophy & Public Affairs* 32 (2004) 2–35.

Robinson, William, "A Church Order: Reformed and Catholic." *The Presbyter* 2 (1944) 5.

Robson, Graham, and Peter McIntosh. *Refreshing the Church Meeting*. London: URC, 1999.

Rousseau, Jean-Jacques. *The Social Contract*. Translated by Maurice Cranston. London: Penguin, 2004.

Routley, Erik. *Into a Far Country: Reflections upon the Trajectory of the Divine Word, and upon the Communication, in Affairs Human and Divine, of the Imperative and the Indicative, incorporating Material used in the Congregational Lectures, 1960*. London: Independent, 1962.

Seligman, Adam B. *The Problem of Trust*. Princeton: Princeton University Press, 1997.

Sell, Alan P. F. *John Locke and the Eighteenth-Century Divines*. Cardiff: University of Wales Press, 1997.

———. *One Ministry, Many Ministers: A Case Study from the Reformed Tradition*. Eugene, OR: Pickwick, 2014.

———. *Saints: Visible, Orderly and Catholic*. Geneva: World Alliance of Reformed Churches, 1986.

Sennett, Richard. *Authority*. London: Faber and Faber, 1980.

Slack, Kenneth. *The United Reformed Church*. Exeter: Wheaton, 1978.

Stanley, Howard S. "A Message from the Secretary of the Union." *Congregational Monthly* (January 1961) 20.

———. *The Next Ten Years*. London: Independent, 1959.

Sykes, Stephen. "P. T. Forsyth on the Church." In *Justice the True and Only Mercy: Essays on the Life and Theology of Peter Taylor Forsyth*, edited by Trevor A. Hart, 1–15. Edinburgh: T&T Clark, 1995.

Tabart, Jill. *Coming to Consensus: A Case Study for the Churches*. Geneva: World Council of Churches, 2003.

Tan, Hwee Hoon, and Augustine K. H. Lim. "Trust in Coworkers and Trust in Organizations." *Journal of Psychology* 143 (2009) 45–66.

Taylor, John H. *Tell Me about the URC*. London: URC, 1981.

Thomas, D. A. Lloyd. *Locke on Government*. London: Routledge, 1995.

Thompson, David M. "Dissolution of the Association of Churches of Christ, 1979." *Journal of the United Reformed Church History Society* 8 (2008) 110–12.

———. *Let Sects and Parties Fall*. Birmingham: Berean, 1980.

———. "Nonconformists and Polity." In *T&T Clark Companion to Nonconformity*, edited by Robert Pope, 89–112. London: Bloomsbury T&T Clark, 2013.

———. *Stating the Gospel: Formulations and Declarations of Faith from the Heritage of the United Reformed Church*. Edinburgh: T&T Clark, 1990.

Thompson, Geoff. *Disturbing Much, Disturbing Many: Theology Provoked by the Basis of Union*. Northcote, AU: Uniting Academic, 2016.

Thorogood, Bernard. *No Abiding City*. London: SCM, 1989.

Tralau, J. "Hobbes Contra Liberty of Conscience." *Political Theory Political Theory* 39 (2011) 58–84.

Tucker, Tony. *Reformed Ministry*. London: URC, 2003.

URC. *Companion to Rejoice and Sing*. Norwich: Canterbury, 1999.

---. *Catch the Vision.* London: URC, 2005.
---. *Manual.* London: URC, 1973.
---. "The Manual." http://urc.org.uk/the-urc-manual.html.
---. "The Ministry and Mission Fund: Principles and Practice (2009)." https://urc.org.uk/images/Finance/The%20Ministry%20and%20Mission%20Fund%20Principles%20and%20Practice.pdf.
---. "URC General Assembly Moderators Comment on New Four-Week Lockdown (5 November 2020)." https://urc.org.uk/latest-news/3640-urc-general-secretary-comments-on-new-four-week-lockdown.
URC History Society. *The United Reformed Church: A Historical Introduction.* London: URC, 1976.
Vine, Aubrey R. "The Nature of the Congregational Ministry." In *The Congregational Ministry in the Modern World,* edited by H. Cunliffe-Jones, 1-16. London: Independent, 1955.
Walker, Williston. *The Creeds and Platforms of Congregationalism.* Boston: Pilgrim, 1960.
Welch, Michael R., et al. "Trust in God and Trust in Man: The Ambivalent Role of Religion in Shaping Dimensions of Social Trust." *Journal for the Scientific Study of Religion* 43 (2004) 317-43.
Weller, John. "Some Notes on the Episcopal Function of Moderators." *COG Newsletter* 3 (1953) 3.
Whale, J. S. *Christian Doctrine.* Cambridge: Cambridge University Press, 1942.
Whitehouse, W. A. "Making the Declaration of Faith." In *Christian Confidence,* edited by Roger Tomes, 13-25. London: SPCK, 1970.
Wilson, Reginald Alastair. "The Problem of Religious Authority in Contemporary Theological Thought with Particular Reference to the Interpretations of John Oman, P. T. Forsyth, and A. E. J. Rawlinson." PhD diss., Columbia University, 1960.
Wisneski, Daniel C., et al. "Research Report: Gut Reactions: Moral Conviction, Religiosity, and Trust in Authority." *Psychological Science* 20 (2009) 1059-63.
Woods, Helen. "What is Amiss in Congregationalism?" *COG Newsletter* 74 (1968) 3-4.
Woolthuis, Rosalinde, et al. "Trust, Contract and Relationship Development." *Organization Studies* 26 (2005) 813-40.
Wyatt, Tim. "Church Leaders Launch Legal Challenge over Lockdown Closure of Places of Worship." *Independent,* November 14, 2020. https://www.independent.co.uk/news/uk/home-news/lockdown-coronavirus-church-places-of-worship-b1722922.html.
Young, Gary. "Authority." *Canadian Journal of Philosophy* 3 (1974) 563-83.

Index

1 Corinthians 12, v14, 4
absentee votes, 73–74, 119–20, 178–79
accountability, xiv, 180, 181, 185–86
Address to the Throne, 92–100
American Constitution (First Amendment), 89
anarchy, 11, 167
apathy, 134, 135–36, 140, 142–43, 202, 209
Apostles' Creed, 84, 87
Apostolic succession, 2, 34, 49, 62, 63, 116
Appeals, 52, 54, 131, 138, 146, 180, 195–96
Areas, 44. *See also* District Councils
Arendt, Hannah, 11–12, 14–17, 30, 114
Argent, Alan, 77–78
Arthur, Gordon, 28, 113
Assembly Executive, 47–48, 55–56, 124, 138, 173–74, 181, 183, 199–202, 206. *See also* Mission Council
Assessment Board, 149, 180
Austin, Victor Lee, 13–15, 20, 23, 30
Authoritarianism, 11, 13
Authority
    "An authority", 18, 20, 21–23, 25, 26–27, 28, 84, 147, 151
    "In authority", 18, 19–21, 22, 26, 28, 147, 151
    as abuse, ix, 23, 24
    charismatic (Weber), 16, 22
    corrupt, 11, 14–15, 23–27

delegated, 20, 48–49, 51, 53, 55, 138–39, 141, 149, 180–81, 206
final, 29, 53–54, 56, 69, 72, 125, 126, 131, 138, 199–200
legal-rational (Weber), 16
object (response), 17–19, 25
of Christ, 2, 5, 62–63, 66, 132, 148, 189
subject (locus), 17–23, 49, 136–37
supreme, 59, 66–68, 70
tradition (Weber), 16
Avis, Paul, 5

Bacon, Francis, 68
Banwell, Harold, 39
Baptist Union, 40, 163
Barrier Act, 86, 129–30, 141
Barth, Karl, 3, 60–61
    Church Dogmatics, 61–62
    proclamation of the Word, 60–61
Basis of Union, A. See *Manual, The*
Bible, 4, 60, 66–70, 71, 77, 107
Bishops, 13, 35, 126, 128, 153–54, 210
Bocking, Ronald, 39, 45, 48
Bradbury, John, xvi, 78–80, 105–6, 164–68, 192–93
    General Secretary, ix
Brexit (UK Referendum on membership of the European Union), 187
Brindley, Nick, 122–23, 200

British Council of Churches, 34
buildings. *See* property
Business Committee, 54–55

Cadoux, C. J., 60
Calvin, John, 3, 67, 112, 162
  Institutes, 103
Camroux, Martin, 46, 76
Candidates for Ministry, 49, 52, 149, 177, 180
Catch the Vision (CTV), 46–48, 50–51, 53, 54–55, 200
Church House, 54
Church Meeting, xi, xii, xiii, 6, 32, 45, 49–50, 72–74, 114, 116–21, 123–26, 129, 137–38, 142, 148, 151, 154–55, 157, 174, 175–76, 181–82, 185, 186, 198–99, 200, 203
Church of England, 7, 35, 38, 90, 103, 154
Church of Scotland, 8, 35, 39, 95, 130, 132, 163, 210
Church Related Community Workers (CRCW), 47, 52, 53–54, 127, 147–49, 150, 154
  commissioning of, 52, 148
Church Unity Commission, 77
Churches of Christ, x, 3, 6, 7, 40–41, 43–45, 76, 84, 141, 146–47, 150–51
Civil Partnerships, 58, 210
Civil War (English), 90–92, 95
Cocks, H. F. Lovell, 60, 63–64
coercion, 15, 17, 23–25, 182
Colston, Edward, 13
Commitment on Human Sexuality (2007), 164–65
Commonwealth, 90–92
conciliarity, 32, 47, 48–58, 112–45, 146, 153–54, 169, 177, 189, 202, 204, 209
concur, 8, 25, 38, 73, 75, 86, 149, 175, 178, 180–81
confession, 29–30, 35–36, 59, 84–89, 104
Confession of Faith. See *Manual, The*, §A.17

Congregational Association, 126
Congregational Church in England and Wales (CCEW), 6, 36–43, 61, 73, 76, 142
Congregational Union of England and Wales (CUEW), 34–39, 77, 99, 127, 142
Congregational Union of Scotland, 6, 44, 76, 132
Congregational-Presbyterian Joint Committee. *See* Joint Committee
Congregational/Church Order Group (COG), 128, 132
Congregationalism, x, 32, 35, 37, 38, 42, 60, 61, 84, 89, 112, 116, 118, 125–26, 164, 165
conscience, 69, 89, 95–96, 160, 161–68
  nonconformist, 84, 161, 163–66
  personal, 58, 167–68
conscientious objection, 43, 162, 166
consensus, 26n36, 74–75, 108, 123–25, 160, 168–72, 178, 179, 181, 183, 186, 199
Consensus Adviser, 170–71
consent, 24–27, 92–94, 101–2
Constitution (CCEW), 35–38, 41
contemporary Church, 2, 5, 8, 9, 10, 33–34, 68, 98, 106, 114–15, 123, 132, 209–11
contract, 24–26, 92–93
Convenors, 54–55, 61, 86n11, 158
conviction
  corporate, 76, 99, 102, 115, 165
  personal, 71–73, 161–68
Cornick, David, x, xv, 7, 33–34, 90n17
Court, x, 8, 125–26, 130–31
covenant, 36–37, 63, 84, 94, 96, 116–17, 119–20, 123–25, 133
Covenant for Unity, 77, 78, 80, 153–54
Covid-19/Coronavirus, 100–101, 140, 178, 187, 188, 191–93, 196–97
Cressey, Martin, 38–39, 56, 113–14

Cromwell, Oliver, 92
Cunliffe-Jones, Hubert, 39, 60

Dale, R. W., 116–17
decision making, xii, 1, 9, 28, 42, 55–56, 57–58, 74–75, 76, 94, 108, 114, 119, 121–25, 133, 136, 138, 142, 144, 152, 160–61, 168–69, 171–80, 182–83, 184, 185, 186, 189, 195–96, 200, 201, 203, 206, 207
Declaration and Address (1809) (Thomas Campbell), 84, 85
Declaration of Breda (1660), 95
Declaration of Faith (CCEW), 36, 61
democracy, 91, 94, 119–20, 190
discernment, xii, xiii, xiv, 2–3, 4, 36, 59, 65, 66, 70–75, 81–82, 103, 119–20, 121, 124, 127–28, 130–31, 136, 139, 146, 148–49, 157, 160, 164, 166, 168–69, 171–72, 177, 178–79, 186, 188–89, 191–92, 193, 197, 198, 208, 211
dissent
    an act of, 42–43, 45, 102, 160, 163, 166, 170, 182
    from the State, 90, 95–100, 162
District Council, x, 39, 41, 44–45, 47, 48, 50–51, 53, 125–26, 129, 133, 135, 139–40, 143–44, 150, 180–81, 204
Dodd, C. H., 60
Donne, John, 83
Downing, Clare, 101
Durber, Susan, xvi, 7
Ecclesial history, 3, 5, 161
Edward VI, 95
Elders/Eldership, 6, 47, 49–50, 54, 73, 75, 86–87, 88, 119, 129, 134, 143, 148–49, 152, 154–55, 169, 173–76, 198–99
Elders' Meeting, 6, 32n1, 45, 49–50, 119, 126, 129, 137–38, 141, 148–49, 155, 173, 174–76, 185–86, 198–99, 208
en bloc business, 175, 184, 185, 189

Episcopacy, 34–35, 128, 146–47, 153–54. *See also* Bishops
episcope, 146, 153, 154. *See also* oversight
eschatology, 4–5, 33, 71, 78–80, 81, 103–4, 105–6, 121
Established Church, xii, 7, 34, 89–90, 95, 100–102, 196
Faith and Order Commission (WCC), 28
Fascism, 30
Figures, J. A., 39
finance, 1, 57, 129, 145, 175, 193–95, 197–98, 205, 207
Fisher, Geoffrey (Archbishop of Canterbury), 34–35, 128
flourishing, xiii, 14–17, 20, 23–25, 30–31
Forsyth, P. T., 68, 69, 75
    Church and the Sacraments, 2, 120
    Moral Authority, 62, 120
    Principle of Authority, 29, 62, 63, 64, 65, 69, 72, 74, 105, 120, 164, 166–68
Free Church Federal Council. *See* Free Churches Group
Free Church of Scotland, 39
Free Churches, 34, 39, 100
Free Churches Group, 34, 97
freedom, xiii, 13–14, 15, 17, 24–25, 27, 30–31, 45, 48, 63, 64–65, 70–71, 89, 92–95, 101, 104, 117–18, 164–68, 210, 211
Friedman, R. B., 16, 18–23
Furedi, Frank, 23, 26n36, 187–88
furlough, 196

Gaunt, Alan, 85–86
Gender Diversity, 54, 176, 179, 183, 184
General Assembly (Church of Scotland), 8, 95
General Assembly (PCE), 42
General Assembly (URC), x, 6–7, 9, 43, 45–48, 51–58, 74, 77, 85–86, 95, 99, 114, 122–31, 134, 137–45, 149, 157,

General Assembly (URC) (*cont.*)
   158, 164, 168–74, 176, 177, 179–81, 183, 184, 185, 190, 191, 194–95, 199–204, 206, 207, 209
   biennial, 47–48, 106, 139, 143, 200–201
   Clerk of, 54–55, 158, 170–71, 191
   Roll of, 55, 191
   Standing Orders, 74, 123–24, 171, 174, 190–91
General Secretary, ix–x
Gerrish, Brian, 3
Glorious Revolution (1688), 90–92
Goodwin, John, 84
Gospel, xiii, 2, 3, 32–33, 37, 53, 62, 63, 65, 66, 68–70, 84, 106, 115, 116–17, 160, 168
Grdzelidze, Tamara, 28, 29
Gunton, Colin, 7, 70–71

Hanson, Malcolm, 86
Hayes Conference Centre, Swanwick, 47
Healey, Tim, 38
Hick, John, 7
hierarchical Councils, xiii, 28, 130–31, 133–34, 148, 195–96, 200
Hill, Craig C., 78–79, 81,
Hobbes, Thomas
   Leviathan (1651), 90–93, 162–63
Holy Spirit, xiv, 3, 28, 36, 53, 57, 59–60, 61–62, 64, 66, 70–75, 81–82, 103, 104, 105, 119–21, 123, 124–25, 129, 30–131, 164–66, 169, 171–73, 178, 180, 186, 190, 192–93, 210
Hooker, Richard, 5
Human Sexuality Debates, 8, 122, 164–65, 168, 210
Hussein, Saddam, 13
Huxtable, John, 7, 34n5, 38, 40, 61, 68–69, 73–4, 77–78, 80, 118, 125, 178, 189

identity, xi, xii, xiii–xiv, 2, 4, 5–6, 9–10, 32, 36, 45–46, 79, 83–111, 112, 114, 119, 132, 136–37, 144, 186, 209–11
inclusive language, 85
Independency, 32, 118, 132, 142, 196
integrity, 162, 164–65, 167
irelevance of structures, 139–41, 202, 204

Jagessar, Michael, 7
Jenkins, Daniel, 115, 117, 119–20, 147–48, 151
Job Retention Scheme. *See* furlough
Joint Committee, 37–43, 45, 60–61, 77, 113, 118, 126
Joint Public Issues Team (JPIT), 163
Jones, J.D., 163

Kaan, Fred, 7
Kaye, Elaine, 121
Knox, John, 67

Law and Polity Advisory Group (LPAG), 206
Lay Presidency, 52, 126, 150, 151n11, 154–55, 192, 210
leadership, 20, 23, 128, 130–31, 134, 146–47, 150, 151–52, 154–55, 195, 198–99, 201
Legal Trusts, 40, 57, 194–96, 197, 206
legislation,
   Charities Act (2011), 195–96
   charity, 100, 197, 206–7
   Data Protection, 196
   employment, xii–xiii, 100, 196, 182, 190, 195–96, 198–99, 205, 208, 210
   Health and Safety, xii, 100, 123, 196
   United Reformed Church Acts (1972, 1981 & 2000), 40, 50–51, 206
legitimacy , 13, 15–16, 17, 20, 25, 27, 101–2, 105, 122–23, 137–39,

140, 172, 174–77, 179–80, 183, 208
Leveson Inquiry, 187
litigious culture, 190
Local Church, x, xi, xii, 6, 8, 9, 37, 42, 45, 48–53, 57, 73, 81, 114–20, 123–26, 128, 129, 131, 132–45, 149, 151–56, 169, 173, 174, 175, 176, 181–82, 184, 190–91, 194–95, 196, 198–200, 202–8
    autonomy, 125–26, 132
Local Ecumenical Partnership (LEP), 79–80, 81
Local Leadership, 134, 150, 154–55
Local Mission and Ministry Review (LMMR), 205
Local Sharing Agreements. *See* Local Ecumenical Partnership (LEP)
Locke, John, 24–25, 63, 90–94, 101–2, 162
    Two Treatises of Government (1690), 24, 90–91, 92–93
Lord's Supper, 119–20, 192
Luther, Martin, 24, 59, 67, 103
    Ninety-five Theses, 103

Macarthur, Arthur, 34n5, 35n10, 38–39, 40n25, 87
MacIntyre, Alasdair, 21–22
MacLeod, A. G., 39
Macphail, W. M., 104
Majority votes, 39, 43–44, 64–65, 74–75, 76, 86, 94, 119, 121, 172, 175, 189, 193
Mansfield College, Oxford, 60
Manual, The, 41, 54, 79, 84–89, 113–14
    Basis of Union (A)
    §A.1, 61, 70, 78
    §A.2, 62
    §A.3, 62
    §A.4, 62, 65
    §A.6, 62, 63–64, 70
    §A.8, 32–33, 76, 78
    §A.9, 33, 65, 103, 106, 110–11

    §A.10, 62, 70, 165–166
    §A.11, 70
    §A.12, 59, 66, 70
    §A.13, 66
    §A.14, 166
    §A.16, 78
    §A.17, 70, 78, 85
    §A.18, 67, 84
    §A.19, 147
    §A.20, 147, 148
    §A.21, 148–49
    §A.25, 49, 150
    Schedule C, 67, 88
    Schedule D
        v1, 44, 72, 88, 102
        v2, 59, 75, 88, 89, 90, 101–2
    Schedule E, 87
    Structure (B)
    §B.1.(1), 49
    §B.1.(2), 51
    §B.1.(3), 57, 129
    §B.2.(1), 49–50, 72, 73, 129, 131, 137
    §B.2.(2), 50, 137, 148
    §B.2.(3), 51
    §B.2.(4), 51, 52, 53, 127, 140
    §B.2.(6), 51, 53, 55, 56, 129–30, 131, 138, 140, 183
    §B.3, 56, 130
    §B.4, 56, 57–58, 130
    §B.5.(2), 58, 131
    Rules of Procedure (C)
    §C.7, 52
Marsh, John, 38
McConnell, Frank, 38
Medium Term Strategy Group (MTSG), 207–8
Members, Church, 6–7, 8, 32, 36, 37–38, 39, 41–42, 43, 45, 49–51, 62, 72–74, 82, 109, 110, 115, 116–21, 123, 125, 126, 129, 133–36, 137, 139–40, 141–43, 144–45, 150, 152, 154–55, 156, 157, 158, 173, 174, 175, 183, 185, 188,

Members, Church (*cont.*)
189–90, 197–99, 202, 203–5,
207–9, 210
memory, 108–11, 144, 208–9. *See also* identity
Methodist Church, 5, 7, 163, 192, 208
Micklem, Caryl, 7, 125–26, 131
Micklem, Nathaniel, 34–35, 60,
Micklem, Romiley, 122–23, 200
Minister
   Auxiliary/Non Stipendiary, 43, 44–45
   Word and Sacraments, xiii, 7, 19, 47–55, 66–67, 73, 75, 86–88, 116, 118–19, 126, 127–29, 147–56, 177, 180–81, 183–84, 192, 193, 194, 196–97, 205–6, 208, 210
Ministerial Disciplinary Process, 52, 53, 134, 165, 180
Ministry and Mission Fund (M&M), 194
ministerial deployment, 128, 194, 200, 205–6
ministerial scoping, 194, 205
Mission Council, 47–48, 55, 114, 130, 157–58, 170–71, 173–74, 177, 183, 184, 185, 189–91, 199–202, 203, 204, 207–8, *see also* Assembly Executive
Moderators
   General Assembly, 47–48, 54–55, 77, 86, 101, 107, 124, 157, 166, 169, 170, 175, 181, 183, 185, 190, 191, 203–4
   Interim, 51–52, 154
   of presbyteries, 35
   Synod, xii-xiii, 51, 52–53, 55, 108, 114, 119, 124, 126–29, 133, 134, 142, 153–54, 155–56, 170, 177, 185, 189, 191–92, 196, 199, 200, 205, 208
monarchy, 12, 91–92, 95–96, 98–99

Nazir-Ali, Michael, 100–101

Neil, Alec, 38
New Genevans, 60
Newbigin, Leslie, 7
Nicene Creed, 84, 87
Nominations Committee, 54, 157, 158, 176, 183–84
Nonconformity, 40, 89, 90, 94–95, 103, 163
Northern College, Manchester, 39
Nuttal, Geoffrey, 84, 90n17, 95n37

obedience, 15, 16–17, 21, 22–23, 24, 25–26, 27, 29, 30–31, 62–63, 66–67, 89, 101–2, 120, 152, 193, 198
Oman, John, 64–65, 68–69, 71–72, 162, 168
Omooba, Ade, 100–101
online platforms, 177–79, 187, 191–92
ordination, 2, 16, 34–35, 52, 63, 67, 87–88, 148, 148–50, 153
oversight, xiv, 50, 51–52, 53, 55, 57, 125, 129, 131–32, 146, 153, 156, 199, *see also* episcope
Owen, John, 62–63

participation, 9, 124, 134, 135, 142–44, 149, 162, 176, 180, 190–91, 198–209
Pay, Peter, 101
Peel, David, 62n12, 67n43, 127–28
people of God, 78, 147–48, 193, 210
Percy, Martin, 110
permanence and reliability, 12, 83, 211
personal authority, 106–7, 146–59
personal episcope, 153–54
persuasion, 15–16, 25–27
Platonic, 15, 16–17, 21, 30
pneumatology, 70–75
Pooler, Norman, 39–40
Pope, Robert, xvi, 75n71, 90n17
power, 12, 14, 15, 17, 23, 55, 80, 91, 94, 96, 107, 117, 138, 210
Presbyter, The, 60
Presbyterian Church in England, 98

INDEX 227

Presbyterian Church of England (PCE), 6, 34–43, 76, 98–99, 104, 130–32
Standing Orders, 98–99
Presbyterianism, xiii, 32, 112
priesthood of all believers, 147–51
Proctor, John, xvi
property
  buildings, xi-xii, 1, 12–13, 40, 41, 49–50, 51, 52, 57, 126, 129, 157, 175, 192, 195, 200, 206
  disposal of, 40, 51–52, 195, 206
  personal freedom, 24, 62–63, 92–93
  rental, 195
Proposals for Unification with the United Reformed Church (1976), 43
Protestant Dissenting Deputies, 96–98, 102, 163
Province. *See* Synod
Public Health, 196

Quakers, 147, 169
Queen Victoria, 98

Reform (URC Magazine), 74, 80, 87, 133, 134, 170
Reformation, Protestant, 2, 3, 5, 7, 32–33, 67, 84, 89, 90, 103–4, 153, 160
Regicide, 65, 90–91, 92
Rejoice and Sing, 87
reliability, 12–13, 83, 144, 211
Rennie, Scott, 8–9, 210
right to change, 80, 85, 102–6, 109
Riglin, Keith, 66, 69, 75, 116, 122–23, 131, 153–54, 200
Ripstein, Arthur, 24
Roman Catholic Church, 5, 7, 67, 100, 103, 112, 128
Rominger, Roberta, xvi, 207
Routley, Erik, 7, 116, 121, 123–24
Rules of Procedure (C). *See Manual, The*

safeguarding, xi–xiii, 142, 196

Same-sex marriage, 173, 184, 200, 210. *See also* human sexuality
Savile, Jimmy, 23, 187
Savoy Declaration, 35, 67, 84–85, 113, 116–17
Scheme for Union, 41, 77
Scripture, 1, 4–5, 59–61, 66–70, 81, 103, 104, 107, 111, 125. *See also* Bible; Word of God
Secretary for Ministries, 54, 180
Sell, Alan, 7, 125, 130
Sennett, Richard, 13, 114–15
Slack, Kenneth, 39
Social Contract (Rousseau), 92–93
sola scriptura, 67
Solemn League and Covenant, 95–96
spheres, widening, 125–26, 130–31, 136–37
Staff Secretaries, 54
Stanford, E. C. D, 126
Stanley, Howard, 35–39, 77
  The Next Ten Years, 35–36, 77
Statement concerning the nature, faith and order of the URC. *See Manual, The, Schedule D*
Statement of Convictions, 39, 41
Statement of Faith, 35, 85–86. *See also* inclusive
Stepwise Programme, 178
Structure (B). *See Manual, The*
Synod, x, xi, xv, 6, 9, 39, 44–45, 47, 48, 50–53, 54–58, 74, 81, 86, 113–14, 118, 119, 124–36, 137, 138, 139, 140, 143–44, 148–49, 150, 153–54, 155–56, 172–74, 176, 178–79, 180–182, 183, 184, 185, 191, 194–197, 199–200, 202, 203–8
  Clerk of, 104, 133, 156, 208
  Presbyterian, 98–99, 104
taskgroups, 181
technology, 115, 123, 177–79, 187, 188, 191–92
Thompson, David, 7, 40–41, 85–86, 88, 100, 104
Thorpe, Kirsty, 7

Toleration, Act of (1689), 95
Totalitarianism, 12
tradition(s), ix, x, xi, xii, 2, 4, 5, 9, 12, 28–29, 32–34, 46, 65, 67, 79, 83, 96, 103, 109, 110–11, 112, 120, 122, 141–42, 146, 161, 162, 190, 192, 198, 202, 210
    antecedent, 33–34, 42–43, 45, 67, 110, 141–42, 198, 202
Treasurer, 54–55, 157–58
Trinitarian, 59, 61, 88, 96
Trump, Donald, 187
trust, 17, 25–27, 107–9, 115, 134, 161, 180–86, 188
Trustees, 40, 55, 57, 195–96, 206–7

uniformity, 4, 32
Uniformity, Act of (1662), 95, 99–100
Union Committee of the Churches of Christ, 40–41
United Free Church of Scotland, 39
United Presbyterian Church (in England), 98
United Presbyterian Church of Scotland, 39
Uniting Assembly, 42

unity, 1, 4, 6, 8, 33, 44–45, 53–54, 69, 72–74, 75–81, 82, 84, 104, 108, 122, 124, 130, 160, 163, 164–68, 169, 171, 186, 197
URC Archive, xv, 73, 118, 125–26
URC Trust, 184, 195–98, 203, 206–7

via media, 5
virtual meetings, 178–79, 188–93
    standing orders, 191

Weber, Max, 16, 22, 188
Welch, Elizabeth, 7
Wesley, John, 5, 103
Westminster College, Cambridge, xv, xvi, 39, 68
Westminster Confession, 67–68, 84–85, 104, 113
Whitehouse, W. A., 61
William of Orange, 92, 95–98
Wilson, R. A., 64–65, 67, 71–72, 105–6
Word of God, xiv, 2–4, 53, 57, 59–82, 103, 129, 131, 160, 168–69, 211
World Communion of Reformed Churches (WCRC), 3
Wren, Brian, 7, 87

www.ingramcontent.com/pod-product-compliance
Lightning Source LLC
Chambersburg PA
CBHW051055230426
43667CB00013B/2305